ABOUT THE AUTHOR'S BOOKS AND WORK

"Nick Jankel uses his unique voice and powerful insights to inspire wonder. His ideas are as relevant to the newest startup as they are to the oldest public company."
Special Advisor to President Obama
Head of White House Office of Social Innovation (Former)

"A glam spiritual activist."
The Sunday Times

"An outstanding framework with powerful tools for self-awareness. Huge impact!"
President, Kellogg Company

"This book is quite amazing. This is the time to switch on and Nick Jankel is a wisdom teacher for this time."
New Consciousness Review

"LOVING IT!!! Actually, tears have streamed down my face more than once already so I just wanted to say thank you for sharing the wisdom you have and creating magic which changes people's lives."
Global Head of Learning and Organizational Development

OTHER BOOKS

Switch On: *Unleash Your Creativity And Thrive With The New Science And Spirit Of Breakthrough*

The Book of Breakthrough: *How to Use Disruptive Innovation & Transformational Leadership To Create A More Thriving World For All*

ABOUT THE AUTHOR

Nick Seneca Jankel is a Cambridge-educated author, philosopher, professional speaker, and transformation catalyst. He is the co-founder of personal and leadership development enterprise Switch On (www.switchonnow.com). Nick develops original thinking, powerful programs, and crucial tools that ensure leaders and individuals of all kinds can transform themselves and their organizations to thrive in the disrupted, networked, and stressed world. He has worked with organizations as diverse as Nike, No. 10 Downing Street, HSBC, and Oxfam and has taught at many universities, including Oxford University, London Business School, SciencesPo (Paris), and Yale University.

Nick hosted a network TV show on BBC as a psychological coach and has been interviewed about his ideas on the BBC World Service, CBS, and Hay House Radio. He has appeared in The Economist, The Guardian, and The Financial Times; and was invited to speak on science and spirituality at Aspen Ideas Festival. Nick obtained a Triple 1st Class degree in Medicine & History and Philosophy of Science from Cambridge University and is the author of a number of books on creativity, transformation, and leadership, including the bestseller, ***Switch On***. Most of all he is a husband and father and loves nothing more than hanging out with his wife and two boys in a field, party, or festival.

Cover design by Jason Anscomb
Brand design by Land of Plenty

Library of Congress Cataloging-in-Publication Data
Library of Congress Control Number: 2017916474
Jankel, Nick Seneca 1974–
Spiritual Atheist: A Quest To Reunite Science And Wisdom Into A Radical New Life Philosophy To Thrive In The Digital Age
Second Edition, September 2018
Los Angeles, United States

Switch On Books
288 pp. incl. index
Philosophy (General) 2. Psychology – Consciousness 3. Religion – Religion and science 4. Memoirs

Printed in the United States and wherever books are sold.

ISBN 978-1-9997315-2-6 (print book)
ISBN 978-1-9997315-3-3 (ebook)
Switch On Worldwide Ltd
London & Los Angeles

www.switchonnow.com

Discounts are available on quantity purchases by corporations, associations, and others.
For details, contact the publisher through the website above.

A QUEST TO UNITE SCIENCE AND WISDOM
INTO A RADICAL NEW LIFE PHILOSOPHY
TO THRIVE IN THE DIGITAL AGE

NICK SENECA JANKEL

A

SWITCH ON

BOOK

THRIVE YOUR FUTURE

For Mémé, who taught me that life is learning

In memory of Salomon, Sabina, Julius, and Ruth

∞

Believe me, I wasn't like this before
Out of my head, unsane, enchanted
I used to be clever like you
I was not hunted down
by this ever-increasing love

Jalal al Din Rumi
Ghazal 1506

ACKNOWLEDGMENTS

I would like to thank many friends, family, and colleagues for their support as sparring partners over the months and years described in this book. In particular: Tom F-M, Angus G, David F, Will P, Lisa U, Kate A, Shaune O, Abby H, Graham H, Fernando D, Stephanie A, Kate E, Alexei L, Jonathan W, Hermy J, Scott V, Jess J, Scott W, Greg W, Jessica J, Monica J, and Richard E for their continued and considered feedback. Eternal gratitude to Alison M, my wife, best friend, co-creator, business partner, and lifetime guide, for all her support, in so many different ways. And my boys Jai and Noah: thank you for giving me the time and space to write this book when all you want to do, quite rightly, is play!

CONTENTS

INTRODUCTION

Do you take the pills offered to you or try out therapy?

Do you risk invasive surgery that might leave you worse off or try alternative medicine?

Do you immunize your kids with a vaccine that parents you know personally believe brain-damaged their child?

Do you stick with an okay relationship or risk everything for deeper intimacy and true love?

Do you have an abortion or have the baby?

Do you stay monogamous, cheat, or try polyamory?

Do you take a job with way less money but way more meaning?

How do you use social media to promote yourself and your projects?

How do you use new technologies like AI and the blockchain?

Do you ensure that your business/organization has a purpose?

Do you invest in a pension or focus on enjoying the moment?

Do you leave your life savings to your kids or give everything to charity?

How do you think public money should be invested to solve society's problems?

What kind of politicians do you vote for to feel safe? To feel inspired?

∞

Choices like these, which may seem like they have little to do with each other, must be made by every one of us each day. What is more, many unprecedented and tricky choices will need to be made by us all as we live, love, and lead in what is certain to be a challenging future. What knowledge and wisdom we use to make our decisions changes the shape of our lives. What we choose in future will determine whether we, our organizations, and our social systems thrive or not in the Digital Age.

When I was fifteen, I decided that the religion I was born into had limited value in helping me answer such questions and make good choices. Instead, I gravitated toward science, which seemed to be full of tangible evidence and hard facts. I became an avowed atheist, convinced that reason was the only path to truth. I threw off the shackles of faith and its tired rituals, scripture, and rules, and became free. Or so I thought.

In the years that followed my conversion to atheism, I roamed the ranges of modern (and postmodern) life seeking certainty in the sciences; seeking sustenance in psychotherapy, travel, and hedonism; and seeking success in the intertwining worlds of corporate innovation and tech entrepreneurship. I found within each of these domains lots of rich insights into how to 'succeed' in life. But science and reason proved to be way more limited than I thought they would be at providing me with a comprehensive *life* philosophy, or *bios*, with which I could consistently make good choices that led to health, happiness and an ability to contribute meaningfully to the world around me.

Although some would see my upbringing as privileged and my life successful, I suffered for many years with both physical and emotional distress: anxiety, depression, chronic pain, and more. I, like most of us, was never given a single second of teaching on how to flourish as a human being in my education. Even the medical and philosophy programs I spent years studying on did not offer a rigorous *bios* with which to engage in the tough challenges of life. By the time I was in my late twenties, I had pretty much everything that I thought was important: my own home; success with the start-up I had co-founded; launching new products (like Microsoft's Xbox), and developing new innovations (like the most successful TV show of all time); and, on paper, I was a multi-millionaire.

But it all came crashing down around the time of my thirtieth birthday. I burned out and had a breakdown. My love life, business, physical wellbeing, and mental health all imploded. I had spent fifteen years living an absolutely atheistic and materialist life but I was missing so much: thriving relationships, a stable sense of happiness, and, above all, inner peace.

It is a sad fact of life today that many, many people find themselves seeking inner peace, intimate loving relationships, and an abiding sense of purpose as a leader and not finding them with ease in our modern world. In this era of vast technological prowess, with virtually the world's entire rational knowledge available to us in an instant on the internet, mental anguish has never been more intense and more widespread.

Depression is now the single greatest burden on health worldwide.[1] Suicide kills more people than war and natural catastrophes put together, and more US troops die from killing themselves than from conflict.[2] Suicide is the second leading cause of death for those between the ages of fifteen and twenty-nine across the planet. These numbers are set to double in the next five years.[3] Anxiety is the fastest-growing illness in those under twenty-one in the UK.[4] A third of British teenage girls say they suffer from depression or anxiety,[5] and there has been a 285 percent increase in girls being treated for self-harm in Britain in just a few years.[6]

Middle-aged people across the Western world are suffering from a massive increase in so-called "deaths of despair", killed by chronic ill-health, suicide, drugs, and alcohol.[7] Addiction to legal opiates kills around 50 people per day in the US alone.[8] 40 percent of older adults in the US say they are lonely (up from 20 percent in the 1980s[9]); loneliness appears to be twice as dangerous to our health than obesity, and just as dangerous as smoking.[10]

Widen the lens and we see that, because of the choices we humans keep making, virtually every ecological and economic system on the planet is stressed to the max. In the last forty years, a full third of arable land on Earth has become infertile.[11] The oceans are acidifying and ice is melting at alarming rates. Reports suggest that one million people in China die each year from air pollution, and that smog in Europe and North America could be more than twenty-five times more lethal than that in China.[12]

It is estimated that, globally, 9 million people die each year from air, water, earth, and buildings that we have made toxic. That means that deaths attributed to pollution are triple those from AIDS, malaria, and tuberculosis combined.[13] For the first time in human history, life expectancy is dropping in developed societies like the United States and United Kingdom.[14] Conflicts over land, resources, and identity are creating serious social and political turbulence everywhere we look.

Something is clearly wrong at the heart of our modern world. When I burned out and broke down, it became evident that something was equally clearly wrong at the heart of me. At rock bottom, I began to search anew for answers.

Driven by physical and psychological pain (like fibromyalgia and clinical depression), and an overwhelming yearning for peace and purpose, I went to India. Developing a peer-to-peer coaching toolkit by day (which has since evolved into a powerful system for change), at night I decompressed from the rollercoaster ride of fast-paced entrepreneurship. Amidst the fuchsia-colored fabrics flapping in the ocean breezes, I would dance until dawn to throbbing basslines.

After one such night, I had an experience so profound that it shook the foundations of my worldview and reoriented everything I knew about life in its wake. At the center was a realization that I was, in some hard-to-describe way, at 'one' with the entire universe, and that the suffering I experienced so often in life was because of a delusional sense that I was separate and alone. It became clear that all the trinkets I had collected as a materialist obsessed with achievement and recognition were fool's gold. Over time, I came to see that what I truly needed had always been waiting for me within.

This quintessentially mystical experience opened the doors of my perception and showed me a place beyond my chattering mind and aching body where I could find the peace and purpose we all long for. I have since learned to return to this place, whether through meditation, ecstatic dance, or loving intimacy, to take refuge. I have also learned ways to harness this 'spiritual' experience to transform 'bad' habits and negative thoughts, and to step up continuously as a leader, lover, and father.

The only problem was that I was, and still am, an atheist. I am a lover of science and a committed man of reason. I have never been comfortable with New Age platitudes or religious superstitions of any kind. So I needed to make sense of the mystical within the context of everything that I had learned up to that point through science and reason. I was not prepared to give up the rigor of reason to embrace spiritual truths without finding a way to make sense of both together.

Turning to the history books, I discovered that the scientific method evolved as only *one* way, among many, of finding out knowledge about the world. Early scientists like Galileo chose to leave out our interior world when they created science because subjective qualities were hard to measure accurately and consistently. In time, because it was particularly successful at predicting the movements of matter, science was put on a pedestal and became seen by many, including most atheists, as the *only* way of providing useful knowledge about life. Spiritual truths were downgraded, and eventually ignored.

Because of this, for the last hundred years or so we have lived in a world with a deeply diminished view of human experience, one that reduces all value to money, material, and metrics. We set out to scientifically explore the further reaches of our cosmos whilst forgetting how to explore our own inner realm. Many activities and substances that could help us access the mystical were suppressed. Science and reason made redundant the shamans and wise folk we needed to return us to truth and help us change. It was then but a hop, skip, and a jump to denying that our consciousness even existed, as many scientists and materialist philosophers do today.

Trained in science, I was led to believe the mainstream views of scientific materialism: thoughts are merely a side effect of the predictable movement of molecules in the brain (and therefore we have no free will); we cannot experience qualities like love or joy because consciousness itself is an illusion; and we exist as a result of a random chain of events, making life meaningless and the universe pointless.

I, like so many of us, had been conditioned by culture to believe that only physical matter was real. I was expected to be critical of, and cynical about, any claim that didn't use the scientific method to provide proof of its veracity. This kept me stuck in a painful double-bind, holding two beliefs that seemed irreconcilable: I enjoyed a deep love affair with science, without which we wouldn't have many wonderful things, from amazing treatments for Ebola, cancer, and HIV, to airplanes, apps, and algorithms that make life better. But I was also steadily more and more aware of, and in awe of, the mystical experience of 'oneness' that my heart kept sensing was real.

For years I suppressed any 'spiritual' intuitions in order to 'succeed' in a fiercely atheistic, materialistic society. I believed, as so many others do, that I had to choose *either* spirituality *or* science; that I could not have both. This created a schism at the center of my being, divorcing my heart from my mind and my feelings from my thoughts until it all became too much, and I imploded.

It is this schism within us, and in the fabric of our societies, that I believe is responsible for most of our individual and social problems. Because scientific materialism and conventional atheism deny our interconnectivity, sense of meaning and purpose, experiences like peace and joy, and even our consciousness, they are incomplete knowledge bases from which to construct a *bios* that allows us to thrive no matter what the world throws at us. So we, as a species, are far from flourishing.

Materialist beliefs about the primary nature of our world are, contrary to received wisdom, not actually hard facts: they are utterly unprovable using the scientific method. They are opinions, just like those that come from religion. These beliefs, untempered by supposedly 'delusional' ideas like love and compassion, have laid waste to all in their path, prioritizing logic over love, and profit over people. The problems that have arisen because of this—from climate change and mass species extinctions right through to the precariousness of so many jobs and the eruption of so many conflicts in our communities—are all driven by a sense of materialist separation instead of 'spiritual' connection.

A preference for reason over emotion has cut off our intuitive and imaginative abilities and locked us into ailments which we no longer know how to heal ourselves from. We have been trapped into believing that either organized religion and its rules are right; *or* that science-driven atheism, with its physical laws, is real. Yet both religious and rational ideologies, when taken to the extreme, prevent us from enjoying our full human birthright to flourish in the face of all adversity.

But it doesn't have to be this way. I have found that the life-changing mystical experience of enlightenment—and with it an abiding sense that we are connected and loved, which has, perhaps unfortunately, come to be labeled 'spirituality'—can fit perfectly well with a love of science and data. Whether we call the sense of oneness and love 'spiritual' or not, matters less (it's not my favorite word, but it will do for now). What matters is that we find a way to feel it and trust it in our bodies, because it is the missing ingredient for thriving more, and suffering less, in the modern materialist world.

Once spirituality is integrated with science into a *bios* that we can call "spiritual atheism", we can all thrive. With a reliable access-point to connection, imagination, and intuition coupled with accurate data from scientific studies about the material world, we can learn how to consistently alchemize suffering into opportunities for more intimacy and trust in our relationships; more ideas and innovations to relieve genuine suffering around us; and wiser leadership to guide our systems to grow in harmony with our planet. In other words, we can make choices that promote love over lack, and connection over separation.

As we will explore together, spiritual atheism also looks able to provide us with solutions to the great paradoxes of modern thought: how to find transcendent morals that we can believe in, and honor, that do not purport to come from the revealed truths of a god; how to get over the split between mind and body that has dogged materialism and medicine since their inception; and how to understand, if never fully explain, how consciousness arises in a warm, wet brain and body.

To build spiritual atheism into a functioning *bios*, I have had to challenge many of my key assumptions about the modern world. Over time, I have allowed my mystical experiences to transform my metaphysics whilst being careful not to relinquish my commitment to reason. As I have found out through this process, it can be uncomfortable to admit that the assumptions that we have built our life or career on—whether about reason, science, religion, or capitalism—may not be entirely accurate or even particularly helpful. I invite you, if such moments arise, to stay open minded and open hearted. Instead of constructing a mental argument to counter what I have said, perhaps feel into your body, into your muscles, into your intuition and imagination, for other truths. Wisdom teaches us that our grasping, grinding minds get in the way of the openness and vulnerability we need to access love, connection, and enlightenment.

It is within the heart, the metaphorical organ of love, wisdom, and connection, and not the head that we experience the profundity of spiritual unity. Here there are no proofs and no hard facts. There are no final answers or permanent theories. But there is insight and intuition. This is why a shift from mind into heart as our dominant way of experiencing ourselves and our world—from control into co-creation, from protection to connection—poses a challenge to many.

I believe that the rewards are worth it. It is not an exaggeration to say that everything that I have ever *needed*—as opposed to the trappings of 'success' that I thought I *wanted*—I have gotten as a result of uniting both science and wisdom within me so I make better choices, and experience more peaceful, love and joyful moments. If you go on the journey to harmonize your intuitive heart with your reasoning mind, and heal any schism between science and spirituality within that might be causing you unnecessary pain and blockage, you may well find your way to everything you need too.

Much is at stake beyond our own personal happiness. I believe that the political frictions, terror, conflict, economic inequality, and environmental turmoil that we face can all be traced back to the schism within that separates us from ourselves, from each other, and from the planet that we rely on for our very lives. I can trace in everything from the rise of ugly nationalism, to the dominance of daily life by consumerism, to this split within our hearts and minds.

As we enter the Digital Age, we need a new narrative and a new Operating System (OS), to help us all engage with the triple threat that faces us all: global risks like climate change, poverty, resource conflict, terrorism, and depression; advancing Fourth Industrial Revolution technologies, like automation, the blockchain, wearables, 3D printing, the Internet of Things, and AI; and shifting customer, employee, and citizen demands, like seeking empowerment, ethics, purpose, diversity, inclusion, equality, and justice.

For a cultural narrative to work it must make sense of our past, shine a light on a compelling and achievable future, and be underpinned by the best knowledge and wisdom of our times. It must help us locate ourselves as individuals within the complexity of our global system and guide our daily actions. It must also be reasonably simple to share, express, imagine, and debate, whilst avoiding underestimating the capacity of people to understand big, important, and life-changing ideas.

I believe some form of spiritual atheism is the bedrock of just such a narrative. It is a new OS with which humankind can thrive in our relationships with each other and with the planet upon which we depend for all sustenance. Spiritual atheism is underpinned by the majesty of modern science without reducing everything to the movements of atoms and what can be proven with a methodology designed to explain only the *measurable* properties of matter. But it does not fall back into faith-based superstition or dogma; and does not cede control to a priestly class, text, or guru.

Most crucially, spiritual atheism reunites the two aspects of our human nature, consciousness and matter, that have been at war with each other for centuries. No longer set at loggerheads, no longer driven to rule or undermine the other, both parts of ourselves can work together so we thrive; and lead others towards this state too. Spiritual atheism sees the scientific and the contemplative traditions as two different, yet complementary and equally valid, ways of seeing, knowing, and changing the world. Science is the most rigorous way we have found to give us reliable and replicable data about the material world of atoms, gravity, and light. Contemplation, whether through ecstatic movement, tantric experiences, yoga or meditation, is the most rigorous way we have found of building up a consistent knowledge-base of the inner workings of our consciousness so that we can reliably experience compassion, peace, and purpose.

Fused together, we can excel at the quintessentially human skill of being able to purposefully change our minds inside, so that we can transform problems that really matter in our world around us. We can master our conscious experience through wisdom practices that look within; and we master our material world through science and technology that look outside. Understood through heart as much as mind, spiritual atheism is a life philosophy that invites us, calls us, to transform ourselves so we can step up as the confident, courageous, and transformational leaders we can all be and so make the world work for all.

Spiritual atheism, as a new cultural narrative and *bios*, balances our spiritual intuitions to contribute to the world with purpose and love with our materialist instincts to get stuff done and keep ourselves and our kin safe. It provides us with tangible and practical ways to recalibrate capitalism so it works for *everyone,* without the need for big government, or forced equality.

In our times of resurgent Christian, Islamic, Jewish, Hindu, and even Buddhist religious nationalism, which is damaging the fabric of our societies, we must find a pathway to open-hearted 'spiritual' values or risk the world being destabilized once again by dogmatic and dictatorial religion. We need heart-led qualities to be placed back into the core of our existence *without* any dangerous religious dogma or corrosive rational cynicism.

∞

Writing this book in the form of a 'philosophical memoir' was not my default choice. It is much, much safer to write a book about ideas in the 'passive' detached voice of the intellectual. This minimizes anything 'personal' within it that people might react to negatively whilst projecting an air of unassailable expertize. But my intuition and purpose, both rarely convenient, kept telling me to make it *very* personal. During many meditative and contemplative moments, I kept sensing that the book would be most useful to you, the reader, if I used some of my narrative, my trials and realizations, to demonstrate what turned me around from the militant, cynical, yet depressed, hurting and anxious atheist I once was. I share my life with you openly because I sense my specific experiences can make 'generic' wisdom become more real, and so make more of a difference to the suffering I see so many people dealing with each day.

Because of this choice, the book plays out in chronological order, showing how I came into contact with the 'ingredients' necessary to bake a 'cake' of spiritual atheism. I have summarized some working principles for a rigorous and useful life philosophy of spiritual atheism, which I have garnered from various domains of life, at the end of each chapter. Take with a pinch of salt everything I say; and test everything with your own critical faculties. I write from within my middle-class, white(ish), and male body and mind. I was born into a relatively entitled life (although one set of great-grandparents were butchers in Essex and another were Holocaust survivors from Romania). In addition, elements of my protective patterns, the habits I developed to deal with life, may have leaked out onto the pages. Please forgive me this and ignore anything that gets in your way of using this book to find the wisdom you need to thrive. If words I use jibe with you rather than jive with you, please try different ones of your own.

I have endeavored to be as relentlessly honest about my supposed 'successes', mostly profoundly partial and utterly illusory, as much as my many, many failures. To evolve the words of the wisdom teacher Nisargadatta Maharaj: spirituality tells us that we are each powerful beyond our dreams and must act now, today, to relieve the suffering of others. At the same time, science reminds us that we are insignificant motes of cosmic stardust, and that the world will be just fine without us. Between these two seemingly polar opposites, a thriving life of love and leadership can flow.

As I have deepened my connection to the oneness, I have come to realize that my projects, including this book and all the ideas within it, are not 'mine' at all in any sense. Everything we create is owned by us all, whether we copyright it or not. We all have gifts, gifts that we need as a species to thrive in the Digital Age. When we see such gifts as public goods, rather than as an individual's private property, we can unashamedly support each other to bring more of our hidden talents to fruition and so increase the flourishing of people and our planet.

In summary, I have done my best to ask and answer the question that has animated my adult life as rigorously as possible with my available knowledge: what life philosophy can help us make better choices and ongoingly transform ourselves and our systems so that we all suffer less and thrive more? This book is not meant to provide the final answers.

I believe that many aspects of the interaction between matter and consciousness will always remain mysterious no matter how much we meditate within or point microscopes at matter. This is why exploring the connection between the two is the mystery within mysticism.

I sense that we don't need all the answers anyway. As the poet Rainer Maria Rilke suggested, we must "live the questions now." If living such questions is of interest to you, then please join me on my personal journey through the modern world to find a *bios* to thrive no matter what life throws our way.

CHAPTER 1

RELIGION AND ATHEISM: SWAPPING FAITH FOR REASON

I remember the day God died (on me, at least). It was a Saturday morning and I was sitting in West London Synagogue, one of the oldest and largest synagogues in Britain. I was listening to a rabbi read prayers that had been sung, and mumbled, in Hebrew for centuries. I had shown up every Saturday for months, actively seeking glimmers of insight to help me process the emotional baggage of childhood and the complexities of teenage life. I was in search of a balm for my troubled heart and mind. However, the words of the rabbi fell flat on my ears. The ancient rituals and writings about the god of Abraham and the Hebrews, seemed of no use to me as a teenager. They did nothing to assuage my inner pain or provide me with a galvanizing sense of life's purpose.

A couple of years before this crisis of faith in the pews, I had been bar mitzvahed in the same temple of worship. This religious ritual is meant to signal that a child has become fully responsible for their own religious life (and the ethics of their actions). I didn't question having a bar mitzvah ceremony but neither did I choose it consciously. It was just what kids did in my community. So it came and went without any genuine contemplation on my relationship with God. As was the tradition at my synagogue, I memorized the part of the Bible, or *Torah*, I had to read so I could perform it without a hitch (though a year of preparation did not stop me from missing out an entire verse, in my nervousness). I did not engage with it as a piece of religious scripture or as a philosophical text. I repeated the ancient prayers, said my piece, and enjoyed the gifts rolling in. I was a Jew because I had been born one.

It wasn't until the following year, when I started a General Certificate of Secondary Education (GCSE) class in Jewish Studies, that I began to fully engage with the questions that arise when one chooses, for oneself, a religious life. The GCSE is an academic qualification equivalent to a high school diploma. Around the same time, I and a cohort of other kids my age were to graduate as students of the religious school that I had been attending, and teaching in, for a decade. In doing so, we would become full members of the synagogue; there by choice, as adults.

To mark the occasion, we were asked to run the majority of a Saturday morning sabbath service with the rabbis in support. I was chosen to write and deliver the sermon. I had a few months to prepare before I was to stand in front of hundreds of faithful congregants and speak my truth. Faced with the prospect of this public test, I began to delve with sincerity into what Judaism, and faith as a whole, meant to me.

Prior to the birth of the Hebrew religion—and from it the 'daughter' religions of Christianity and Islam, which together account for more than four billion people out of the seven billion or so on the planet—many scholars of religion believe that most tribes engaged with, worshiped, and sacrificed to many gods and spirit entities. But in the deserts of the Middle East, the tribe that would become the Hebrews shifted from an interest in many divine beings or energies to a belief in *one single* god. Because the name of this god could not be fully known or said, the letters YHVH were used whenever he was mentioned (pronounced "Yahweh"; or "Jehovah" in the West). This was the birth of the monotheistic Jewish faith, and the old gods were denounced as "false idols". These old gods eventually became many of the demonic forces warned against within the three great Abrahamic faiths.

This happened roughly between 800 BC and 300 BC in a period that has become known as the Axial Age, a term coined by psychiatrist and philosopher Karl Jaspers.[15] The Axial Age is described by scholars as a period of immense change in many societies across the globe that led to the complex, religiously-inspired cultures we see today. With the Axial Age innovation of Yahweh, the divine became singular: the ultimate cause of all being. Over time, as more and more people worshiped this god, Yahweh became more and more separate from the profane world of his mundane Creation. Yahweh was above, humans were below, and any sense of interconnectedness between the two faded. By the time the teachings of Judaism were passed to me, the prayers lauded an entity that was all-powerful, yet seemed to have very little to do with me. Whatever truth this religion may have had when it first arose in human history, thousands of years of organization and ossification had obscured it.

I recently visited the Israel Museum in Jerusalem, where a rather fine archeological exhibit features artifacts from thousands of years of worship in the Fertile Crescent. According to the museum's literature, even after the Axial Age invention of a singular God, people continued to worship the local pagan gods alongside Yahweh. Over time, there was a push by the powerful to centralize worship of YHVH in Jerusalem, where the religiosity of the people could be controlled by the great and good of the time. A great temple was built, where the rites and rituals of the people could be closely monitored. When the temple was destroyed, first by the Babylonians and then by the Romans, the observance of the 'correct' rites and rituals of the Jewish religion became even more crucial in order for it to survive the diaspora. The Ten Commandments were born soon after; rules to control behavior. They were soon followed by literally hundreds more regulations about how and when to eat, wash our hands, bathe, touch each other, and much more. Today, priests of the Abrahamic religions issue rules about everything, even which foot to use when entering and leaving a restroom.

For a religion to become organized, its codes of conduct and worship must be formalized into rules. The religion can then be scaled and distributed just like any product or service. If this does not happen, the religion must depend on its worshipers' own ideas and ideals of what it means to be religious, which limits the capacity for scale and control. Rules, in the form of temple doctrine, holy scriptures, and sacred rituals, allow for greater spread, but also less freedom. Rules are always a product of their time, fitting the ways of the world from which they emerge.

For example, a rule forbidding Jews to eat shellfish in the middle of a desert, where it would be difficult to keep crab and shrimp fresh, may once have been a smart way to promote survival. But the world is ceaselessly changing, and almost all religious rules become outdated. The rule banning contraception in the Catholic Church is a poor fit for a world in which overpopulation and sexually transmitted diseases might lead to the destruction of us all. As for religious rules against homosexuality, gender fluidity, abortion, and any other form of life choice—pfff. And what more can be said about the horror of priests abusing children in their care; and religious groups covering up child abuse in their communities?

From time to time, wise people arise in a faith and try to reform the rules. If Jesus existed historically, I believe he was a Jew who attempted to rejuvenate the old ways and bring new life to the faith of Yahweh. He wanted to ensure there was a fit between the rules in the Bible's Old Testament and what the contemporary world needed to thrive. Judging by his sayings, he was intent on refocusing the Hebrews on love, compassion, and community as elemental to a good life. But then came others who transformed his wisdom teachings into the rules and regulations of the organized Christian Church. They anointed him as the Messiah, the Son of God, as opposed to a wisdom teacher with fresh insights relevant to his times. Teachings were again replaced by dogmatic rules, just as they had been when Judaism spread from the Temple. The same thing may have happened again when Mohammed's insights were turned into the Koran and Islam became institutionalized.

Judaism, Christianity, and Islam, which all drink from the same monotheistic well, each took the foundational idea of one god and fused it with local traditions to build unique yet overlapping philosophical and theological systems. It is the differences in the rules they encoded to spread the word—their religious dogmas and doctrines—that have led to serious fighting among and within them, resulting in untold numbers of deaths. With the rise of the great religions of the Book, no longer did each person get to seek their own truth. Those in power defined Truth for all, using the words in scripture as evidence that their rules were right. Whilst rules can help the ruled feel safe and comfortable, lessening confusion and reducing the cognitive effort needed to make decisions each day, they also usually become a form of mind control that is used to grab and keep power.

It was in the interests of both religious priests and local royalty (kings, emperors, and caliphs) to turn wise insights into doctrine, stories into scripture, and useful habits into rituals, because then they got to decide who was following the rules properly and who was not. As soon as there are religious rules written down, one group can always claim that their way of observing the rules is more accurate, puritanical, or 'true' than any other. Those in power get to define who is devout and who is a sinner. If anyone resists the power of those in charge, they get labeled as heretics and can be dealt with effectively. They can be excluded from society, have their property taken, and be generally blamed when things go wrong. Whoever controls the narrative has the power to decide who deserves God's love (maybe heaven awaits them)—and who is naughty and going to hell (or prison).

Since the Axial Age, priests have used religious rules to rise to the top of the power hierarchy. In fact, the word "hierarchy" literally means "rule by the sacred". Power and organized religion have become inextricably intertwined. Hierarchy was a vital step in organized religion, as without it priests did not have the luxury of doing their god-focused work—praying, studying sacred texts, carrying our sacrifices, and so on—because they had to spend their time trying to survive like everyone else. In order to move beyond subsistence farming, priests needed someone else to provide for them. By ensuring that worshipers felt obligated to sacrifice food and other riches to one god (or many of them, as in ancient Egypt), a surplus of wealth was created that allowed priests to engage in religious study and worship, which in turn reinforced their power.

As a teenager on the threshold of adulthood, I sat in synagogue listening to the rules and they felt totally redundant to me. Was this God really interested in whether I put a prayer upon my doorpost, refused to eat pork, or washed my hands before eating? Wasn't living with integrity and honor, compassion, and empathy more important?! I began to question not just the rules but the whole power structure of religion.

What may have accelerated my growing disenchantment was that I could understand most of what the rabbis were saying, since the services in my Reform synagogue had as much English within them as they did Hebrew. I was free to analyze the content. Take this typical English quote from the *Siddur*, or book of prayer: "We acknowledge to You, that You are our God and the God of all generations, forever and ever. Rock of our lives, shield of our salvation." As a young man deciding whether to lead a religious life, I was hoping to find spiritual nourishment in words like this. Even now, with more of an understanding of different spiritual traditions, and skills in decoding the surface level of such phrases to find their mystical meanings, these words do absolutely nothing for me.

I spent most of my time searching for some kind of transcendent truth in the primary creation story of the Jewish faith: the covenant, or sacred agreement, that God made with Abram (or Abraham; the extra "ha" in his name was added after the pact was made), the first *bona fide* Jew. It is this covenant I was supposed to have reaffirmed, and taken responsibility for, with my bar mitzvah experience.

The deal, told in the book of Genesis, was simple: Abraham and his descendants were to worship the one God, Yahweh. They were to renounce all other gods, such as Ba'al of the Canaanites. In return, Yahweh would make them the chosen people. He would protect them and care for them and give them the land of Canaan to settle in for all time. This promise is repeated many times in the earlier parts of the Old Testament. Moses led the Hebrews to Canaan to make good on the promise of the covenant. There are many different flavors of Jewish faith, but most agree that this is the key to it all. In fact, Jewish boys are circumcised eight days after they are born to symbolize this covenant with Yahweh. Ouch!

Circumcision. It is one of the oldest religious rules in Judaism, and one that has given me most cause for reflection. Each year, thousands of highly educated Jews subject their children to this ritualized, rule-driven wounding (Muslims do it too, when the child is a bit older). My first son was circumcised, even though I had been an atheist for many years by the time he was born. I made this decision not out of religious faith, but because it's just what Jews do, even if they are not religious. I rationalized this act to myself as something to do with wanting my son to have the same shape and form of member as me so he felt 'normal'. But when the bleeding from his little penis did not stop, and he had to be rushed into hospital and an IV line put into his tiny toe, knowing I had done this to him by choice was agonizing. Even if we think we are free of religion's rights and expectations, they can be so deeply encoded in our orientation to life that they maintain a power over us.

So embedded was this religious rule, passed to me with the power of thousands of years of conditioning, that choosing *not* to circumcise my second child was still extremely hard for me. His mother and I studied the scientific data before we made our decision. Many physicians suggest it is traumatic, that it can be remembered by the child and may permanently alter the brain.[16] Some, including the august American Academy of Pediatrics, say the medical benefits outweigh the costs.[17] So even with the latest scientific data, which is confusing and contradictory, we still had to make a positive choice ourselves using our own reason (and intuition).

To return to my educational program at the synagogue, I realized that in order to be part of the Jewish religion by choice, I had to buy into it all. I had to believe that God was there to protect me as one of his 'chosen' people. I had to worship him as omniscient and omnipotent. I had to remake the covenant between him up there and me down here. But I couldn't push away the feeling that this covenant made no sense at all. The idea that a tribe of desert-dwelling nomads was somehow specially chosen—for what, persecution, neuroses, and sardonic self-effacing humor?—seemed like wishful thinking, particularly given the suffering of so many.

My paternal great-grandparents were wiped out in the Holocaust (we recently laid commemorative stones for them outside their home in Berlin). My grandfather himself was rustled out of Berlin by the *Kindertransport* initiative in early 1939. My maternal grandmother, a brilliant and generous woman who has inspired me to be curious and to learn as much as possible all my life, had to escape from Nazi soldiers who had commandeered her house in Bucharest, Romania. If our God had the powers to intercede, as he apparently did when parting the Red Sea to allow his people to escape Egypt to the Promised Land of Canaan, why did he not intercede during the Holocaust?

The idea of a personal god, a god that can intervene in life and to whom we can pray for favors, made no sense to me at all. What was more, the Old Testament's father-like God seemed angry and capricious all the time. The stories of burning bushes, vengeful acts, murderous tests, and feisty angels did not provide me with poetry to open up my heart. Quite the opposite: it caused me to shrink away. I had enough anger in my own life and didn't need any more.

I was beginning to read psychoanalytic and socialist theory—both pioneered by Jewish atheists Sigmund Freud and Karl Marx—and my critical faculties were developing. The concept of people exalting a male father figure, treating him as if we were lucky to have been blessed by him, seemed like psychological weakness. It appeared to reveal our deep need for a strong parent to tell us what to do. I was turned off by a patriarchal, shame-inducing system that provided people an opiate that seemed to reinforce social inequality and mass disempowerment.

The philosopher of religion Rudolf Otto describes the religious experience as a *mysterium tremendum et fascinans*.[18] A mystery that we are curious about and drawn to (*fascinans*) but also terrified of (*tremendum*). I was neither fascinated by, nor afraid of, the Abrahamic god. I was actually repelled by talk of power and obedience. There was little in the religious services that enabled me to find any sort of transcendence. God was always on the outside, not found within.

The Hebrew word *kadosh*, which forms a very important prayer in the Jewish liturgy, is taken to mean "holy". However, its literal meaning is being separate, apart, other. Right from the start, in Genesis 1:1, the most important ground rule for the monotheistic Abraham religions is laid out: "In the beginning, God created…" From the get-go, the Abrahamic God exists *outside* of his creation. He created the world and is therefore separate from it. It is this apartness, this separation between me and Yahweh, that has always been the main barrier that has prevented me from connecting with any Abrahamic religion.

Back then I did not feel seen, heard, or loved by this separate, almighty God. I felt zero connection at all with the prayers, the rituals, or the paraphernalia. The practice of worship and the study of the Bible seemed fundamentally useless in dealing with the trials and tribulations of my teenage life. Religiosity didn't seem to produce any transformations in my heart, nor did it satisfy my yearning for meaning, love, truth, and connection. The mainstream technologies of the Abrahamic religion, like colorful ceremonies, community activities, and collective mumbling of prayers, were comforting in a kind of homely way. But in terms of easing my growing angst, the whole thing was a fail.

What I wanted were ideas and activities that could liberate me from a growing sense that there was something wrong with me, that I somehow didn't belong, a feeling many, if not most, teenagers have at some point as they grow into young adults. I was intrigued by the *mysterium*, the mystical side of the Jewish tradition, collected together under the name Kabbalah. I found glimpses of it in sayings by Jewish mystics snuffled away at the back of the prayer book. Here I sensed a source of the fullness and ease that I yearned for. Maybe, within the famously strange stories and difficult texts, there was a pathway through the nitty-gritty of everyday life. But as a young teenager I had nobody to show me a path to the mystical. I asked two respected rabbis for help, but they offered me no insights, not even a book to read. With no Google and no online, the path seemed shut to me.

It was time for the graduation service from the religious school. I stepped up to the pulpit and, rather than committing myself to God, I proceeded to critique faith with fiery yet inelegant atheistic notions. I can still see the confused congregation staring back at me as I expounded a precocious teenager's view of atheism in a temple dedicated to the covenant of the one God with his chosen people. I shudder with the naive arrogance of it. Thankfully, my family and the community as a whole were quick to forgive me.

I had come out as a non-believer, and so began a period of my life guided solely by reason and rationality (or so I wishfully thought). Everything about atheism appealed to me. Atheists reject the superstitions of religion and see no need for a belief in a personal god. There is no deity in the atheist's world, whether a white-beard-in-the-sky male Lord or an earthy and fecund female goddess. Atheists resist religious rules of any kind and are deeply suspicious of claims that a text is the revealed word of a god, as opposed to a myth or narrative written by human hand.

Atheism, as well as seeming to be intellectually right, had the added benefit of connecting me more with my father. At that time in my life, I only saw him during school holidays, three or so times a year. My parents divorced when I was two, and he had moved away from London when I was six or so. He was an ardent atheist and socialist. By cutting through religious dogma, I had found a way to kindle an intellectual touchpoint between us.

Atheists believe that using the faculty of reason irrevocably leads to the conclusion that faith is false and religion a lie. This was famously summed up by German philosopher Friedrich Nietzsche when he proclaimed: "God is dead. God remains dead. And we have killed him."[19] God was a casualty of the Enlightenment of the seventeenth and eighteenth centuries.

However, this cost us terribly, according to the German philosopher Ludwig Feuerbach. After centuries of being subjected to organized religion we had become "alienated" from our own human essence. As believers, we had projected our most important subjective qualities, like power, love, and compassion, onto the Abrahamic god. This god then ruled over us and we lost our humanity in the process.[20]

Marx went on to develop the concept of alienation in his critique of the political and economic structures of capitalism. He saw that money, industrial scale, and the profit motive had alienated human beings from each other. People clung to religion to ameliorate the suffering this caused. Religion was, for Marx, "the sigh of the oppressed creature, the heart of a heartless world, and the soul of soulless conditions."[21] I felt the false promise of religion acutely myself at the time. Marx's insight was elemental in my rejection of religion and I became more interested in politics.

After the Enlightenment, we progressively renounced the falsehoods and fantasies of religion in order to embrace the secular and the scientific. Rational ideas bested the dull and dusty rules in bibles and prayer books. After many years of struggle against the power of religious institutions, *logos* (logic and reason) crushed *mythos* (beliefs contained in stories and myths) and left us intellectually emancipated. As the sociologist of religion Max Weber put it, "the fate of our times is characterized by rationalization and intellectualization and, above all, by the *disenchantment of the world.* Precisely the ultimate and most sublime values have retreated from public life."[22] We swapped out enchantment by faith, magical thinking and the, sublime for enlightenment with reason, rationality and science.

As religion was challenged, government became a distinct and separate domain of activity from religion. With the separation of Church and State, millions of people were liberated to worship whomever they chose—or not worship at all. This division between the religious and the political was so important after the French revolution that the principle, called *laïcité* in French, is the basis for Article 1 of the current French Constitution (this principle is causing much public debate in France as French Muslims, who want to wear clothes that match their Islamic faith, are not allowed to in the public sphere). With secular values embedded at the core of the ideal of the State, nobody could be put in prison for not going to church anymore. With this freedom of conscience, atheism went mainstream, especially in intellectual circles.

Charles Taylor, a Canadian philosopher of religion, believes that, for the first time in human history, atheism is the default option for the majority of the educated.[23] Today in the United States, the number of people that categorize themselves as having no religious affiliation at all, called the "nones," has risen from 15 percent to 20 percent in the last five years or so.[24] 59 percent of young adults who attend church regularly when they are kids drop out as adults. In the UK, census data has shown that the number of babies born as Christians in Britain is dropping by about 10,000 a week. If that rate continues, the Christian religion will be over in the UK by 2067.[25]

Atheism has had a major impact on society. Data seemed to show that a rise of atheism as a mainstream belief is linked, positively, to a country's social progress. According to a massive Gallup poll that interviewed over 60,000 people worldwide, countries that are *least* religious generally score higher on the Social Progress Index, which measures how good a country is at delivering on basic human needs.[26] Although we must be careful not to equate correlation (two factors show up together because of an unknown link) with causation (one factor directly causes the other), these statistics are fascinating.

Atheism seems to empower technological and political progress. Rationally then it would be natural to assume that as societies evolve, religion dies out. Except it doesn't: the number of Christians in China will double in the next six years.[27] The number of Muslims worldwide is set to rise by 73 percent, to 2.8 billion, in 2050.[28] Rationality may have disrupted religion from its prime position as an arbiter of truth, but it hasn't gone away by any means.

Atheists must, therefore, still account for the continued, and in some places rising, phenomenon of religion. They usually turn to science to do so. Charles Darwin was not an atheist, but his theory of evolution through natural selection is used by atheists to explain why religious faith still exists. The logic is that religion must have once had a role in helping us survive to pass on our genes but is now a primitive and vestigial left-over, like a cultural tailbone. At best, religion is seen as a tool that helped us play nicely together; a social glue that helped us work collaboratively to survive.[29] Interestingly, the word religion may derive from the Latin *religare*, meaning "to bind tightly".

Another scientific explanation for religion is that it is a by-product of the evolution of conscious awareness. Consciousness helps us plan for the future and so survive better in the present.[30] Since brains can imagine the future, they can also dream up gods: fictions that give comfort but also cause people to kill each other. In essence, reason sees religion as a lie that, at best, is useful and can help us live together in harmony. At worst, it is the cause of all our ills.

New Atheism, the most extreme form of atheism which became popular with the rise of thinkers like Richard Dawkins, goes way beyond a disbelief in god and scripture to state that *everything* to do with gods and religion is damaging and dangerous. [31] To a New Atheist, anything that cannot be investigated scientifically, and proven by the scientific method, does not exist and so must be a lie. I drank this nuevo atheistic Kool-Aid like a thirsty boy that had spent too long in the Negev desert. I believed that religion, and with it, all forms of spirituality—for as a New Atheist I did not see a difference between the two—is bad for society and must be fought tooth and claw by freethinkers, like the one I hoped I was becoming.

∞

Though I happened to be intellectually able as a teenager, emotionally I was in way poorer shape. I had been mercilessly bullied at school for years, a source of constant anxiety and despair. My self-esteem was lower than Barry White's voice, and I was cripplingly shy. I was fast approaching 250 pounds in weight and loathed myself for being obese. I had never dealt with the divorce that rocked my young life; I constantly fought with my mother and stepfather; and I was unable to communicate much at all with my father. On top of this, I was dealing with all the usual questions of an inquiring young mind: Why are we here? What is the point? How do I engage with this thing called life?

Being a New Atheist, I believed that science and logic were the only routes open to me for reliable knowledge about my life and to guide me in the world. So I turned (and was pushed just a little by my well-meaning mother) toward a thorough investigation of my inner life within the atheistic system of psychoanalytic psychotherapy. I began my first encounter with Sigmund Freud's grand attempt to make the analysis of our psyche, or soul, into a science; an experience that was to open my mind, if not my heart, to what lay beneath.

SPIRITUAL ATHEISM PRINCIPLES:

- Be free from any rules, hierarchies, and dogma that have been used to control us and dominate society; and which can block our genuine empowerment, joy, and liberty.
- Realize that old rules, customs, and beliefs can remain embedded within our bodies, minds, and choices long after we think we are free from them.
- Seek principles for wisdom, happiness, and thriving over rules from the past (which quickly become out-dated in a fast-changing world).
- Consciously develop our critical thinking skills so we can analyze and interpret the world free from the rules and belief systems of others.
- Appreciate that the moral foundations of compassion and charity that many religious traditions teach can be a powerful driver of active citizenship; and can prevent us from becoming nihilistic and self-centered.

CHAPTER 2

PSYCHOLOGY AND PSYCHOTHERAPY: THE MIND AND ITS DISCONTENTS

For three years, between the ages of fourteen and sixteen, I obligingly trundled off to my psychotherapist's home every week. These sessions with J___, an expert in his field, were my first, but not my last, experience of Freud's "talking cure". I say talk, but often there was very little of that involved; being an old-school sort of therapist, if I didn't broach a subject, J___ would say nothing and we would sit in an awkward and costly silence for most of the requisite Freudian fifty-minute hour.

I did not walk down the road to his house with a skip in my step. How many teenagers want to swap out after-school TV and shenanigans with friends for a deep analysis of their mind and its discontents? This was not play therapy or art therapy either. It was traditional, subdued-lighting-and-dark-wood-panel psychoanalytic psychotherapy, the kind where your therapist burrows deep into your unconscious mind to analyze *ze real problems wit you.* However, it did promise a god-free way to explore , and perhaps tame, my inner demons.

I was not in short supply of them, struggling as I was with the after-effects of my early life experiences. As the fat kid at school—there is always one, and I was he—I was bullied by kids and teachers alike. I was also regularly criticized and shamed by some of the key adults in my life; and was spanked more often than anyone would like, a practice shown by science to increase the chances of kids having mental health problems.[32] Research has also shown that social exclusion, bullying, and shaming hurt our brains in the same place, and with the same intensity, as physical pain.[33] Sticks and stones break our bones; words break our hearts and minds. Psychological pain can last an entire lifetime, even turning into physical ailments if not addressed.

What hurt most at the time, though, was that I didn't have a girlfriend. All I wanted was to feel loved and wanted, but I was not to enjoy that for many years to come. I became paralyzed with fear around girls, convinced my obesity made me unlovable. This reinforced my growing sense, which had begun years earlier when I was a child of divorce, that there was something wrong with me. This belief was to hang over me for years.

My many sessions inspired me to pay attention to the ceaseless marvels of the human mind and the profound challenge of how to understand ourselves. Engaging with psychoanalytic theory gave me a valuable introduction to the power of self-awareness and the importance of our past in our psychological health. It helped me understand the fact that our hidden issues within will cause us problems in our everyday life until we resolve them. I was fascinated by the field and went on to study it a few years later.

The rise of psychology and psychoanalytic theory has normalized the process of getting to know our own mind and what lies beneath everyday consciousness. It is now acceptable to try to heal psychological pain by talking about our experiences, feelings, and beliefs, instead of relying solely on drugs and other more extreme medical interventions. That may not seem like a big deal, but talking through our problems, though presumably a mainstay of human culture since tribes began, has long been marginalized. By the time we entered the Victorian age, way before psychotherapy and counseling, cognitive behavioral therapy, and life coaching become mainstream (even if they still have social stigma in some circles), dealing with mental anguish was typically either the preserve of an "alienist", the forerunner of today's psychiatrist; or it was a problem for a priest. The alienist would try to cure you with a stay in a madhouse or a frontal lobotomy.[34] The priest might try to cure you with prayers if you had fallen from grace, or with an exorcism if you were thought to be possessed by demonic spirits.[35] Everyone else with the kind of chronic, low-grade mental suffering and emotional stuckness that is endemic in our society today had to suck it up and get on with it.

As the Enlightenment dawned, people began to pose theories about what caused psychological maladies, but psychology was a long way from being a discipline, let alone a science. This changed in the middle of the nineteenth century, when researchers began experimenting with various tools to uncover the hidden causes of certain diseases. In particular, there was a lot of interest in decoding the phenomenon of "hysteria", a condition of 'excessive' emotion. Hysteria, a profoundly misogynistic term if ever there was one, was derived from the Greek word for "womb". Assumed to be an exclusively female disease, the Ancient medic Hippocrates believed it was caused by movement of the uterus.[36] This chimed with the reigning view amongst Victorian men: that women were irrational, which is why they were not given the right to vote by their oh-so-rational husbands, brothers, and fathers until well into the twentieth century.

Sigmund Freud started out as a young doctor working in Vienna with Joseph Breuer, a physician who had successfully treated a hysteric called

Anna O by asking her to describe precisely what she was thinking and feeling before a fit. Anna O called this experience her "talking cure", a term that has stuck to psychotherapy ever since.[37] Breuer sponsored Freud to go to Paris to study with French neurologist Jean-Martin Charcot, who opened a specialist clinic at the Salpêtrière Hospital in Paris in 1882.

The clinic quickly became a mecca for anyone interested in the emerging field of psychology. Both Charcot and Breuer were experimenting with hypnosis, a promising technique for treating hysteria. Freud believed it could accelerate the 'cathartic', or cleansing, process of talking things out. He theorized that hypnosis could provide evidence that humans held memories and ideas of which they were not conscious. He started to experiment.

Some trace the roots of hypnosis back to ancient Greece, India, or Egypt, but it was the German Franz Mesmer who popularized the practice in Europe in the eighteenth century.[38] "Mesmerism" is still used as a pejorative term for hypnosis. Mesmer achieved cult-like status by using hypnosis to treat patients with hysteria in dramatic stage shows. He turned hypnotic induction into a theatrical art form. However, he also developed a wildly speculative theory about what was happening to patients under hypnosis, claiming that magnetic forces were the driving power that created both health and disease (as well as planetary motion and the tides). His ideas about "animal magnetism" were discredited as nonsense by the scientists of the day, and many dismissed hypnotism as bogus, too. These negative associations still cloud the perception of hypnotism.[39] I use some of the principles and practices of hypnotherapy regularly, but it took many years to be able to use it (and write about it) without feeling intellectual guilt.

Freud experimented early in his career with both the straightforward talking cure and hypnosis to treat his patients. He used them as tools to tease out what had been "repressed", as Freud termed it, inside the psyche of his patients: memories and thoughts that were undermining their happiness and health. The cathartic release of these dark materials became the fundamental goal of therapy. But Freud soon abandoned hypnosis and its snake-oil associations. He developed what he believed was a more rational, intellectual approach to the talking cure called "free association", which became the core of psychoanalysis.

In free association, patients are encouraged to make connections between memories, symbols, and emotions, but without going into a hypnotic trance. This process is meant to allow the psychoanalyst to help the patient release repressed matter in the unconscious, or what Freud called the "id", According to Freud, the id contains our primitive and instinctual drives and our hidden memories and traumas. The point of therapy is to resolve the conflicts between our id and other parts of us within.

The concept of repression is essential for understanding the way we develop psychological conditions. The theory is that we repress painful feelings and thoughts, pushing them deep into our unconscious, as a defense mechanism because they are too awful or shameful for us to consciously engage with. Our hidden instincts and urges then drive self-sabotaging behaviors and addictions. To keep our memories and desires repressed takes up a lot of energy, leaving us exhausted and perhaps even depressed.

When I started psychoanalytic psychotherapy with J___, unbeknownst to me, he was seeking to find and cleanse away repressed memories and feelings that he believed were the cause of my teenage angst. But the rational, talking process did not seem to work well on me. I never once cried in any of the sessions. I kept feeling dark inside. The drain on my energy from negative feelings and memories from my earlier childhood, as well as daily abuses from bullying, depleted me often. This would be followed by good times, during which my childlike exuberance shone through. I oscillated between these periods regularly, as many of us do. My inner world was still full of the innate human curiosity and joy we have as children. It often exceeded the sadness and disappointment; but the blue periods got darker and lasted longer over time.

I believe that part of us, what I have come to call Control and Protect Mode, wants to protect us from having to experience again the inevitable disappointments and frustrations of childhood. This protective part of us wants to control a scary world as best it can. It causes us to attempt to be certain about what is right and wrong, so we do not feel out of control. It learns a set of rules to keep us safe. These rules prioritize protection and control above all else. We invent our own rules and mimic those of others. The rules are manifested in our behaviors, beliefs, and emotional habits. They are designed to protect ourselves from either a lack of loving attention (when extreme, called neglect); or too much painful attention (when extreme, called abuse).

As we grow into adulthood, we keep on using the old rules and habits to deal with the challenges we face. They become conditioned into our nervous system as "patterns" that we use many times a day to get by. Here are three patterns that I developed as a teenager: I ate to feel loved and in control, a habit exacerbated by a Jewish culture that uses food as a proxy for love. I learned to be 'smart' so I was successful and could outfox bullies. And I developed a 'funny' persona, the Greek term for "mask", so that I would be liked. These habits, and many others, were in my rulebook for dealing with life.

Such habits and patterns may work to keep threats at bay when we are kids, but they start to fail as we grow up. What once protected us from feeling hurt or threatened now starts to sabotage our potential, causing more problems than it solves. Eating too much food, being a smarty-pants, and acting like the school joker may have worked when I was ten to help me feel OK, but by the time I was sixteen these habits were leading me to a fail. I was fat. I was seen as arrogant, even though inside I was a crumbling mess of insecurities. At the same time, people didn't take me seriously because I was always joking around.

We've evolved so that the protective part of us dominates our lives because it is vital in keeping us alive. It is the essence of our drive to survive. In early childhood, the anxiety of feeling separate from our parents, which is an inevitable and necessary experience as we grow into individuals, can feel like a threat to our existence and so generates patterns. Control and Protect Mode is always looking for threats to our existence, whether real, like an oncoming car, or imagined, like a workplace slight. When we feel threatened we enact whatever protective response we have learned or created. Stress, anxiety, and uncertainty—hallmarks of modern life—all trigger protective patterns. We repeat patterns for the rest of our lives unless we learn how to master, but not control, our own biology.

Control and Protect Mode's role is to keep us alive. It takes its role very seriously and it will defend us at all costs. So Control and Protect Mode resists interventions, like psychotherapy, that try to get it to stop defending and start relaxing. Control and Protect Mode does not do this because it wants us to be unhappy, but because it must use the rulebook created when we were kids to protect us from any perceived threat to its own activity. To enjoy the benefits of self-transformation we must be able to get out of Control and Protect Mode, somehow, so that we can let go of the old rules long enough to have insights that help us heal. The kind of therapy I had both at school and later, during and after university was not able to show me how to do this. So I remained stuck, defending myself against the change I yearned for.

This is why meditative or hypnotherapeutic interventions are so powerful: they drop beneath the radar of Control and Protect Mode and engage with others parts of our consciousness. In fact, Freud is said to have admitted that hypnotherapy techniques were easier and quicker to apply than talk-driven psychoanalysis because they can get around our resistance to transformation.[40] However, when he gave up on it, all that was left was words and analysis. Because the therapy I had was all talk, the 'smart' protective pattern in me could defend me from the ideas of my therapists. So I resisted change.

How defensive we are in general, and particularly in moments of uncertainty and doubt, seems to be largely dependent on the quality and strength of our initial relationships with our parents and other loved ones. One of the key tenets of modern-day psychotherapy, brought to the fore by intellectual heirs of Freud such as therapists Alfred Adler and John Bowlby, is that the connections we form (or don't) with our caregivers create templates with which we then approach all relationships later in life.[41]

Our childhood experiences, particularly those in which our sense of love, trust, and safety are first generated, set the tone and tenor for every subsequent interaction. If our early relationships don't leave us feeling safe, secure, and 100% sure that we are totally lovable, it is hard for us to build intimate and open-hearted relationships as adults—or teenagers. As I found out so clearly in my attempts to find romance, if we have an unlovable template within, we will find it hard to be loved by others.

According to Bowlby's Attachment Theory, positive early attachments provide a lasting imprint of security in our relationships.[42] With these firmly forged, we can explore the world feeling safe and connected. But if we experience anything other than a secure attachment, because our early caregivers cannot or will not give us the love and safety we need in the way we need it, we have challenging relationships with others until we find a way to transform the templates within. We will find it hard to achieve intimacy, and be vulnerable with people, because our attachment imprints activate defensive patterns: characteristic emotions, thoughts (usually negative beliefs about ourselves, others, and the world), and behaviors. We employ such patterns to deal with moments of insecurity and doubt in later relationships, romantic or otherwise. The tragicomedy is that our patterns are usually both ineffective and inappropriate, as they are based on an old set of outdated rules rather than being responsive to the moment.

Given how long it took me to be able to have lasting and loving relationships, it is likely that I had a wonky attachment template for love and connection. My parents had a tempestuous relationship by all accounts, full of upsets and betrayals of trust on both sides. There was an unpleasant battle for custody during my early years. My mother, with whom I am now extraordinarily close after years of mutual effort to create an intimate and supportive relationship on both sides, revealed to me a few years back that she had had trouble bonding with me in my first two years of life. She was often frightened of me and my needs. This is the exact time period in which my core relationship template for life was generated.

Such maternal ambivalence and inconsistency is more common than many might think and, in my case, led to me having elements of ambivalent, and also disorganized, attachment: I craved connection with people but also pushed them away because I did not fully trust that safety, love, and attention would be there for me. The habits that I developed to get attention would often fail, leaving me confused and broken.[43] This patterning was to arise for many years in my intimate relationships. Those with attachment challenges like mine are also more likely to be bullied.

Check. Because I did not have a secure base from which to explore the world, any sense of diminished status in a group of my peers would usually lead to intense emotions like panic and despair.[44]

The real kicker for my happiness and self-esteem was when my father left London for a new life up north. Admirably, he left the ad industry to become a social worker and probation officer, which required a massive salary drop that made London life tough. I went from seeing him every few days to just visiting him in the school holidays. Here I saw absolute confirmation of my burgeoning belief that I was the one who forced other people away because I was bad/wrong/evil. The profound loss of my father, and the feeling of abandonment that came with it, drove a painful wedge into my heart.

I watched how other people around me dealt with their own lack and pain, and I mimicked it. I started eating food, often a Jewish proxy for love, like it was going out of business. I wasn't allowed candy at home, so I ate it in secret, at school and after school. I ate (and, over time, drank alcohol, smoked, worked, and much else besides) to paper over the pain. I ate to abuse a body I thought was worthless, rejected, abandoned. I ate to feel free. I soon felt like an alien from Planet Fat who had found himself in the Land Of the Skinny. Kids used to call me "Roland", referring to the fat kid in a legendary school-based drama series called *Grange Hill* that was on TV in the early eighties in Britain. He was an obese no-hoper, bullied by everyone. Like him, getting changed in the locker rooms for sports was a moment of daily dread.

The feeling of not belonging, first felt within my family and then reaffirmed at school, persisted long into adulthood. I was alienated from my body for years. I stayed in my head, full of cleverness and craziness in equal measure. I didn't have an empowering narrative to make sense of what had happened to me as a young child. Instead, like many kids of divorced parents, I blamed myself: it feels safer in Control and Protect Mode to blame ourself than it does to perceive our parents to be at fault, and therefore that they are incapable of ensuring that we survive.

This sowed the seed of a punishing lack of self-love. Quite simply, I believed, deep down, that I was in some way bad, even evil. Because of this, my experience of connection to myself, others, and the world as a whole was full of doubt and anxiety. Even my close friendships were haunted by the fear I would be excluded, mocked, and rejected, as I had been so many times before. I was perpetually on tenterhooks, sure that what little safety I felt would all come tumbling down in an instant. I became hypervigilant to verbal threats and social exclusion. I was trigger unhappy.

For years, I would walk into a meeting or nightclub and assume that people were mocking me, teasing me, or just did not want me there. I would mind-read, as psychologists call it, assuming I knew that someone was putting me down without checking with them or reflecting on it. I would then act the part, becoming dismissive, arrogant, or needy in my attempt to protect myself from the perceived threats.

Our patterns are shaped by our parents' patterns. Theirs are, of course, shaped by imprints from their childhood, as they do the best they can with their beliefs and baggage. Patterns get recreated from generation to generation. They can get passed down as family beliefs about life, or as coping strategies displayed by our elders that we end up mimicking. Patterns can even be expressed through our genes. An emerging field of science called epigenetics has suggested that stress can influence how DNA gets expressed. More shockingly, these changes in DNA expression seem to be able to be passed down to kids and even grandkids. One study has shown that survivors of the Holocaust can pass on a heightened stress response from the trauma they experienced during life to their children.[45]

According to Dutch psychiatrist and pioneering PTSD researcher Bessel van der Kolk, trauma is what happens when an experience overwhelms our biology's capacity to deal with it effectively, in the moment. The result of this failure to process in the moment is that traumatic experiences stick around in our body: viscera, nerves, and brain. They alter the way we process and recall memories. And they keep us repeating patterns as a way to defend against anything that looks like it might traumatize us again.[46] Many of us have had traumatic experiences that have been encoded within our cells, which then trigger patterns with us. We pass these patterns, and possibly even the trauma, down to the next generation.

Whatever the specific history, most families have gone through very challenging times, leaving an indelible mark on us all. Whether stressful experiences of famine, oppression, or emigration, we are all impacted by the long past. Most families pass on powerful, yet ultimately destructive, patterns for dealing with life to the next generation: negative beliefs, persistent moods, abusive behaviors, addictive habits. Which means we all have to find a way to transform them if we want to flourish as times change.

The Greek word for thriving (as opposed to pleasure), *eudaemonia*, means having friendly demons within. I desperately wanted psychotherapy to help me transform the nasty demons inside me into friendly ones. But the field's focus on analyzing words rather than understanding the entire mind and body seemed to make this transformation impossible. Freud's disdain of anything irrational seems to come from his desire to make psychoanalysis a science. Psychoanalysis literally means the splitting into pieces (analysis) of the soul (psyche). Freud, like many early psychologists, saw the mind as a scientifically explorable domain that could be studied in the same way the natural world could be by a physicist.

Freud was an uncompromising atheist who had, like me, been put off by the Jewish faith of his birth. He believed that religion was a neurotic belief that we fabricate to overcome the fear of our own death (and the reality of our vulnerability in nature). It was his view that I echoed in my sermon. In his book *The Future of An Illusion*, Freud hopes that science will replace the delusions of faith with rationality and reason. Perhaps encouraged by a craving to be respected as a genuine scientist himself, he excised, or perhaps exorcised, much of the transformative wisdom out of both the theory and practice of psychoanalysis.

This is evident in how serious the process usually is. Psychotherapists distance themselves from their clients much as scientists remain detached from the atomic particles they study. The therapist becomes an objective observer of us, the subject of the therapy. During three years we spent together, my first therapist never disclosed a *single* thing about himself or his life. There wasn't even a photo or *tchotchke* in his treatment rooms, either. Nothing to suggest that he was just as vulnerable and flawed a human being as his patients.

I believe that Freudian psychoanalysis got carried away with rational analysis of the mind—and with forging elaborate theories to explain it—instead of engaging in the rich joy (and pain) of being alive. But there was one psychoanalyst, though, who tried to break out of the rationalist box. This endlessly fascinating thinker, the Swiss doctor Carl Jung, was the first major breakaway from Freud's inner circle. His oeuvre forms a rich, holistic exploration of the multi-dimensional nature of human consciousness. He challenged Freud's science-loving ways, suggesting that Freud's theories were confined by an "outmoded rationalism".[47] As such, Jung advocated placing genuine transformation—a change of body and heart as much as mind—into the core of therapy.

Jung believed that we all have a "shadow" within us: his word for painful emotions and the protective patterns we cover them with (as well as the parts of us that are amazing, but that we cannot accept because we have low self-esteem). This shadow is outside of our conscious understanding of who we are. My shadow included the ideas that the divorce of my parents was my fault (and that I therefore repelled people); that my mom didn't connect with me early on because I was unlovable; and that I should act in various defensive ways to protect myself and get the attention I craved.

Transformation occurs when we take this "dark side" and shine a (loving) light on it. We process the painful shadow and transform it into a sense of strength and empowerment. We recapture the wasted energy that is caught up in repression and the qualities of our character that we have denied. Over time, we integrate the energy and qualities within our transformed selves. We take those pesky demons and we love them so much that they eventually stop trying to protect and control all the time, and become friendly: our best buddies, in fact.

∞

Toward the end of my first three year course of therapy, it was time to choose what I was going to focus on as a career. As a kid, my parents and grandparents were constantly inspiring me with their acts of generosity and service to society. Charity, *tzedekah,* is a core moral principle in Judaism, and my folks always did a lot of charitable work. Being of service was built into my cultural and familial DNA, so I wanted to do something that was of value to society. I was okay at science so becoming a doctor seemed like it would fit the bill.

Inspired by therapy, and perhaps because it had not worked in the way I hoped it would, it became clear to me that I wanted to know more about the human mind. I assumed that the best way to do this was to be even more scientific and rational (as opposed to developing a sense of intuition and wisdom) and so I aspired to become a psychiatrist. I vividly remember the moment I received an embossed letter from Queens' College, Cambridge, offering me a place to study medicine there. Someone had seen potential in the fat, four-eyed loser I saw myself to be. However, before I could go 'up' to study science, the letter asked me to take a year out. Perhaps they thought I could do with some maturing.

I took them up on both their offer and their suggestion. I had been devouring novels about China, so thought I would explore the Far East, but all the programs that I contacted were full at that late stage. I don't remember how, but I found out about a little-known organization that sent high-school kids to what seemed like deepest, darkest Africa to teach. They had a couple of spaces left on the program, so I and one of my best mates signed up.

We had no idea what to expect, as we had done very little research on the country or the program. It sounded exciting and extreme, so we went for it. Without training of any kind, the next thing we knew we were being hired by Robert Mugabe's government in Zimbabwe to teach science in remote rural schools. This was shortly after a dreadful civil war had finished that had pitched the minority whites, who ran the country, against the majority black population, who were excluded from power and wealth.

I would soon be teaching the children of guerrilla soldiers in a part of the world that would leave me a changed man.

SPIRITUAL ATHEISM PRINCIPLES:

- Be aware of the many unconscious and often hidden causes of suffering, 'stuckness', and stress within us. This subjective content includes traumatic experiences, pain/fear memories that have been repressed, and the stories we tell that limit us. These will cause suffering in the form of mental anguish, physical pain, chronic health problems, addictions, repeated relationship crises, and reduced leadership capabilities until we address them.

- Seek to always recognize and release repressed inner content when it arises in everyday life. Until we learn how to do this elegantly, and can effectively integrate the results into a stable way of being as we develop, we will always be locked into self-sabotaging habits that diminish us and other people.
- Realize that we all create and mimic protective patterns to ensure we feel safe, cope with chaos, and survive the toils and trials of life. Even if they sabotage us in later life, they have logical reasons to exist when formed: protection.
- Take full responsibility for our experiences of life and the protective patterns of thought, emotion, and behavior we use to navigate it. Our stories, moods, and habits will own us until we own them.
- Actively seek to release old pain, trauma, and disappointments from our bodies and minds. Protective patterns can only be let go of and transformed when they are no longer needed for safety and survival.
- Understand that everything may not happen for a reason. However, everything can be harnessed for a reason: for our growth, transformation, and expansion.

CHAPTER 3

TRAVEL AND ANTHROPOLOGY: MY HEARTBEAT BEGAN IN AFRICA

My trip to Africa did not get off to a promising start. The creaking and squeaking old plane that took us from London to Harare, the capital of Zimbabwe, was crammed with passengers. A few hours into the flight, there was a technical problem with the plane and we landed in Italy. A few hours later, we were forced to make an emergency landing at a military base in an unknown African country. We looked out the window and watched as soldiers streamed towards the 747.

Gulp.

Finally, the pilot advised us that we had landed because we had run out of fuel. With the air conditioning turned off, we were sweltering in our seats, but we were not allowed off the plane. Then the water ran out, causing everyone to become a little delirious with thirst. It was a fitting welcome to the often vaudeville-like vagaries of African travel. Thankfully, within a few hours, our tumbledown plane was back in the air, and we reached our destination soon after.

Africa. They say once she has gotten under your skin—once you have been seduced by her deep, red dirt—you can never shake her loose. I was, eventually, utterly smitten by her and her charms. Traveling alone in other people's cultures, all over the world, would also become a consolation for me. However, my first few lonely months away from home were absolutely dreadful.

The program I had joined was a ramshackle affair, with little organization and even less pastoral care. Within a few days of arriving, I was driven in a pickup truck on the road towards Mozambique and dropped off in a rural village in the northeast of the country. Another brutal civil war, in which a million or more people died, was in its last stages less than a hundred miles away. All I had to accompany me into this former British colony was what would fit into my backpack. I was shown to a dark room with hole-pocked concrete walls.

The place reeked of paraffin, the cooking fuel of necessity in the bush. There was no electricity for thirty miles. There was no running water, either. Everyone got the water they needed each morning from a pump in a field near the school. And the toilets: al fresco "long drops" thick with mosquitoes. It was a long, long way down, as I discovered when my wallet fell into the darkness one day. At night, I would listen, melancholy, to the BBC World Service on a small battery-operated radio that caught and lost the signal multiple times an hour. The nearest payphone was ten miles away along a dirt track that few cars ever went down.

My new roomie, the first of my life, was an intense African man in his thirties. He greeted me with hardly-disguised disdain. He turned out to be an ardent Marxist-Leninist, a position I had some sympathies with, who had recently returned to Zimbabwe after studying socialist politics and education in Fidel Castro's Cuba. He was no lover of white capitalists, especially, it seemed to me, young, spoiled ones like I was (though he is not alone in that). He spoke stilted English and didn't seem remotely interested in connecting with me—in fact, the sight of me seemed to enrage him.

Given that his people had been recently brutalized by a white supremacist regime created by the descendants of British colonists, this was utterly understandable. However, this did not help the eighteen-year-old version of me, full of triggers around being rejected, feel safe and happy in my new home.

The school day started at 8 a.m. and I usually graded books by candlelight until 8 p.m. As many discover, teaching is not easy. I had taught kids at Jewish religion school, but that was just a hobby. Now I was having my first true taste of the difficulty of leading scores of kids towards a better way of thinking about themselves and the world. While most people on the program taught English, I was required to teach science—concepts such as the industrial process of making steel and the central mechanics of cell biology—to my students in a language that they were simply unable to read, write, or speak well. English was the official language of both the school and the country, and the Zimbabwean government aspired to British standards of education even as they were busy building a fiercely post-colonial and quasi-socialist society.

The brilliant Brazilian post-colonial thinker and educator, Paulo Freire, suggested that no educational system can emulate models from colonial oppressors and still be empowering.[48] I found this to be true. My kids were utterly uninspired to learn what I had to teach them. It seemed useless to their everyday lives but it was the only content I was allowed to impart. Struggling to connect with them and perform as a teacher, I fell back on the only template for education I knew, which was that of a British school. I used the techniques my teachers had used to get their students to listen and, perhaps, learn: I made them leave the class or write lines on a blackboard if they were misbehaving. Few of these charming Victorian-era educational approaches worked to engage or educate. I could not reach my students in a way that felt meaningful. The rational content didn't reach them, and neither did the petty punishments I mimicked.

The books I graded each night were mostly full of incomprehensible sentences. Occasionally a correct answer interrupted the uniform sea of red crosses. Most of the kids could barely afford the school fees, let alone exercise books, so their homework was given to me on scraps of paper from the bags that ground maize, the staple food source in the country, came packaged in. For this work I was paid about $100 per month, a prize salary in Zimbabwe. Most teachers had to use it to support their nuclear and extended families.

It was hard to keep track of who I was teaching and who I wasn't. Kids came and went from my classes depending on whether their parents had the money for school that week or not. Maintaining their attention and creating a fertile learning environment in the class was not easy. Although pupils enrolled in my class were supposed to be between thirteen and sixteen, some were in their twenties. They had not yet finished school because of illness, poverty, or both. Many towered above me, sometimes ten years older than I was. Some walked an hour or more each way to get to school and back. Some had to shuck maize or plow dirt before they set off and after they got home. They were often exhausted and in need of sleep. It was a challenging experience for everyone.

Outside of school, village life began to draw me in. Within a few months some of my keenest pupils invited me to meet their parents who lived in the surrounding villages. I remember my first time socializing within a traditional circular mud hut, about a forty-five minute walk from the school. I entered and was greeted by an entire family beaming with pride. A fire had been built in a depression in the center of the circle, and the billowing smoke caused me to cough. We conducted initial greetings done through a confused medley of hand signals, as the parents spoke no English.

I was offered a clay pot to take some food from. Without electric lights or even candles, which were too expensive for most people in the village, it was too dark to see what I was picking out from the pot. I peered through the shadows to see a chicken's head in my hand. Adroitly, I hoped, I snuck it back in the pot. Next out was a chicken's claw. I didn't feel I could reject another piece for fear of offending my hosts, so I forced myself to nibble around the edges for the next hour or so while we shared the meal.

My excited student acted as an interpreter so we could exchange jokes and learn a little about each other. Afterward, as he walked me part of the way back to my village, he told me that one of their very few chickens had been slaughtered to honor me. I returned home deeply moved, feeling truly honored, respected, and seen. I was also damn hungry.

Not everyone was quite so friendly, though, which triggered more patterns around social exclusion. I felt particularly self-conscious when I walked past the local bottle store, where a bunch of forty-something men hung out looking as haggard as pensioners. A bottle store is a bar and liquor store that is often the social hub of many villages in southern Africa. When I walked past the men would sneer at me, perhaps a symbol of the unwelcome return of the white man. When they had money, they drank bottles of lager. When they were down on their luck, they drank cartons of a stinky home-brew called *chibuku:* a thick sludge looked, and tasted, to me like a drunkard's vomit after eating a large bowl of porridge.

I found out from my teacher colleagues that these men had been freedom fighters during the civil war. They had fought for their country's independence against the well-equipped military forces of white-minority Rhodesia. It had only become Zimbabwe after independence in 1980. The

British government, Rhodesia's former colonial master, had supported majority rule, but the white Rhodesians had declared independence from the UK in the mid-sixties. The war, which was mostly played out in the bush in which I was now living, had been long and brutal. Some nights I would drink a bottle or two at the store, looking into the eyes of these wasted veterans, seeing how much anger still seethed in their hearts. I wish I'd had the wisdom and wherewithal to offer them my compassion, my solidarity, and my apologies. I guess they just saw me as another foreigner colonizing their space.

Ever since Bartolomeu Dias circumnavigated the Cape of Good Hope in 1498, firing the starting pistol that set off the race to colonize every corner of the planet, pretty much every non-European country has been forced to engage with the long-lasting, and usually deleterious, impacts of imperial domination. Often using both religion and science as a justification, the powers of Western Europe clambered over the globe to grab land.

The religious rationalization, driven by the salvation doctrine of Judeo-Christian theology, was that there was an urgent need to convert the heathens so their souls could be saved. The scientific rationalization was that it was the duty of the smart and rational Europeans to liberate inferior cultures from the dark ages.[49] Colonists really believed they were bringing the efficiencies of the modern world to the natives. This narrative was still being played out by many white former-Rhodesians I met. I would hitch rides with them back to my school, and they'd hold forth on how insane I was to teach the 'blicks.'

Of course, the real impetus behind the Victorian "Scramble for Africa" was that the European powers wanted to carve up the continent between them so they could extract resources, become more wealthy, and build up their military prowess. The veterans of the war for Zimbabwe were living evidence of how long the wounds from such a project take to heal. Whenever I walk around the grand cities of Europe, looking at the mighty banks and government buildings, I picture the colonized men and women whose backs were whipped, limbs amputated, children stolen, and lives diminished to carve out the stones and pay for the construction. The impact of this violence was still being felt in the villages I visited across southern Africa. Its impact can also still be felt in most North American cities too.

Imperial colonialism was a naked display of the "will to power", the term Nietzsche used to describe the drive to dominate other people and the planet. Encouragement to colonize is found in the Book of Genesis: "And God said, 'let [man] have dominion over the fish of the sea, and over the fowl of the air, and over the cattle, and over all the Earth, and over every creeping thing that creepeth upon the Earth'." Built into the Judeo-Christian worldview is permission to own and use nature (and supposedly 'lesser' races) for our own needs. Heirs to this will to power, rational science and industry saw India, Africa, and America as laden boughs, full of resources, ripe for the plucking. Unhampered by love and compassion, an activated Control and Protect Mode can easily fuel a limitless hunger for power over others and nature itself.

Frantz Fanon, a man of mixed race born in the French colony of Martinique, was another great post-colonial thinker who wrote many books on the psychological impact of colonialism. A descendant of African slaves himself, his works burn with brilliant indignation. The most famous, *The Wretched of the Earth*, is a seminal study of the dehumanizing logic of colonialism.[50] He saw such enterprises as purposefully setting about to transform native peoples into objects (like those that science studies) of economic value for their imperial masters. Using threats, laws, thievery, and violence, colonization forced millions, perhaps billions, into mental and physical slavery. Fanon suggested that colonization also enslaves the colonizer, with both master and slave locked in a neurotic grip that makes all suffer.

Fanon, a psychiatrist who treated both colonists and indigenous people alike with innovative therapies, believed that the trauma of colonization could only be healed through violent revolution. The hope of a society-wide catharsis transforming colonial inferiority into nationalist empowerment is what brought Robert Mugabe (and many other post-colonial big men) into power. But even with revolutionary socialism taking root in Zimbabwe, the inner psychological trauma of many of its freedom fighters remained unhealed. The angry revolution that Fanon prescribed had done little to create the prosperity and peace people wanted.

A few years after I left, the conflict re-emerged and, transmuted into social and economic warfare, went on to rip apart this beautiful country once again. As I knew personally, upset driven by pain keeps coming up, in one form or another, until it is released. This is why violent revolution rarely, if ever, leads to lasting peace. Just down the road in South Africa, Nelson Mandela, who consciously chose to cleanse his psyche of anger through spiritual practices during twenty-seven long years of political imprisonment, showed us that finding peace within can lead to peace without.

As a young adult, my own emotional pain consumed me. Around this time, the walls of protection I had erected so firmly in my mind to keep the baffling and bewildering world at bay came crashing down. I had been reading *Zen and the Art of Motorcycle Maintenance*, by Robert Pirsig. Rejected by more publishers, more times, than any other bestseller, it has since sold millions of copies. The narrator drives across the United States from East Coast to West, reflecting on deep philosophical topics, in particular the tension between rational and romantic (irrational, emotional, creative, and spiritual) ways of seeing the world. Toward the end of the book, the hero goes insane from his intense philosophical deconstructions.

This schism between rationality and wisdom within our society, and within most of us, had been preoccupying me more and more as I realized that rationality was a fail for thriving in Zimbabwe. My intellect was not helping me find intimacy with a girl, nor was it helping me connect with my pupils or the local culture. As I read the book, with just the stars, the radio, and exercise books for company, I started to lose it, too.

Walking back from the bottle store one evening, I fell to my knees on the dirt, right next to a puddle; rains had finally arrived to quench the drought. I peered into the pool that reflected the dark night sky and felt as though I was staring into the abyss of insanity. The appeal of diving in abyss and giving up trying to make sense of life, of myself, was profoundly seductive. To be able to let go, to be crazy . . . aaah, what a relief that would be. Staring into that puddle, I felt the infinite immensity of the universe. It felt like I was as important in the grand scheme of things as a mote of dust in a shadowy corner of a long-forgotten room.

Without faith in God or something bigger than me to make me feel significant, I felt totally inconsequential, and it was terrifying. However, I held on. I chose to crawl back from the abyss and return to the task of living, gnarly as it was. The existentialist choice to truly live, fully responsible for my own existence, had been made. The rest of my life has been shaped by the decision I made that night to never succumb to despair, no matter how tough things got. I got back to my knees and chose life. I also chose Africa.

At the start of the program, I was not really interested in African culture. I was in such a hurry to get out of the village at the end of a school week that I could not wait to jump on the bus into Harare on Friday afternoons and hit the capital. I would meet up with other Brits to eat Western food at a Western-ish hotel. There was only so much *sadza*—maize meal boiled in water—I could eat before craving something more familiar. As there were only two buses a day out of the village, to make my weekend plans work I had to skip out of class twenty minutes before the bell rang. I would be all ears, waiting to hear it chugging toward the school along the sandy road. My desperate run for the bus, overweight as I still was, was usually accompanied by the joyous whoops and catcalls of my amused students.

But once I chose to get stuck in, strange, wonderful changes started happening in me. I started syncing with the rhythms of a rural community uninterested in the relentless drive for rational efficiency and productivity characteristic of my world back home. Up until now I'd been wallowing in the feeling that I was stuck all alone for a year in a tiny African village, five thousand miles away from everything I knew, teaching kids stuff they couldn't understand and weren't interested in.

Then something snapped in me and I decided to embrace the 'weirdness'. I got into local life and chose to contribute to it. I started staying home on the weekends rather than racing out to the city. I was soon invited to soccer matches that our school team played with other schools. I had never watched a soccer game in my life at that point, much less played. Back in London, I could not have been less interested in the sport, but the way it brought this community together each week was a marvel. Inside of the shared celebration on and off the soccer field, I fell in love with Africa for good.

The team, their friends, some teachers, a few parents, and various hangers-on would all pile into a huge open-top truck, used to transport building materials during the weekdays, to travel to another school. The truck would labor up and down hills, churning through sand-covered roads, for hours until we arrived. Then the lads would play. Every time we scored a goal, a bunch of my smiling-eyed pupils and I would rhythmically dance onto the field, drums pounding, in a tribal rite of jubilation. Then we would dance off again.

We laughed. We giggled. We connected. We began to understand each other. I engaged with them as equals, instead of within a teacher-student (or master-slave) dynamic, a great relief to me (and I imagine to them) given that I was only a year or two older than most of them. In the evenings I would go to the bottle store and dance to local *jit jive* music played on a terrible stereo at distorting volumes. It was here that I learned, even though I was still overweight and punishingly shy, that I, like every human alive, could dance. More than that, I realized that dance was (in) my soul.

It is hard to share in words what a seminal realization this was in my life. The beat of the drums and the defense-less warmth of African humanity captured my heart and moved my feet. No longer stuck in my head, I felt my heart beating with life. For the first time I discovered a glorious sense of physicality: of the movement of muscles and the joy of engaging playfully with gravity. The delighted bottle-store ladies, who challenged local propriety by drinking and partying rather than being stuck cooking and cleaning at their homesteads, showed me how to shake my ass with African panache.

I began to release a few psychological defenses, especially those that had kept me away from places like dance floors, where I risked being laughed at for being the fat loser. I was transforming, and it was happening by way of "irrational" means: dancing with people, playing with people, being with people. I had thrown off, to some degree at least, the sensuality-repressing mantle of Judeo-Christian culture. And I was loving it.

I also began to really enjoy all things rural. Up to that point my home had been London, one of the greatest but also most hectic places on Earth. I had never seen myself as a nature person, no matter how many rock faces and mountain sides my climbing-obsessed father had made us mount at the crack of dawn. I believed myself to be a city slicker, a ranger of the concrete jungle. Yet here I was, way past the boondocks, and I was thriving in harmony with nature. More and more I would take comfort in the endless plains and find solace in the feel of sand and rock on my skin. I would walk out into the bush alone and unafraid, reveling in the emptiness. I was well and truly out of the city, which had an impact on me both physiological and philosophical.

I started to relax: to really chill out and unwind my mind. As I did, I began to experience the warmth of the utterly uncynical locals. I was no longer so ready to assume such people disliked me or hated me when I walked into a room. Control and Protect Mode did not need to be activated so often now that I felt more appreciated for who I was. There was no need to always be cynical, knowing, and funny. In fact, acting that way kept getting in the way of my relationships with people utterly uninterested in the concept of cool.

In the African bush a powerful part of me was able to come more often to the foreground: Create and Connect Mode. This part of us all yearns to connect with others, with the natural world, and most of all, with ourselves. When we know how to access it within, we can also find a limitless source of love, self-healing, and creativity waiting for us. This part of us is wise and wants us to grow. But it won't be in charge of our choices until we find a way to ensure that Control and Protect Mode feels that we are safe. That means we have to find a way to feel secure enough to let go of our protection patterns and controlling ways. This is perhaps our greatest task as individuals.

Surrounded by people who took me as I was, a loved human being who was part of their community, I started the very long process of learning how to find my way to Create and Connect Mode. The lightness and naivety of the place brought out the lightest, most playful, and most naive version of me. I finally let my social defenses down long enough to have moments of intimacy for the first time in my life. My new African friends and I would hold hands as we walked up the sandy track to the bottle-store or hung out in the bus station in the local town.

Initially I found this man-to-man touch intimidating, and I laughed at it. It burst my Western bubble of self-protection. Then I realized how intoxicatingly beautiful it was. While I had been doing psychotherapy as an individual to work on myself, my Zimbabwean friends had been dealing with their issues through interactions with each other. Experiencing a sense of brotherhood, of unity, within this unhurried and unworried community began to chase out the upsets of my childhood. My wounds began to scab over in the shared meals and moments of simple village life.

The people who lived in the huts around me, who seemed so very different from me, became a mirror in which I could see more of myself, my true character. I could see the joyful core as much as the frayed edges. Seeing our humanity reflected in others' can accelerate the process of our own becoming. The process goes two ways, though. To truly connect with other people, we have to open our hearts and minds.

When traveling, it is all too easy to get stuck in an arrogant, colonial-style mindset in which we look down on, unconsciously, the indigenous population and their eating styles or timing differences. They are turned from living, breathing people into Others to be waved at and marveled at, at best, and oppressed and exploited at worst. The original colonists defined their greatness in contrast to the perceived feebleness or strangeness of the Other, be it Indian, African, or Native American. This is done out of weakness, not strength. But wise travelers, liberating ourselves from the defenses of imperialism, can discover more about our own vulnerabilities and strengths by connecting with an open, vulnerable heart. This is why I fell in love with traveling alone.

Traveling with Westerners makes it too easy to stay in the bubble which defines itself against the Other. Truly independent travel, without tour operators and cookie-cutter hotel rooms that could be Marriotts in Minnesota, Manchester, or Mogadishu, flings us into settings that are profoundly unfamiliar and which challenge us to rise to them. By diving in wholeheartedly, we get to transform our hearts within. I believe that the purpose of anthropology—the study of human culture that I went on to research avidly and practice later in life—is not just to analyze other cultures like a scientist studies atoms. It must also be to engage with people to help us make sense of our own lives as well as theirs. The opportunity with travel of any kind is to achieve *mutual* growth through interconnection and inter-being.

Anthropology's main research tool is ethnography, which literally means "writing culture". It is centered around a practice called participant observation, which entails hanging out with others in their huts or hospital rooms in an attempt to experience their world. At the same time, the anthropologist also attempts to remain true to his or her own world, and be aware of unconscious beliefs and biases.

In this experience of being both part of a culture and at the same time apart from it, the anthropologist translates what we, he or she thinks is happening in one culture into language and metaphors that make sense in the other. Anthropologists connect as deeply as possible with their subjects while maintaining a boundary that allows them to stay grounded in who they are. They dance between the two cultures, attempting to render the alien familiar and turn the opaque into clear insight. They must always maintain an awareness of their unconscious desire to 'other' the culture they are studying: seeing them as exotic or primitive in a bid to raise their own profile, power, and status. I came to understand this in Africa; and was utterly humbled by the warmth of the culture I was lucky enough to stop a while within.

Another technique within ethnography, made popular by the brilliant anthropologist Clifford Geertz, is called "thick description".[51] We engage with what seems like a small phenomenon, but within it we glimpse a profound epiphany about a culture. One such phenomenon fascinated me during my time in Zimbabwe. At first I thought it was simply a verbal quirk of people who spoke limited English. Pupils and fellow teachers would often say "Sorry Mr. Nick" whenever I hurt myself, made a mistake, or dropped something.

Initially, I was taken aback. "It's not your fault, so don't take the blame", I would explain as rationally as I could. I remember wondering whether this was a hangover from a more servile mindset after centuries of colonization. But I came to realize, as I opened my heart and my mind, that they were not trying to take the blame, apologize out of fear, or look good as individuals. Instead, they were sharing in my frustration as if they were part of me. They were making it clear that what I perceived as my frustration was actually *shared* frustration. My pain was their pain. How insanely beautiful is that?

What I was picking up in that humble sentence, spoken so often in that little pocket of the African bush, was the indigenous Bantu philosophy known as Ubuntu. This can be summarized by the phrase "I am because you are". Although I only experienced a slice of it, it changed me at the deepest level of my being. The experience of being at-one with others, even without knowing it, began the long process of resetting my relationships. Ubuntu is a lodestone that can guide us into genuine comm*unity* in a modern world that tends to force us apart.

Archbishop Desmond Tutu explains: “You can’t be human all by yourself. A person with Ubuntu is open and available to others, affirming of others, does not feel threatened that others are able and good, for he or she has a proper self-assurance that comes from knowing that he or she belongs in a greater whole and is diminished when others are humiliated or diminished.”[52] This relational way of understanding being-in-the-world stands in stark contrast to the modern tradition that sees each of us as islands entire unto ourselves, as the poet John Donne put it.

We in the modern West see ourselves primarily as individuals, discrete and alone, while Africans consider themselves part of an interconnected whole. It is easy to feel afraid, needy, and greedy as a lone player when we feel scared and alone. Control and Protect Mode sees everything as separate and atomized so we need to fight for what we want. However, it is far less existentially agonizing to feel part of a whole that loves you, cares for you and, in some way, actually *is* you. This is how we see the world through Create and Connect Mode.

To be seen as one with each other is a balm for every suffering person. I believe most Western people yearn for this feeling in the deepest recesses of their being. In that little African village, which had gone through centuries of Western oppression and arrogance, the powerful non-rational culture of Ubuntu helped me finally experience myself as unified with the great web of life. Rather than bullying, mocking, or teasing me, the Africans I met that year and for years after—whether in Zanzibar or Cape Town—bestowed on me the greatest gift of their culture: they saw me as part of them, even though I was white, male, Jewish, and British. But I would not have been able to appreciate the gift, or even recognize it, if I had kept the same attitude of separation and otherness that I arrived there with.

African cultures, as well as all other indigenous and usually non-rational cultures across the planet, have essential wisdom that we have lost or misplaced in the West. This wisdom has the potential to help us recalibrate our sense of self and restore the health of our social and economic systems. Sadly, most people in the developed world do not take the time to even consider that a place like Zimbabwe has anything much to teach us.

I am deeply grateful that I had the opportunity to be cloistered away from individualistic advertising, consumption, productivity, and achievement during my time in Africa. I experienced a different orientation to life. When I tried to shove Western science and Anglo-Saxon grammar down the throats of my pupils, I lost connection with them. It was only once I opened my heart and put aside the rational agenda I'd been brought there to deliver—to fill their minds with scientific content from their former colonial masters—that I reached them. And we both learned in the process.

During my time in Africa the imprints of pain that had been etched into my nervous system as a child began to be smoothed away. The schism within me was on the mend. But although Ubuntu helped me considerably, I was not in Africa for long enough for it to help me fully unwind a quarter of a century of internal tightness. I was also utterly oblivious to the way the magic of connection was healing me and would not have known how to continue it if I had wanted to. It takes years of sustained effort to integrate our Jungian-style shadow into light; and we have to understand the process of transformation if we want to do it continuously.

It is incredibly challenging to integrate the transformations that take place during travel—around the planet or within our own consciousness—into our everyday thoughts and habits. Without learning how to rewire our habits, we return to old patterns of protection and control all too easily. I had little idea how to create Ubuntu for myself. The feeling of being connected, of being in it together, emerged from time to time in my joyful moments. But back then I knew of no way to choose the feeling consciously. It was not embodied within me.

∞

I entered Zimbabwe as a privileged boy from a wealthy London suburb with a lot of philosophical confusion and more than a few psychological issues. Inspired by the lessons the remote village had taught me about human interconnection and interdependence, I left more humbled and aware. But I soon had to shrug off Africa's warm embrace and return to Britain to go 'up' to a cold and windy Cambridge exactly a year and a day after I had left. Walking the streets of the medieval university town, for only the second time in my life, I discovered that it was a bigger culture shock than the African bush was.

Just as I had arrived in the Zimbabwean hut feeling discombobulated and alone, I found myself in the same state on my first day as an undergraduate. I came armed with enough ethnic art and crafts to festoon even the largest student digs. I was shown to a tiny room at the bottom of a Victorian-era staircase by an Edwardian-era porter. I sat on the bed. I looked around at the wooden panels and my new medical textbooks, and all I could think of was how much I missed that cockroach-infested hut and long-drop toilet. As I wistfully remembered the sounds and sensations of Africa, I was utterly unaware of the intellectual and emotional cyclone that was about to hit me.

SPIRITUAL ATHEISM PRINCIPLES:

- Be open to non-Western ways of experiencing and understanding the world, like Ubuntu, that might offer us unique and essential insights into what it means to be human.

- Travel not to escape into exoticism or to appropriate the trappings of Other cultures but to transform ourselves in deeply respectful relationships with other people and nature. All the while, avoid projecting onto other traditions, cultures, and individuals the idea that their wisdom is better than ours; or that we need their aesthetics and accessories to thrive.
- Dance, move, and connect with our bodies, as much as our minds, to release repressed pain, break down protective patterns, and transform trauma to find peace. Living fully embodied lives—developing ever-increasing awareness of, and mastery over, our inner experience as a single, unified 'bodymind'—is critical to personal transformation and thriving.
- We have everything we need within our bodymind to feel free and at peace at any moment, no matter what is happening around us.
- Build nurturing communities that foster the optimal conditions for shared healing, thriving, and joy through daily open-hearted connections between individuals. Within such loving and connected communities, our protective patterns can dissolve quickly as they are no longer needed for safety and survival.

CHAPTER 4

SCIENCE AND MATERIALISM: PRAYING AT THE ALTAR OF ATHEISM

Cambridge is one of the birthplaces of modern science. One can piece together a decent history of the subject by taking a look at its alumni. Francis Bacon, a resolute Christian and the grandfather of what we now call the scientific method, was there in the late 1500s. Isaac Newton developed the laws of motion there. Charles Darwin studied there before writing his treatise on evolution. Ernest Rutherford split the atom there. Crick and Watson discovered the structure of DNA there. I felt suitably humbled.

Now it was my turn to be inducted into the scientific project. Here I knelt at the altar of atheism and prayed to the elevated ideal of Reason. For three intense years, I attended lectures three times a day, wrote two or three essays on complex science subjects each week, and had one-on-one supervisory reviews with experts to go over each essay. There was nowhere to hide. As I went on a steep learning curve I began to understand science in a way I never had before. I learned that it is a way of studying nature—through such techniques as experimentation, measurement, and the publication and review of articles by our peers—in order to create reliable, consistent knowledge about the material world around us and inside us.

Using this methodology, science has had amazing successes, from defining the elemental particles of nature to working out how bodies reproduce through DNA. Almost all of the technologies that we rely on every day exist because of the progress of modern science. It has increased the average life expectancy in the West by about thirty years since 1900.[53] Perhaps the most important insight science has contributed to our understanding of human life is the theory of evolution. Charles Darwin, the originator of this theory (although there have been many other contributors to the Modern Synthesis), believed that our ability to adapt to change was the key to survival. He stated, towards the close of his masterwork *On the Origin of Species*, that "better adaptation in however slight a degree to the surrounding physical conditions will, in the long run, turn the balance." In other words, we either fit the world as it changes, or we fail.[54]

When we feel ourselves starting to fade and fail, we need to transform. For example, at medical school, the sheer pace of learning overwhelmed me. I had to adapt, very quickly, or I was going to drown in an ocean of knowledge. Prior to this moment, I had been slapdash, never doing things properly. This was a sign of low self-esteem: why bother doing something well when everything you do, and the person you are, totally sucks? But this pattern was starting to cause me problems. Luckily, my "careless" habit wasn't covering over a deep wound so I was able to become more rigorous through cognitive choice. This was not the case with many of my other patterns. Powerful protective patterns need emotional transformation before behavioral change can occur.

As I began to practice science in the dusty, wood-paneled laboratories, I begun to understand much more about what makes science such a sturdy foundation for building a reliable and rigorous understanding about much of our world. Before the seventeenth century, your friendly neighborhood Aristotle scholar or your unfriendly neighborhood bishop had the power to tell you what was right and wrong based on philosophical or religious dogma. Kings, aristocrats, and the Church controlled almost all the money and the land. Your local lord could order you to go to war to fight on his behalf. Your local priest could excommunicate you from the community or decide you were going to heaven. Priests were the only ones who could read and understand the Bible (in Latin or Greek), so they told people what to believe and how to live their inner lives. Amazing as it may be to us now, it wasn't that long ago that people who didn't go to church could be fined, have their property confiscated or even be imprisoned.[55]

Against this backdrop, a group of (sadly, mostly) men all over Europe began to study nature in a new way, freed from many of these medieval limitations. They managed to challenge the elites' claims to the absolute truth and offer a method of study that eventually anyone, from any background, could employ (at the start, science was not massively accessible, since only those who had time and money to spare could do it). It caught on and cascaded through the world, shifting everything in its path and rendering most other ways of understanding life parochial. Science has since replaced centuries of dogma to become the dominant way of being right, and so of making choices, in the modern era.

Every historian of science has a different opinion of how and when it started (and so what 'science' really is). Some point to ancient Greece, where proto-scientists like Aristotle and Archimedes were investigating nature as precisely as possible. Other historians point to the great advances of the medieval Muslim world, which brought us algebra, chemistry, and coffee. The majority contend that the advent of western science may have begun with the Greeks, but only reached full maturity in modern Europe.

Charles Taylor thinks that the "great invention of the West was that of an immanent order in Nature, whose workings could be systematically understood and explained on its own terms."[56] Such science was agnostic on whether there was a god behind all the creativity in nature. As a form of knowledge distinct from superstition and magical thinking, it relied on the development of a sense of reason that was disengaged and disconnected from the subject matter it was studying.

As this form of knowledge-building emerged and went mainstream, the Scientific Revolution of the sixteenth to eighteenth centuries occurred. Since then, tens of thousands of scientists have made it their business to measure every mandible, identify every ion, and chart every quark they can get their hands on.

One of the first scientists to achieve legend status was Galileo (the narrative of his battle with the Church set up an early belief that religion and science are utterly incompatible). His careful observations of the moons of Jupiter landed him in the hall of fame. But before he could see these moons in the starry firmament, he had to first build a telescope powerful enough to see that far. New technology and craftsmanship have always been core to scientific discovery.

Once Galileo had built a piece of kit powerful enough to see Jupiter clearly, he could finally observe the planet's moons as they moved in space. What he saw empirically, *with his own eyes* (albeit magnified by the lenses of the telescope), challenged the dogma of the day and changed the world. According to Holy Scripture, God made man the center of the universe, so it followed that the planets and sun must orbit the Earth. But Galileo's telescope showed something very different. Having gone over and over his calculations so he was sure the measurements were correct, he stated with the certainty that comes from seeing something for oneself, that the moons of Jupiter orbit the planet and both Jupiter and Earth orbit the sun. He had proved, *with data*, what Copernicus had suggested with his "heliocentric" model of the cosmos.

This new form of truth, based on empirical evidence—evidence from repeated observations—disrupted both religious and Aristotelian beliefs out of the market. I think it is hard for us modern folk, having been born into a truly science-loving world, to understand just how much the many scientific revolutions since then have changed our mindsets and culture. Consider our view of comets, for example. For centuries the spotting of a comet, a stream of light exploding across the sky, would inspire religious awe. They were seen as divine portent that revealed the pleasure or wrath of god, causing people to wonder at what he up there might be communicating … and to whom. Many felt a sense of fear and foreboding about the unknowable when they saw such phenomena.

Then, in 1705, the Englishman Edmond Halley published a testable scientific prediction that a comet would appear fifty years later, in 1758. He used the laws of physics devised by his contemporary, Isaac Newton, to create a hypothesis that the comets seen in 1682, 1607, and 1531 were in fact the same object orbiting the sun. When, on Christmas Day, what we now call Halley's Comet did appear, it was the first major public proof that this newfangled thing called science was not just interesting, but powerful too. It could predict the future!

Early scientists were exuberant. One wrote, "The universe beholds this the most satisfactory phenomenon ever presented to us by astronomy; an event which, unique until this day, *changes our doubts into certainties*, and our hypotheses to demonstrations" (my italics).[57] In other words, up to that point, science was still not sure of itself, and religious faith and folk conventions held as much sway. But with Halley's prediction, science *proved* itself more reliable than Aristotelian doctrine or Christian scripture for telling us how the physical world works.

Divinely ordained rule by the powerful now began to look a bit suspect. Enlightenment thinkers, *philosophes* like Jean-Jaques Rousseau and Denis Diderot who set about challenging orthodoxy with élan, took the opportunity to fiercely critique the aristocratic political system and knock the priests from their pedestals. Reason and science had finally gotten the upper hand. Freeing as it was, it soon became the gold-standard for all knowledge.

Scientists embraced a new view of the universe as a mechanism—one with inner workings as predictable and knowable as those of a clock. Figure out how the clock works, and you have unlocked the secrets of the universe; you can explain, and perhaps also control, everything. Scientists began to put themselves in the position of being all-knowing, wrenching power over nature and people from the hands of God. The logical conclusion of this is the scientifically inspired tenet of New Atheism: only truths about the material world, proven beyond all doubt by science, should be used to guide our lives and our societies as a whole.

Although science gives us a very important way to understand the world, it can't tell us everything about our lives because it has much more trouble understanding subjective experiences inside hearts and minds than it does heart muscle and brain neurons. For example, very recent neurobiology studies have discovered two major neural networks that play a large part in our everyday thinking. However, the research is of minimal value unless we bring in other forms of knowledge and wisdom.

Scientists have begun to study the brain/mind by putting people in fMRI scanners. To discover insights into different types of human thought, particularly understanding what happens when we are thinking analytically as opposed to creatively, they have started scanning the brains of rappers and jazz musicians, both virtuosi of improvisation. To explore what is happening in the moment of creation, they ask research subjects to improvise new content, like jazz music or rap rhymes. Then, in contrast, they ask them to perform material they have created in the past.[58]

Through these studies they have identified a powerful brain network called the Cognitive Control Network or Executive Control Network, which dominates us when we are solving familiar problems with existing rules (and so relying on our patterns to control the world). I *sense* that this correlates with what I call Control and Protect Mode. There is also another network, the Default Mode Network or "daydreaming" network, which allows us to create new solutions to problems as they emerge in a changing world (without which our species would not have been so successful). This seems to correlate with what I call Create and Connect Mode.[59] One of the key pioneers of the research, Rex Jung, has speculated that people who are locked into one brain network or the other, at the edges of the normal distribution curve, are either psychotic (extreme creativity) or autistic (extreme control).[60]

Neuroscience can tell us a lot about how the materiality of our brains (neurons) changes when we are in different modes. But it is way more equivocal when it comes to telling us *how* to switch between modes, what value each has in life, and the experience of them in the moment. Science can tell us that we shift into different patterns of brain activity with certain stimuli or tasks. But we need something more than science to tell us which one is ideal—and so a fit—for any given situation. This is because science is designed to be valueless; and making choices mean giving more value to one thing than another. By turning the scientific data into wisdom principles, going from brain network language (provable) to how to modes and switching modes language (unprovable), the value to practical life increases—but it moves away from hard facts.

By the time I was looking at brain scans, with a few years of proper science behind me, I begun to grok that science, so good at predicting the movement of atoms and the physical survival of species, was much less helpful when helping us thrive through the nitty-gritty realities of life. This is because human beings are not clocks and cannot be 'fixed' or 'engineered' like clocks can be. We are evolving, living biologies that can feel and think; as well as objects that have *some* mechanistic properties. So although I was doing well in the *material* world of test scores, my inner emotional life was still a mess.

I had fallen for a student who was in the same lectures as me. Happily, for the first time, my interest was returned—though not for long. With unhelpful patterns still beavering away trying to protect me from disappointment, I fumbled my way into disaster. I had finally kissed a girl—yay!—but within days my ambivalent/disorganized attachment templates began to fire and I torpedoed any chance of a lasting relationship. After it was over, I sank into the blues once again.

My best friend at the time, a fellow medic who was heavily inspired by the mystical Indian philosophies of his culture of origin, wrote me a letter stating that if I could only realize how "infinite" I was, all my loneliness would cease. But the idea of limitlessness meant nothing to me as a committed atheist. It seemed obvious that I was limited by the skin that covered my flesh and bones and kept me separate from everyone else. I could not compute what he was trying to tell me so I went back into atheist psychotherapy. It alleviated the intensity of the heartache a little, but, once more, did little to get to the heart of the matter. My wounds were in the domain of love; but the methodology never touched those parts of me.

My feelings about myself were filled with shame and pain. It felt like the rest was just an act. With intimacy still elusive, I began to look for proxies for the love I wanted. It was here that I started to get serious about being 'cool'. I had not owned a pair of branded sneakers before the age of twenty, but I began to see hipsterdom—from collecting rare vinyl records to wearing retro clothes—as a passport to being liked (if not loved). This was to become a dominant new pattern for over a decade—distancing me further from the intimacy and connection I most yearned for. Being 'cool' is a protection which ultimately pushes people away.

I was by now attending classes in psychology, the scientific study of human minds, which I hoped would be of more use to me personally than the rest of the medical sciences I had engaged with. This branch of science had kicked off around the same time Freud was studying in Paris. Wilhelm Wundt, the first person to call himself as psychologist, opened the first laboratory dedicated to the subject at the University of Leipzig in Germany in 1879. He wanted to study human consciousness—our subjective experiences of life—using rigorous and systematic scientific techniques. "The exact description of consciousness is the sole aim of experimental psychology," Wundt wrote in his introductory textbook.[61]

Soon Wundt and others realized that consciousness is a very hard thing to study in ways that yield reliable and consistent *scientific-style* results. Everything is a bit woolly, which puts the lovers of hard data off. So for a century or more, experimental psychologists moved on to more measurable and quantifiable topics that could be studied in labs more easily. So I learnt very little about my conscious experience from psychology!

Consciousness, of which there is no agreed-on definition, is darn tricky to study scientifically because the scientific project was never conceived to answer questions about our consciousness, like how to have a life of meaning and to be happy. In fact, science developed over time to *avoid* such questions as much as possible. Early scientists, like Galileo, had discovered that some things are easy to measure and some are not. And the scientist can get better results, more easily, by focusing on easy to measure qualities.

In the study of particles, for example, one can calculate their size, energy, mass, speed, direction, and shape with accuracy. Scientists call these the "primary qualities". Such properties stay the same even when different scientists measure them. They seem independent of the mind of the observer. Because these properties are relatively simple to measure precisely, whether through telescopes, measuring tape or lasers, we can carry out successful experiments that tell us accurately how they change. Does a certain chemical reaction increase or decrease the mass of a substance? Has the particle accelerator changed the speed or spin of an electron? How many genes from one species show up in another species' genome? Using mathematics to play around with the measurements—the data—we can build strong, testable theories about how the primary qualities of physical objects work.

What of the things about the world that are not so easy to measure? Color, sound, and taste, for example, exist largely in what Galileo called the "sensible body", within the embodied experience of the observer. So they are less easy to quantify objectively. This is even more true of rich and complex experiences like "love" and "meaning". So such aspects became known as "secondary qualities". Scientists, following the lead of ancient Greek thinkers like Democritus, who floated the idea of the atom, made a bold step and decided that science should only study the primary qualities, not the secondary, because the secondary qualities lead to softer data. Soft data make prediction harder, which means scientists make less certain 'progress' when studying them.

Galileo wrote on this matter, "I think that if one takes away ears, tongues, and noses, there indeed remain the shapes, numbers, and motions, but not the odors, tastes, or sounds; outside the living animal [our conscious biology] these are nothing but names".[62] In other words, secondary qualities are in the mind of the perceiver, not 'out there' in matter. Writing later, the British empirical philosopher John Locke dismissed the secondary qualities as being "nothing in the objects themselves but powers to produce various sensations in us".[63]

The French polymath and devout Catholic René Descartes, for many the godfather of modern life because he helped place truth in humanity's hands and not in God's, furthered the distinction between primary and secondary qualities. He called things that show up with hard primary qualities *res extensa*, or "extending, material stuff"; and things that perceive the sensations of the secondary qualities *res cogitans*, "thinking stuff".[64] This set up a dualism at the core of Western thought. Crucially, it allowed the perceptions, emotions, and biases of the observer—the scientist—to be removed from the measurements. Thus focused on matter alone, science was able to become "hard".

With its metaphysics sorted, science now needed a method for gathering data and turning them into reliable knowledge. Descartes' contemporary, Francis Bacon, suggested a process that, with many refinements, has become what we now call the "scientific method".[65] Through repeated measurements of matter, a scientist can generate a hypothesis about how a certain material works in the world. She can then make good predictions about what will happen in the future if specific primary qualities, like mass, energy, or direction, are changed.

These predictions, like Edmond Halley's, are based on the available data, not on opinion. They should be valueless, with as little human perception as possible. The scientist then designs experiments that test the predictions to draw highly probable conclusions. Over time, the scientist develops a theory to explain what she has observed over repeated experiments. She publishes her thinking and data in a journal where her peers can comment on and critique her work. Her results can be made available to other people to check independently. Others can try to replicate the results. The theories that change the least over time become "laws of nature": hypotheses that we see as proven and inalienable truths about how the material world works.

With this method in place, knowledge could never again be accused of being 'soft'. Knowledge—*scientia*, in Latin—became rigorous, hard, certain, true. Enlightened 'progress' gathered pace as scientific knowledge led to improvements in our machines, our productivity, and our physical health. Theories grounded in observations replaced endless arguments about whether people should believe in Aristotle's theories or Biblical scriptures. Debate was replaced by detailed investigations. Guesses were replaced by calculations. Humans could now 'prove' things about the world. However, it is vital to realize that because of this methodology of constant experimentation, *all* science is provisional. Virtually every scientific theory you hear will be altered or replaced in the future.

Modern science is, by its own design, a science that can tell us a lot about the material elements of our universe, for example, our height, weight, GPS location, and genome. But if we want to study thoughts and feelings, like how it feels to read these words and apply them to life, things become a lot tougher. To study them scientifically we must always rely on people's subjective experiences of themselves, full of bias,[66] to determine what numerical level of happiness or stress they are feeling.

Many of the studies that form the foundation of psychology attempt to measure secondary qualities by having subjects respond to surveys and questionnaires. But the shifting and fickle nature of subjective experience can make the data questionable. Since we are all organisms not automatons, and our thoughts are influenced by hunger, desires and mood, it makes much of what we think we are feeling unreliable and subject to bias. The shocker is that this is equally true of those doing the science. In an analysis of hundreds of studies on the impact of soft drinks, juice and milk on human health, papers funded in some way by the food industry were six times more likely to produce favourable or neutral findings than those that were not!

To make matters more challenging, most psychological studies use as their subjects Western, educated people from industrialized, rich, and democratic countries. These subjects are known by the acronym WEIRD. So the results are not necessarily representative of people in, say, Africa or South America; or even from marginalized groups in the West. The conditions of the studies also throw into doubt the value of the insights. For in order for such research to be considered scientific, any variables that might confound the data must be removed. Therefore, the vast majority of the "facts" from experimental psychology come from experiments done in clean, neat laboratories with little "noise". Such sanitized conditions are utterly unlike our messy, chaotic, busy lives and so the data may not hold up in the complexity of real human experience.

As a result of these challenges, psychological studies are much more difficult to replicate than experiments in a field like physics. In a 2015 investigation, almost 300 psychological scientists from across the world attempted to replicate more than a hundred already-published studies in experimental psychology to see if they could be repeated. Remember, replication is one of the criteria for "good" science. More than 50 percent of the experiments failed to provide the same results.[67] This has precipitated what has become known as the "replication crisis" in psychology.

What most people don't realize, including many New Atheists and scientists, is that all scientific truths, even those that form the bedrock of "hard" fields like physics, are probabilistic, as opposed to absolute. Statistical methods are always used to determine whether the results of an experiment are "significant", or a product of random chance. If your analysis of your data reaches a certain probability value, a p-value, you can claim you have made a statistically significant scientific discovery. This can lead to publication in prestigious journals, lucrative funding, and high-profile awards. But however much acclaim you receive, even if it's a Nobel Prize, your discovery is still premised on probabilities—not certainties.

Since it is so challenging to create hard facts about anything other than hard material (and even these can be challenged by people using different experiment designs measuring different metrics with different statistics programs), matter and the primary qualities have become way more respected in our secular scientific societies than consciousness and the secondary qualities. This is why most scientists, intellectuals and technocrats are materialists: they believe that only matter exists and that the secondary qualities are irrelevant. Materialism sees everything in the universe being reducible to the movement of matter or energy (Albert Einstein taught us that energy and matter are effectively the same). Materialists believe only in what we can measure with our senses. This bias has transformed our world into one which lionizes matter and disregards consciousness.

However, materialism is not the only game in town. During the Enlightenment, there was a strong school of thought that challenged materialism. It stated that as everything we know—data, statistics, theories—is filtered through the subjective experience, we cannot ever be sure that what we measure through our senses with science is absolutely true. Proponents of this view, like Bishop George Berkeley, are called "idealists". They believe that not matter, but *consciousness*—in the form of human will, or universal spirit—is the ultimate foundation of all reality. This common-sense insight casts some doubt on the value of the opinion that physical matter should be seen as the foundation of all reality.

The conflict between materialists and idealists has been a central animating debate in Western philosophy for the last few hundred years. The materialists, emboldened by the successes of modern science, are currently in the ascendant, as they have been for some time. In society, objective facts related to matter are generally considered more important than subjective experiences. This is what most of us are taught, whether explicitly at school or through absorbing the materialist assumptions that underlie the modern world.

The degrading of our inner experience in favor of what we can measure in the physical world has not happened without resistance though. Philosophers of the Romantic Movement, like Wolfgang Von Goethe and Ralph Waldo Emerson, tried to fight back. To them, as well as many wisdom teachers and artists today, it is clear that materialism can tell us *a lot* about how atoms and molecules work, but can tell us very little about how to have specific experiences, like feeling happy or free.

In other words, it is way more limited than most scientists like to admit. Materialists are no better than anyone else at figuring out how matter in the brain generates the conscious experiences we have, the thoughts we think (that allow us to practice science in the first place), and the feelings we enjoy. Materialists have no idea why we dream. They have very little idea why some things are alive and why some are not. There is no agreed definition of a gene or even a cell, because such definitions are in our consciousness, as concepts, as much as in hard data. Materialist scientists can't even agree if butter or red wine are good or bad for our health.

From the moment Democritus, Galileo, and the rest of the gang laid down the foundations of science, two related problems arose for materialists to answer. The first is the "mind-body problem" and the second is the so-called "hard problem of consciousness" (a term coined by Australian philosopher David Chalmers). The problems stem from a separation of matter and consciousness, making some really important questions all but impossible to answer rationally: How and why does "mind stuff" arise from "material stuff"? How do matter and mind interact? And if consciousness is not the same as matter, then what the hell *is* consciousness?

So far, materialism has failed to answer these questions in any coherent way. To materialists, the only element of our mind that exists is nerve cells firing. In practice, this means only measurable events like molecular channels in neurons opening, allowing ions to cross cell membranes propagating an electrical signal, are real. Everything that comes after—the secondary, subjective experiences that philosophers call *qualia*—don't qualify. Some influential philosophers, like Daniel C. Dennett, appear to go so far as to claim that even their own conscious experiences (through which they have ideas and write books) are an illusion![68] Some make a less strong but still hard-to-fathom case; matter is primary, and consciousness is an epiphenomenon that somehow magically emerges from inert physical matter. Nobody has explained exactly how.

For most materialist thinkers, there seems to be no such thing as free will. Our mental experiences are *caused* by a collection of nerves firing; so our decisions are predetermined by the movements of molecules. Our minds cannot impact biological processes in our bodies in any way, because matter comes first and mind stuff either emerges from it or doesn't exist at all in any real way. But empirical science tells us that the reverse is true. The "placebo effect", where changes in what patients think about pills leads to healing, is one of the most well-documented phenomena in science. It has been observed thousands of times across all kinds of diseases and conditions.[69] The mechanism for how our beliefs, in consciousness, can change our physical biologies cannot be explained by materialism.

There is a chasm between materialist explanations about the world and our rich experiences of it. Yet these major philosophical issues are not well known to the public, or even to many scientists, since most are not expected to study the philosophy of science. Therefore people continue to believe that materialism is the answer to everything. Another word for it is "positivism": the idea that we can only be positive about things that can be observed objectively and verified through the logic of the scientific method. This way of viewing the world has aggressively expanded into every part of life. Insights from wisdom, morality, and other modes of knowledge have been cast aside. New Atheists believe that science, seen through the materialist's lens, is the last word on *everything:* no exceptions. This stance, called "scientism", seems to be Control and Protect Mode that has run amok.

∞

At medical school I learned the objective facts about every material nodule in the chambers of the heart but was still ignorant about how to heal my own. Attending lectures on psychology had given me zero mastery of my own psyche. I rode my familiar rollercoaster of emotions, up and down like a yo-yo, as I reacted to the world around me with old habits and moods. One minute I believed that everyone in a room was staring at me and disliked me (narcissistic neuroses); the next, that nothing I said or did mattered to anyone (nihilistic neuroses). I was still a virgin at the end of my second year at college. The shame I felt about this was even greater than my ongoing loneliness. I became more protective than ever, hiding the generosity and caring that comes naturally to us all because revealing them only opened me up to hurt and disappointment.

Empathy, compassion, and love are all deeply tied to healing. But nobody at medical school gave us any insight into how a physician can heal themselves. I was still traumatized, often depressed, and a walking relationship disaster, and yet I was expected to be a healer.

As a rationalist, atheist, and *de facto* materialist, I assumed that there was nothing better out there than science. My mind wouldn't allow me to engage in any wisdom that materialism didn't tell me was a proven way to succeed in life. Yet even as I prayed at the altar of atheism as fervently as the next scientist, my curiosity about other ways of knowing the world had not gone away. I won a number of prizes during my time there. One was a £20 book token. I bought with it an illustrated copy of the *Zohar*, one of the central texts of Jewish mysticism.

Sadly, the wisdom within this tome did not do much for me at that point in my life. Create and Connect Mode may have taken me into the bookshop, but Control and Protect Mode stopped me from reading the book. It actually took me another ten years to pick the book up and engage with the ideas within it. In the meantime I kept it hidden away on a shelf, evidence of my guilt as a traitor to rationality, atheism, and materialism.

There was one place in my life where I did allow irrationality, even ecstasy, into my everyday experience: on the dancefloors of the exploding rave scene.

SPIRITUAL ATHEISM PRINCIPLES:

- Be ready to use empirical observation, reason, and the scientific method to overcome our human biases in order to find out reliable information about the material world of 'primary properties'.
- Realize that scientific studies that analyze human beings are probabilistic rather than absolute. They are necessarily insulated from real-world

settings in order to focus on specific causes and effects. Therefore they always offer partial not total truths.

- Remember that science finds it hard to provide proven facts about conscious experience, the 'secondary qualities' of our inner world. Because of this, it has tended to prioritize easy-to-measure external matter as more 'real' than hard-to-measure subjective or interior experiences. Over time, conscious experiences have become dismissed and diminished as less important than matter and material.
- Embrace the evolutionary imperative: we either adapt to the fit the world as it changes; or we start to fade and fail. This demands that we are able to continuously transform old patterns—emotions, ideas, and habits—in order to adapt to fast-changing realities. We cannot be fully adaptable and creative when we are locked in our protective patterns. If we remain stuck within our patterns, we will suffer unnecessarily.
- The evolutionary nature of our world means that all projects and principles—whether about matter or consciousness—will evolve over time and unfold in time.

CHAPTER 5

MUSIC AND ECSTASY: SPIRIT IN THE RAVE

As luck would have it, in my late youth the UK was the global epicenter of the emerging rave movement: a social revolution that was bigger than punk, and more accessible than the flower power of the sixties.

My first taste of a rave was just before flying off to Zimbabwe. I went to two legendary London clubs. I returned to them many times in the years that followed, but those first nights left an indelible mark on my being. I walked into cavernous rooms packed full of people moving and connecting in ways I had never witnessed before. This wasn't like our tame local club nights, where Top 20 chart music was spun as we all got drunk. This was a phenomenon.

Waves of people were pumping, grinding, hugging, smiling, sweating, gurning, and grooving, all in a chaotic, beautiful human synchrony. Electronic bleeps and tweaks played us like violin strings until we reached an orgasmic, orchestral climax. The steamy, sultry sweat seduced us to break free of everything that held us down.

A radically diverse smorgasbord of people—rich and poor, black and white, men and women, young and old, hipster and mainstream—melted into a sea of unity. I was blown away by the music, the magic, the movement, and the intensity of the moment. I let go of self-protection and experienced pure connective joy on those dance floors. I fell head over heels in love with it all.

Raving, for me, was about a lot more than hedonism. It was, and still can be, a massive social movement that aimed to bring about genuine community, social justice, and psychological emancipation in the guise of partying.[70] When I hit my raving peak in the mid-nineties, newspapers were reporting that over 2 million people every week were going out and raving (many of them taking the drug MDMA). Soon, global "superclubs" like the Ministry of Sound and Cream came into being. Mega-star DJs like Fat Boy Slim and The Chemical Brothers reached commercial maturity, influencing scores of others in every creative field. Places like Ibiza and Goa, New York and Manchester, became world-famous centers of club culture, attracting millions of people to their sun-kissed or snow-tinged parties. The rippling impacts of this cultural tsunami are far from over. Stores on well-to-do main streets and chi-chi hotels on high-end rivieras alike are influenced by the dance music aesthetic.

Dance music culture seemed to me at the time like the freshest, funkiest thing imaginable. It felt like nobody had ever partied this way before. However, the desire to come together and get out of our heads and into our bodies did not start in nineties Britain. Neither was it new in the disco-crazy New York of the seventies, nor in the music halls of fifties London or the jazz joints of thirties Harlem. As cultural historian Barbara Ehrenreich writes in her book *Dancing in the Streets: A History of Collective Joy*, human beings have been dancing together, generating shared moments of joy, since at least the time of the Greeks, and probably since the first cave-dwellers tapped two stones or bones together to lay down a beat.[71]

When I joined the rave scene I became a *bona fide* member of a species whose original art form is, I sense, dance, for it needs no tools other than our "bodymind" (for, not being a dualist like Descartes, I do not distinguish between mind and body). Dancing, whether alone or in a sea of people, is worship of life itself. When we dance we get to experience the pure potential, the irrepressible bliss, of just being here right now, together in a unity of diverse bodyminds.

Nietzsche thought that dance as worship was first seen in the West in Greece, where people moved rhythmically in praise of the god Dionysus. This deity was (and still is, for some people) the representation of the miracle of aliveness. Dance like the Greeks did in their Dionysian celebrations and we can transcend the limitations of self, of I and Me, and enter a realm where rationality and logic no longer hold sway. Nietzsche surely got it right when he said that we should only believe in a god (or a DJ) who can dance.

Dancing, I no longer felt like a playful human locked into an alien's obese body. I got out of my head and got into my entire bodymind. The more I danced, the more I found myself in Create and Connect Mode. For a few hours on the dance floor I was outside the prison of negative self-talk and I was ecstatic, free.

The Greek word *ekstasis*, the root of the word "ecstasy", means to be outside of ourselves (in other words, out of our heads). It usually refers to the experience of transcending the mundane state of subjective self-consciousness. We shift out of a linear, logical mindset and slip into a connected form of consciousness instead. Such experiences, when integrated, can expand our horizons and help us access a form of everyday

Ubuntu that breaks us out of our self-imposed boxes of logic and reason.

When we are in ecstasy, however we get there, we are outside of the box we created for ourselves with all the rules and habits of self-protection. Ecstasy can be triggered by dancing as well as hypnotherapy, rituals, meditation, breathwork, tantric-style sex, fasting, feasting, dancing, sweating, saunas, intense exercise like long-distance running, exhaustion, depression, psychedelics, and, simplest of all, spontaneously as we wander around, and wonder about life.

Materialism, as the study of primary qualities in matter, is not much interested in such phenomena. It is not easy, and perhaps even impossible, to make sense of ecstasy from the materialistic position. The temptation is to dismiss the feeling out of hand or put it down to an exotic brain state—drug- or disease-induced. But right at the birth of psychology, ecstatic states were being systematically studied by one of the founding fathers of the subject, William James.

James' landmark book, *The Varieties of Religious Experience,* uses the rigor of science to understand why altered states show up in so many different settings.[72] In spite of his book's title, James did not limit his studies to traditional experiences of divine rapture. He studied the lives of some of the greatest thinkers in the world and discovered that they all shared a common experience: moments of unconventional, non-rational states of consciousness that took place during periods of deep concentration, whether during work, or while walking in nature.

Contemporary scientists have also studied such experiences happening in the lives of many people, calling them "flow" or "in the zone" states. In one study, researchers found a "dramatic and compelling" correspondence between the experiences reported by hundreds of elite athletes and those described by mystics.[73] Rather than disregarding states of ecstasy as wacky anomalies, James viewed them as having a purpose and value. He believed that they occur not to signal that something is wrong, but to point to something true about the world we live in. Although they feature heavily in certain spiritual traditions, such the Vodou traditions of New Orleans and Haiti, these special states are not religious miracles or magical thinking. For James they were a normal part of human life.

Another early pioneer of psychology, Frederic W. H. Myers, systematically gathered enormous amounts of empirical evidence about human capabilities like ecstasy that could not be—and still cannot be—explained by conventional materialism.[74] Through his research he developed a model of the self that was picked up by William James, although it was scorned and discredited by many who came after. Harnessing this model, James proposed that ecstatic states are a form of "cosmic consciousness" in which people experience an intense but non-religious union with the universe itself.[75]

Carl Jung further built on this idea with his theory of the "collective unconscious",[76] holding that all humans share an unconscious well of wisdom based on collective experience. States of cosmic consciousness, like those that arise in ecstasy, allow us to tap into the collective unconscious to learn and grow as people. Carl Jung was such a big fan of hypnotherapy, dream work, and creative imagination techniques precisely because he saw that they enabled people to reach states similar to ecstasy, where they can harness wisdom not available in rational thought. While Freud focused on analyzing the psyche using logic, trying to use Control and Protect Mode to understand something beyond it, Jung wanted to get people out of their box and into Create and Connect Mode.

Jung saw the value in entering a mindset in which we cannot control everything.[77] In Create and Connect Mode, we can gain wisdom that can help us transform the most powerful of our protective patterns. Extremely creative and connective states can give us insights into our emotional hang-ups and help us explore our shadow without shame or resistance. Without this kind of elemental creative and empathic thinking, transformation in life, love or leadership cannot occur because we are biologically locked into patterns and rules.

According to Mircea Eliade, the great Romanian student of religion, the first reliable route to the kinds of "transpersonal" insights and ideas that come to people in ecstasy—things we could not know from our own biographical personal life—was shamanism.[78] Eliade suggested that a type of person akin to a shaman has appeared in virtually every traditional culture on the planet, including our own in the West. The shaman's job is to help us communicate with something outside everyday consciousness—whether we call that our true self, nature, or the spirit world—in order to help individuals and communities solve problems.[79]

Shamans use ecstatic states, whether induced through "movement medicine" (aka dance) or "medicine plants" like ayahuasca and peyote, to help people release protective patterns and so adapt to thrive in nature. These trips out of the usual headspace bring new insights and information that are of value to both the individual and the tribe. I have seen people enter shaman-induced trance states like this during *macumba* rituals in northeast Brazil, and in conference centers in Birmingham, and it is something amazing to behold.

The experiences of ecstatic flight and freedom I had on the dance floor have stayed with me to this day. I came alive then and I come alive now. I hear a few bars from a house, funk, or disco classic and I get rushes of energy up and down my spine—a powerful judder of connective re-alignment—calling me, demanding me, to move. And within the fellowship of the rave, sharing water bottles with and hugging random people, I felt seen and appreciated—witnessed—by other human bodyminds. It's profoundly self-actualizing to move intimately with a complete stranger, all defense mechanisms dropped. Dancing with each other helps us overcome the despair of the routines that permeate modern life. We join together in rhythmic harmony to escape the "terror and horror of existence" that Nietzsche said arises once we kill off God.

Today, many of our communities no longer have shamans, wise women in power or transformational leaders. I believe this is contributing to the devastating problems we face as a society. In our uber-rationalist culture we have lost access to the ecstatic and the sublime. We make do instead with a pale hedonistic imitation, attempting to get out of our heads through sex, revelry, and drunkenness. With this ersatz ecstasy we go up just to come down again, often with a hard landing.

With *genuine* ecstasy we experience something much more expansive. We get past our usual sense of having to fight the world to survive. We become bigger than the guy or gal who does the dishes, returns emails, and worries about making the rent. We break out of our perceived limitations and connect with something unlimited. This then helps us make our corner of the world that bit better for everyone in it.

My experiences have taught me that we all yearn for ecstatic connectivity in the core of our being. I imagine this is why humans have been finding paths to ecstasy for millennia. As Greek rationality exploded into the world, people would flock to Eleusis, near Athens, to be initiated into ecstatic practices called the Eleusinian Mysteries, which are likely to have involved a shamanic substance, called *kykeon*, to induce ecstasy. Plato could well have been one of the initiates, as he alluded to them in numerous texts. He saw them as inspiring human reason rather than limiting it.[80]

Over in Crete, in the Bronze Age civilization of Minos, people were dancing in "ecstatic movement" to bring about an epiphany: a sudden moment of realization. Again, judging by artifacts found in Minoan archeological sites, such dance is likely to have involved some kind of "juice" that induced ecstasy.[81] Even as we look to our Greek forbears as paragons of logic and reason, they were getting out of their heads regularly and intentionally to engage fully with the mysteries of life.

But today's rationalists and atheists, heirs to a partial and selected heritage of Greek thinking that promotes logic and downgrades the ecstatic, see any form of transcendent experience as suspicious, whether glimpsed in a political rally, an impassioned football game or a charismatic gospel service. I believe they feel threatened, worried that easing their rational grip on reality will leave room for chaos to disrupt their control and power.

The State constantly fears that it will be toppled by an ecstatic mob. The Church fears that giving people direct access to the sublime will put them out of the job of being God's representatives. Scientists fear that allowing for other ways of knowing the world will undermine their status as purveyors of truth. These elites scramble to suppress the methods we use to go beyond ourselves in ecstasy. As soon as someone develops a new way of accessing ecstasy, whether through hedonism or healing, the system attempts to crush it with fear-mongering, scorn, and criminal prosecutions.

In the rave scene, the use of the psychoactive substance MDMA was one such method that the elites quickly moved to suppress. MDMA—called "Ecstasy" on the streets because it helps people feel love and connection in the place of fear and constraint—was first patented in 1913 in Germany by Merck, but it lay forgotten and unused for over half a century until the chemist and culture-hero Alexander Shulgin rediscovered it in the 1970s. Soon after, a loose network of psychotherapists began to use it as a substance to help with their work, particularly in relationship therapy. It was nicknamed Adam because it facilitated a return to Eden, where people could be innocent and trusting again. It was soon banned by the authorities.[82] Likewise, lysergic acid diethylamide (LSD), a powerful hallucinogen, was banned even though around 40,000 people had been given it as a therapeutic treatment in the middle of the century.[83]

Making MDMA illegal wasn't the only measure the government took to crush our movement: they also tried to outlaw our music and gatherings! In the early nineties, laws were enacted by the Conservative British Government to crush the burgeoning rave scene. The establishment realized that tens of thousands of revelers feeling ecstasy together constituted a threat to their highly ordered political system. The tabloid newspapers sensationalized the parties, igniting a wave of panic among the curtain-twitching moral majority. We began to see squads of police cars driving around fields, housing estates, and warehouses where raves were held, attempting to stamp out parties before they even got off the ground.

A couple of years after my first experiences in the clubs of London, the government voted in the Criminal Justice Act to kill off our youth culture for good. This infamous piece of legislation was an attempt to define, and so control, dance music itself. Any gathering of people listening to music that was "wholly or predominantly characterized by the emission of a succession of repetitive beats"[84] could be shut down, even on land owned by the people having the party. The status quo fought to crush the joy before we could rise up together, in unity and shared hope, to change things. By defining our music and gatherings as unlawful, the government thought it could stop us from dancing. But we just organized better and kept the rave going in festivals, house parties, and licensed clubs. We still are!

Even in New York City, another global epicenter of celebration through movement—where break-dancing, salsa, disco, and house were all either formed or perfected—there are less than a hundred venues, out of 22,000, that can legally allow people to dance. Many of those are strip clubs and concert venues, leaving a handful for wholesome and healing worship of life itself. I was myself stopped from dancing in a bar in the Lower East Side one night, and was struck utterly dumb by it. The city's cabaret laws originated in a seemingly racist desire to suppress the dangers associated with the Harlem jazz clubs of the 1930s.[85] Driven by fear of the Other, the Control and Protect Mode of the anxious white man and woman is continuously seeking to crush the ecstatic. But despite constant repression, the human need to join together in ecstasy ensures that collective dancing never dies.

Each week I melted into the bass and beats carried away by movement and music. Dancing for twelve hours or more brought me into increasing awareness of my body's potentiality. I found within the expressive arcs of rhythmical movement a sense of a quickening, as my bodymind became liquid spirit. As this potency ripened in me, I started to relax more in social settings and my sensitivity to perceived slights began to dissipate. Intimate conversations with strangers were easier, and I developed a much deeper empathy for people from all walks of life.

I would find myself invited to the homes of "randoms", people I met by chance on the dance floor. Some lived in council estates (social housing) in desolate inner city areas; others owned posh country houses. It mattered not. I would ask them about their desires and dreams, their fears and loathings, with childlike vulnerability. After we came down from a night of ecstatic dancing, our hearts were wide open. Control and Protect Mode was on pause. A sense of connection and creativity, of Ubuntu, reigned.

With armor dropped, people shared who they really were with me, and I with them, and I harnessed these rare moments of truth (as well as time spent in hundreds of focus groups that I would end up running all over the planet) to understand more about myself and the human condition.

If only such feelings could have stayed with me after those long nights were over. As had happened with Ubuntu when I returned from Africa, I didn't know how to bring about the sense of connection and creativity for myself. Although ecstatic dancing helped me expand my awareness, life remained challenging, for I had no idea how to access the "liquid spirit" back home at the ranch (and could barely remember the liquid feeling at all). The gains I made in self-love, wisdom, and collective joy on the dance floor did not translate into major transformation in everyday life.

As soon as I was back to the humdrum of everyday life, my constant companions—the voices of doom and gloom—returned, too. They were incredibly noisy, spitting out criticism after criticism with abject self-loathing. In fact, in the days after going out clubbing, I would often find myself more depressed and in a darker mood than before because I was so depleted of energy and the neurochemicals of joy. My self-esteem would tank and a sense of despair would spike. The Tuesday after the Saturday before is not called Suicide Tuesday in club culture argot for nothing.

The biggest challenge of ecstatic experience is that if we don't have an internal path to what we can call "connective consciousness", we can get hooked on external substances to get the feeling of joy. If the cell receptors in our brains start to habituate, we can become psychologically dependent on external factors for our own happiness. Because our brains adapt quickly to pleasure, we need to seek out ever more hedonistic experiences to keep the high.[86] As soon as the high wears off, we are left back in the company of the demons within us.

Unless we have mastered the ability to bring ourselves to a state of joy, we can be locked in the phenomenon know as the "hedonic treadmill". Whether the high is from drugs, fancy handbags, or Michelin-starred restaurants, if we don't find a way to jump off the treadmill and feel good for ourselves, we get addicted. I became a little hooked into hedonism myself. I had no techniques for integrating the insights from connective consciousness into normal, toast-and-tea, life. I wanted to be transformed by what I saw through the wide-opened doors of perception, but had no life philosophy through which to make sense of any of it.

∞

I found more clues to a working life philosophy during my final year at university, when medical students were given the opportunity to study a subject of choice. Most medics chose to spend this year going deeper into one of the sciences. I decided to delve into philosophy. I converted my major and joined the Department of History and Philosophy of Science (HPS).

What I discovered in just one year blew my mind. The thinking was so exciting that I would often wake up early, certainly for a student after a weekend of raving, and run to the library to gorge on ideas. Philosophy is often seen as an academic field stuck in ivory towers, but when it is applied in a practical way, it is one of the essential tools for living, leading, and loving to our fullest potential.

Philosophy, which literally means "love of wisdom", is not just an academic career but an everyday tool to help us clear out old assumptions and so transform ourselves and our world. As the philosopher Ludwig Wittgenstein suggested, it is the very job of philosophy to liberate us from the bewitching lies that flow into every stream of human thought. More than anything else I studied formally during twenty years of high-end education, philosophy helped me understand myself; as well as gain the confidence necessary to penetrate beyond the shiny surfaces of life to find the hidden order of things.

SPIRITUAL ATHEISM PRINCIPLES:

- Be open to engaging in non-rational, shamanic, and ecstatic experiences that can help us enter 'connective consciousness': in which we feel that everything is connected and everyone is our ally. They can be used to heal, empower, and unite us.
- Realize that ecstatic/mystical states can be a natural and essential part of everyday life. The connective consciousness that results can be used as a critical tool for both personal transformation and social change.
- Harness mystical, ecstatic, and shamanic experiences wisely—as tools for growth and transformation rather than just hedonism and escapism. Ensure we integrate the insights from such experiences fully into everyday life; and be vigilant for protective patterns that drive us to use these experiences to go too far, too fast; or to become psychologically or emotionally addicted.
- Avoid projecting onto the potions, practices, and people of mysticism and shamanism the power of inner transformation. Conscious experiences of joy, unity, and inner change lie innate within us all, at all times. Substances and shamans can open the doors and point out the path—but we can get there on our own by turning within.

CHAPTER 6

PHILOSOPHY AND POSTMODERNISM: DECONSTRUCTING EVERYTHING

Almost everyone else in my philosophy program had already spent their first two years grounding themselves in the history of Western thought. I had sixteen weeks to both catch up on the entire canon and learn the new content for the third year program. I needed foundations—from the ancient Greek Heraclitus right up to the modern German Heidegger—and I needed them fast. So I speed-read my way through a lot of books. I would often work late into the night, hundreds of small Post-its stuck around my desk, trying to build a map of human knowledge for myself.

Piece by piece, with more than a few false starts and plenty of moments of terrifying confusion (which can still arise now), I started my journey to understand some of the beliefs upon which our world is built. Rather naively/arrogantly, I thought this project might take me a couple of years. It ended up taking a couple of decades.

Although the teaching in the program was, for me at least, neither inspirational nor clear, being an official student of philosophy gave me the permission I thought I needed to really think, rather than just taking other people's word for it. I initially assumed that studying philosophy would give me some answers about why we exist, that it would help me find the point of life. But I found that the analytical kind of philosophy that was popular in Britain and America did not do it for me.

Instead, I fell in love with continental philosophy, which, along with understanding our existence and conscious experiences, is interested in the dynamics at play when anyone—priest, scientist, or philosopher—says they have the Truth. The philosophy I studied made an important point: don't just believe what people say. Always seek to understand *why* they are saying it: how it serves their desires, be they conscious or not. Penetrate to the hidden order of things *before* you start drinking the Kool-Aid. So I began to question everything, including what I had been told about science by professors of science.

Whether we like it or not, science has become the gold standard for what is right or wrong. What started out as a tool to find certain facts about the physical world has been applied to pretty much all fields of research. Proponents of scientism, who think this a wonderful win for reason, point to the eradication of diseases, the lengthening of lifespans, the reductions in infant mortality, and much more to claim this has been an unmitigated success. They tell a story of scientific progress as a triumphant march towards ever-more certain knowledge and absolute truth. Along the way, the story goes, stupid superstitions like the belief in god, magic, and ecstatic states have been rendered obsolete. This narrative has become so embedded in our minds that it is hard to see that it's a story, rather than simply *the way it is*.

Studying the history and philosophy of science—including medicine, physics, anthropology, psychology, psychoanalysis, and even the law—allows us to remember that science can be studied with a critical eye and not just accepted as the truth. Part of Karl Marx's greatness was his willingness to subject every aspect of the modern world to criticism. This impetus was embraced by a group of mainly German philosophers that came to be called the Frankfurt School. They criticized reason as a totalizing philosophy that denies others elements of being human. Even though reason dismantled superstitious faith, it then became an unquestionable authority itself. The philosophers of the Frankfurt School harnessed "critical theory" to show that rationality has become reified into a new god which seeks dominion over all. Our "fully enlightened earth radiates disaster triumphant" (they weren't talking about spiritual enlightenment). They pointed to the mechanized efficiencies and rational violence of the twentieth century to show what happens when "instrumental reason" reduces everything to data, measurement, and metrics.

Other thinkers studied the history of science, as well as anthropologically observing how scientists actually do science in a lab, to show that science does not progress in a rational, neat line towards absolute Truth; slowly filling in the gaps of knowledge as more 'facts' are discovered. Instead, as Thomas Kuhn demonstrated in his landmark book *The Structure of Scientific Revolutions,* science evolves through major, non-linear breakthroughs that depend on consciousness as much as the data.[87] This challenges the idea that science is simply a mirror of nature.

To describe what happens when science undergoes a major change in theory, Kuhn came up with the notion of a "paradigm". He suggested that all scientific actions, from switching on an MRI scanner to pipetting a chemical solution, happen from within a paradigm: a way of thinking about the world that makes sense of it. In other words, scientific knowledge is as much created by our thoughts as it is discovered by neutrally investigating nature. Our lens, our frame of reference, distorts as much as it reveals.

During business as usual, one scientific paradigm rules over all. But experiments may eventually turn up data that don't make sense. At first, these contradictory results are rejected as "anomalies"; since they do not fit the reigning paradigm, they are discounted. For example, evidence related to the placebo effect is regularly ignored by people who are wedded to the paradigm that biological healing cannot be influenced by the mind.

However, when enough anomalies build up, the old paradigm eventually must be discarded, and when it is, a scientific revolution happens. The data are remixed into a new paradigm that fits the evidence better. For example, for centuries Isaac Newton's classical mechanics theory was the reigning paradigm in physics. Scientists across the planet believed that Newton's laws were the last word on (the) matter. Yet eventually, Quantum Mechanics emerged, a new paradigm that is better than Newton's for studying and describing very tiny things. However, anomalies were showing up for years before people changed the paradigm. This is why the quantum physicist Nils Bohr jested that science progresses one funeral at a time. The old guard has to die, or at least retire, before a new one can emerge with their scientific revolution.

This is huge, because it suggests that *all* scientific ideas sit within a paradigm, and are not simply value-free facts about "the way it is". Materialism is just one way, among many perhaps, of making sense of data. Perhaps other ways of knowing the world may also be useful and valuable. Perhaps ecstatic experiences, studied by William James and facilitated by Carl Jung, have validity even if we cannot understand them from the viewpoint of materialism. In essence, this kind of history and philosophy of science showed me that materialism, privileging primary qualities over everything else, is a metaphysical, and therefore philosophical, *choice*. It is not the one and only Truth.

Once we grok that *all* knowledge is formed within a paradigm, a profound, and potentially both life -and world-changing realization emerges: if paradigms are somehow chosen by our minds we can, perhaps, "unchoose" them consciously. We can learn how to use a shift in consciousness to change paradigms so that we can think new thoughts. We can choose to feel, think, and act in new ways that help us see, imagine, and invent the future rather than be stuck in the past. If we want to lead transformation, in any field of human endeavor, we must become masters at this paradigm shifting. When a paradigm shifts, we have a breakthrough: a transformation in our consciousness that ushers in a transformative solution to a problem that matters in the material world.

In my final year, I had such a breakthrough. I met a woman in a dank cellar deep underneath an ancient college. There a small gang of people from across the university held a mini-rave most Monday nights. Feeling happier than ever, I had enough belief in myself to ask her out. We hooked up and begun to date. It was an explosive love affair but it only lasted a short period before my relationship templates—so ambivalent about trusting another—managed to tank it. I finally had lost my virginity (what I thought I wanted); but didn't get the intimacy I really needed.

For years after, I would come on strong, creating a love-whirlwind to win a woman over, before retreating behind a wall of self-protection as the fear of being hurt kicked in. I became addicted to the chase. I learned how to optimize the whirlwind of romantic seduction to persuade people to fall for me. But I had not learned yet how to love with an open heart and without defenses. This pattern let me feel lovable rather than actually allowing myself to be loved. I call such ambivalent relating the "pushyoupullyou" pattern. I pulled people towards me only to push them away. I stayed a love addict for many years. I had had a breakthrough; but I had not integrated it into my life.

Just as it took me years to have a real transformation in my ability to love without conditions or walls, it usually takes a long time for scientists—even those working on breakthroughs themselves—to fully let go of their old paradigms to allow the shift to happen. This foible is built into how our brains work. We hang on to old patterns and mental maps because their familiarity offers safety and structure, something Control and Protect Mode craves.

Letting go of our paradigms, even for a moment, feels profoundly risky. We feel it as a threat to survival. So unless we learn how not to be afraid, we cannot let go of old patterns (habits, beliefs and moods). Control and Protect Mode holds on to old patterns even if they aren't working anymore. The mode we are in, whether creative or controlling, is driven by the emotion-processing part of our brain (within what scientists call the Salience Network).[88] So being able to have, and lead, paradigm shifts depends on emotional stability, not just reason.

Much of the focus of my work has been centered on how to accelerate this process of transformation more easily. The more our paradigms and mental maps fit the world as it changes, the more we thrive in leadership, love and life. We don't suffer unnecessarily, or cause others to suffer, because we are hanging on to old paradigms that are no longer a fit.

One of the early historians of science and a key influence on Kuhn, Gaston Bachelard, proposed that the history of science is a story of individuals having such transformative experiences. He called this kind of change a *rupture épistémologique* or "epistemological break". We shift from one paradigm or to another. One of the greatest proponents of this kind of thinking, and the most cited author in the humanities, is the French philosopher Michel Foucault. He proposed that everything we think to be true only looks that way because we see the world through an "episteme", a knowledge "frame" or "lens". When we change lenses, we engender paradigm-shifts.

Foucault showed that every claim to truth comes from within an episteme; we cannot help but see and think within a paradigm. While an episteme helps us make sense of the world, it also locks us into a specific way of thinking that may not be useful or empowering for us or others. In fact, Foucault believed that many scientific epistemes are used to control and dominate people.[89] Control and Protect Mode likes to grip tightly onto epistemes—like materialism—that promise an increased capacity to control and dominate the chaos inherent in life. It loves paradigms which offer us power, fortune and fame (which it thinks it needs to be safe). This causes untold suffering to others (and the planet).

A popular episteme loved by materialists is the medical model of disease. This paradigm sees all illness as being caused solely by problems with the physical machinery of the body: all disease is reduced to problems with molecular mechanisms which can be 'fixed' with drugs or surgery. I discovered just how limiting this episteme is the summer before I started in the HPS department. Still caught in a *wanderlust* driven by the desire to get away from myself, I spent four hot months in India. I was ostensibly there to study Ayurvedic medicine (indigenous Indian medicine) on a scholarship. I confess that I spent most of it engaged in hedonistic travel, moving all the way from Ladakh on the Tibetan plateau down to Kerala in the south.

The Rajiv Gandhi Foundation had given me wads of rupees (literally) that I worked out was a budget of £3 per day. I spent a pound or so on accommodation and roughly a pound on food. Then I had one pound remaining for either bottled water or transport, but not both. Stuck in the naive invincibility of youth, on the days when that pound was spent on bus journeys, I drank the local water. I can still see the small rooftop worker's cafe where I downed a cup of water that instigated a "sliding doors" moment in my life.

An hour or so after lunch I started to feel very ill. Thus began three days and nights of bloodstained delirium. Feeling I was near death's door, I crawled on the floor to the front desk. There I begged someone to call a doctor. The rest remains vague. A doctor came, but I was unable to speak with him. He gave me a handful of tablets that were so big that they seemed apt for an elephant. Clearly one or more of them worked, or I would not be writing this. My illness, probably severe amoebic dysentery, cleared up.

Thinking I was cured by the drugs, I set back off on my travels. But in the days and weeks that followed, I started to feel excruciating pain across my back and neck. I assumed it was physical aching from sitting at the back of buses as they bumped and jolted over potholes across the Indian subcontinent. On my return to the UK, the pain had still not eased. I went to the doctor to get it checked out. I was referred to a series of specialists who investigated me for material problems: damaged discs, scoliosis, ankylosing spondylitis. But nothing checked out.

The doctors I saw told me it was not serious, and I was urged to assume a very British stiff upper lip. But the pain was so intense that I couldn't pretend it wasn't there. What I discovered, after two more years of exhaustive tests and dismissive doctors, was that I had contracted, or acquired, a condition called chronic pain syndrome, or fibromyalgia. It is likely the dysentery triggered the syndrome in ways that the medical model does not understand. This paradigm has turned out to be all but powerless to treat this agonizing condition that affects 5 million adults in the US alone.[90] Lady Gaga is the most vocal sufferer of it. She has cancelled tours because of the pain (and she has a team of people to support her). The drugs I was prescribed, which I dutifully took for years, did little to ease the pain.

What makes such a condition particularly challenging to have in the West is that medics operating within the medical model are notoriously uninterested in treating pain. Unlike, say a tumor, which has obvious primary properties to grapple with that can be measured on an MRI scan and cut away with a scalpel, pain is impossible to measure objectively. Since it is a secondary quality, its severity and importance are constantly underestimated by doctors.[91] The lens of materialism distorts their perceptions and they downgrade pain to an after-thought, which it never is for the patient. Just as many materialists/atheists see consciousness as an illusion, many see pain as not really real.

Foucault taught the importance of "excavating" such epistemes to explore the beliefs upon which they are based. Once we dig in, we are more able to emancipate ourselves from limiting assumptions. His "archeological" study of concepts such as madness, medicine, and sex demonstrated that the scientific 'facts' that our world has been built on can be challenged. In fact, they *must* be questioned if we are to become truly free because they often hide agendas of power and control. As philosophers of life, we must dig until we reach the hidden desires and power plays that, unconsciously or not, underpin every belief society holds.

When we do this we find that most 'modern' ideas about human beings, most 'truths' that shore up the status quo, help certain people win. This is as true of science as it is of politics and religion. The win might take the form of a comforting sense of psychological certainty, and feeling right. It might lead to winning funding grants, or attaining positions of prestige. In each case, knowledge can be used to gain, and then hold on to power. Foucault called this nexus of the two "power-knowledge".

The use of knowledge to gain power is hard to spot when rationalists (and they are often militant atheists) use fancy words, impenetrable numbers, and exhaustive evidence to declare that science is the truth. The use of complex statistical mathematics and technical terminology can disguise the power plays that is happening. This isn't always a malicious act. Many people use their privileged access to knowledge to dominate others unconsciously, whether in boardroom shenanigans or seemingly innocuous pub conversations. This is what Control and Protect Mode has us do to feel safe and in charge.

But when scientific knowledge is used to create "norms", those who do not fit in are often rejected or abused. One can be praised or shamed for being above or below average in intelligence or weight. A website can refuse us a loan based on a calculation of our value, driven by averages and algorithms.[92] These science-driven measurements and rankings are a form of control. When people see the world purely in materialist terms, never stopping to consider secondary qualities like feelings, and dreams, they can easily transform our rich subjective selves into scientific objects. Multifaceted, complicated individuals are reduced to their primary qualities, so they can be analyzed, explained, and eventually dominated.

It is tempting to think that religion has been the chief cause of such domination, but science—purposefully untethered from love and compassion in order to be objective—has led to suffering for untold multitudes. Science has been used, whether consciously or not, to destroy love, communities, and hope in virtually every place on our planet.

Soon after Charles Darwin published his work on evolution, the theory was used by Social Darwinists to support the idea that the strong, powerful, and rich in society have a natural right to win over the weak. This power-knowledge is still being used to justify the ideologies of free-market capitalism and political conservatism. Darwin, who believed that sympathy and love were key to evolutionary survival,[93] did not coin the phrase "survival of the fittest": the right-wing philosopher Herbert Spencer did.

Hitler also drew upon evolutionary theory to form his political ideology, holding that weak ethnic groups had to be destroyed to return humankind to its rightful evolutionary path. The Jews were seen as a "nonrace" that corrupted the natural, scientific order of things, and they had to be removed.[94] The rational and logical conclusions of such scientific racism were the death camps and murder squads of the Nazi regime.

I have seen for myself the horrifying reality of the impact of scientific racism on flesh-and-blood human beings. My father took my sister and me on a family heritage tour of Eastern Europe. We entered Poland to visit Auschwitz. Coaches buzzed in and out, taking hordes of tourists on tours of the camp. I wandered off on my own, needing some space to reflect. I stumbled across a mound of children's eyeglasses that lay quietly in the tall grasses. They had been thrown there years before when kids were unloaded from trains, and then gassed. I had thought I was done grieving for this unmeasurable act of violence that ripped a gaping hole in the fabric of my family, but I cried floods of tears as I looked at those glasses in the grass.

Eugenics was not simply a Nazi perversion of science either. The exclusion of Jews and other undesirables was inspired by the successes of the Jim Crow laws in the United States.[95] In fact, German scientists worked with their American contemporaries to provide the evidence needed to support Nazi policies.[96] The Jim Crow laws, which were in place in the majority of the US long before the Nazis created their Nuremberg Laws, were a scientifically justified apartheid system. They legally separated African Americans from European Americans on the basis of what were considered to be rational and scientific 'facts' about race. This power-knowledge allowed white people to dominate black even though the American Civil War had been fought to end such inequality.

It was not just in the south that science was used to dominate and control. From the 1900s to the 1970s, around 60,000 supposedly 'unfit' people were forcibly sterilized across the US to prevent 'feeble' offspring from being born. 20,000 of these were in the shiny, happy state of California. Their right to give birth, to enjoy the process of raising children, was taken from them by the government based on the science of the time.[97]

Science has also been used to enact violence on those considered mentally ill within the medical model. In the 1940s and 1950s, 40,000 or so people in the United States were given frontal lobotomies to 'cure' them of psychological challenges that may or may not have been caused by mechanistic breakages. The damage done to their brains and psyches was made infamous by Ken Kesey's book *One Flew Over the Cuckoo's Nest* (since turned into a movie starring Jack Nicholson). Many of those lobotomized were gay,[98] which, until 1974, was officially considered by the American scientific community to be 'abnormal' and so a mental disorder.[99] This was of course underpinned by the best science of the time, so it seemed rational within the paradigm.

All this, and much more that we may never know about, is why Foucault demanded of proponents of scientism, "What types of knowledge do you want to disqualify in the very instant of your demand, 'Is it a science'? Which speaking, discoursing subjects—which subjects of experience and knowledge—do you then want to 'diminish' when you say: 'I who conduct this discourse am conducting a scientific discourse, and I am a scientist?'"[100]

When people use science to fulfill the ambitions of Control and Protect Mode for certainty and domination, people usually suffer. Science doesn't have to be a form of power play, though. The British philosopher Bertrand Russell pointed to a distinction between science driven by the will to power, enacted from within Control and Protect Mode, and that carried out from within Create and Connect Mode, driven by a deep "love of nature", as he put it.

Russell believed that, as the Enlightenment dawned, connection and curiosity animated the pursuit of science. He acknowledged other ways of knowing, noting that mystics and poets sought knowledge not for power over others, but for empowerment. Alongside other truth-seekers, scientists were inspired to investigate nature because they were in love with the world. But as we know, science was eventually taken over by people who wanted power over others and over nature itself.[101] As Russell said, "the lover of nature has been baffled, the tyrant over nature has been rewarded".

Francis Bacon, the pioneer of the scientific method back in the seventeenth century, believed that there was no need to worry about anyone abusing the power of science. He held that our scientific prowess would be governed by "right reason and true religion".[102] But atheist scientism has progressively rooted out the value-systems of religion to leave us morally adrift, as Nietzsche pointed out so powerfully. We now believe that 'good' science is value-less; but that leaves us as leaders without morality to temper the what science says is 'normal' and what is not.

When Bacon's contemporary Galileo split primary and secondary qualities apart, I do not believe he thought that secondary qualities were less important than primary ones; he just didn't think we could rely on them to do science. Compassion, morality, and values were removed from the practice of science out of concern that these secondary qualities would affect the objectivity of the scientific method (which they can do). As a consequence of killing off God and embracing atheism, positivism and scientism, we lost any firm foundations about what is right or wrong. Lobotomies and gas chambers were a direct result.

Science is fabulously successful at telling us about what exists in the material world of physics, from gravitational waves in space to the forces that hold together our atoms. The chances are that the laws of physics will apply to your body for all the time you are alive (and as you decompose, too). But it can only offer conjectures and speculations about the complex, often non-rational, inner life of human being. Scientific probabilities can indicate what might happen if we live our lives in certain ways, say with purpose (or with pain). But science can't tell us what that means, how it will feel, or how to make it happen.

Science can never be the *sole* guide for how to live because to make it objective, all subjective opinions and personal values had to be taken out. Science is therefore valueless and meant to be so. Hence there is no philosophically valid way to move from statements that describe how matter is in the physical world (no matter how positive we are about their veracity) to statements that prescribe how reality should be for human beings. When we leap from making scientific observations about what *is* occurring to thinking about how people *ought* to live their lives, we commit the "is-ought fallacy", made famous by the philosopher David Hume.

We must all move out of 'is' and into 'ought' at some point in order to make decisions as leaders (and parents), whether in our own lives or someone else's. To do this we must leave the realms of empirical science and enter philosophy of some kind, even if we don't like this and just want to stick with "the evidence". If we try to apply scientific method into arenas in which it cannot be used, we risk enacting violence on the very real human beings who have to deal with the consequences of outdated medical, political, and economic paradigms.

Since the modern world is effectively run by people using "evidence-based" science to execute their jobs—this includes economists, lawyers, psychologists, doctors, policy professionals, and politicians—we need to pay careful attention to what we are told. It is incumbent on us to find out exactly what is and isn't being said when a person utters words like: "This project is right because of this logic and that evidence".

We must do this vigilantly, whether on a small scale, such as by questioning the medical interventions our doctor recommends; or on a larger scale that could impact thousands, when we must make decisions as leaders based on incomplete data sets. There is always incomplete data about such a fast-changing world. We must employ what Aristotle called *phronesis*: practical philosophy that helps us surface the assumptions upon which beliefs are built and so make decisions that lead to more thriving.

We, too, operate from within a certain paradigm at all times. This is what the anthropologists realize when they try to study an other human culture from within their own. Materialists think that by removing subjective experience from the scientific method, they have also removed the problem of bias. But the work of Bachelard, Kuhn, Foucault and other sociologists, historians, and anthropologist of science shows us that this is never entirely possible. Everyone interprets the world through their own paradigm, which is heavily influenced by their education, psychological development, and life experience.

When I began to study philosophy, I was still wedded to the materialist paradigm, though I didn't know it was a paradigm. I assumed it was just the truth. But after I discovered the way science works, I realized that materialism's privilege on truth was suspicious. This epiphany launched me into an epistemological breakthrough that changed my life. I began to free myself from the mental slavery of materialism. But this was not as immediately liberating as it might seem.

Much of this philosophy, doubting and deconstructing reason and science, is called "postmodern". Postmodernism is very good at telling us what is *not* absolutely true. But it is less good at telling us what *is* true, providing us with a foundation to flourish with. It is relatively easy to deconstruct anyone's claim to truth in flashy postmodern turns around the intellectual dance floor, but constructing a new paradigm to ensure we thrive is not so simple.

We can critique the ideology of positivism, but then we are left sinking into an abyss of nihilism. It is easy to poke holes in the arguments of others by exposing their assumptions and revealing their biases. It is much, much harder to create a philosophy that can withstand the assaults of fellow intellectuals and act as a meaningful guide for how to live. People trained in critical theory, whose Control and Protect Mode has discovered the thrills of using deconstruction to 'win', love nothing more than to knock it down.

Our brains and bodies want certainty among the chaos. If they don't get it, we can feel lost, confused, and fearful. The Enlightenment displaced God and Aristotle from their central role in organizing the world. With Descartes' famous idea that *cogito ergo sum* (I think, therefore I am), the rational mind was coronated in their stead.[103] But reason, taken to its logical and skeptical conclusion in the form of postmodern philosophy, casts suspicion on everything (including itself).

We thought science could replace God with logic and hard evidence. But science was designed from the outset to be partial, focusing on primary properties and getting rid of secondary qualities (like moral values and subjective feelings). Because we destroyed the idea of a transcendent god that defines good and evil, we no longer have any firm footing—agreed-upon cultural values—upon which to make decisions.

Science, materialism, and atheism have it that we are an accident of evolution (albeit a marvelous one). The universe is seen as a dead machine with a bunch of static mechanical laws to govern our physical reality. Nothing has any objective value over anything else, other than perhaps the fitness benefit of a mutation. With this paradigm, science has been incredibly successful at studying the material world but much less successful at understanding our inner world. There is a huge paradox here: science is carried out from within a *mental* paradigm that lies within human consciousness. Yet materialists say there is no such thing as consciousness. Therefore no scientific facts discovered through conscious experience should exist. Help!

Nietzsche summed up our (post)modern malaise when he wrote, just after pronouncing that we had killed God with reason, "how shall we, murderers of all murderers, console ourselves? That which was the holiest and mightiest of all that the world has yet possessed has bled to death under our knives. Who will wipe this blood off us? With what water could we purify ourselves? What festivals of atonement, what sacred games shall we need to invent?"

Postmodernism, which transforms everything of certainty into irony, shows us that every act is good or bad only because of the paradigm through which we see it. Therefore all acts are relative to their cultural context. We cannot judge people for doing things that their paradigm says is okay, even if this means promoting Female Genital Mutilation. This is an urgent issue for us all to grapple with. Without a clear meaning-making system with values within it, we have no firm basis on which to make either personal or collective decisions. The resulting nihilism is not an easy reality to flourish within. I was stuck inside it for years as I believed relativism was the ultimate truth. I thought nothing could come after postmodern deconstruction. I was wrong.

Philosophy's job must be to create hope and meaning as much as cast aspersions on other systems or ideals. As the thinker Jordan Peterson says in his online videos:[104] "The best you can do with postmodern philosophy is emerge nihilistic, at best. The worst case is that you're a kind of anarchical social revolutionary who is directionless apart from that you want to tear things down. Or you end up depressed". A philosopher cannot just tear down other people's ideological towers. Upon the rubble we must build lighthouses that shine a beam on the future and guide people to a place where they can thrive.

Without religion to make meaning and with science no longer the sole arbiter of my truth, I was thrust into an existential dilemma. I thought I had to choose between dogma of some kind (religious or scientific) or living with the knowledge that everything I said or did was ultimately relative and thus meaningless. I got lost down this rabbit-hole for years. I can still feel the emotional memories of existential confusion, doubt, and panic that reverberated within me for a decade.

Having spent a year deconstructing the paradigms and claims of medicine and science, I was no longer convinced it was the right path for me. I viewed the materialist medical model as being powerful in many areas of disease, but direct experience of pain and depression suggested it was less useful in my interest area: mental health and psychological healing. The philosophy I was exploring had helped me see that much of our mental suffering is caused by paradigms and beliefs, secondary qualities that can't be addressed with medical interventions.

My path was bifurcating. Everything came to a head, as so often happens in life, by a full-blown crisis. As I explain in *Switch On*, a crisis is nothing to be feared when we can consciously use it to transform ourselves. The Greek word literally means a "turning point". I did not know this then. All I knew was that my body was wracked by gnawing pain all the time. Some days it reached such a fever pitch that I could attend to little else. Until I got very committed to self-healing years later, excruciating muscle pain was my everyday reality. Often the pain was so intense and insistent that I fantasized about slipping a stiletto knife under my shoulder blades, the ground zero of the pain, and cutting the muscles out. Sometimes I didn't want to stop at the shoulder blades.

The pain was taking a toll on my mind. This was exacerbated by the epistemological rupture I was undergoing and the confusion that comes when old paradigms break down. I started having fierce panic attacks, waking up in the night gasping for air as I stared out into the emptiness of nihilism and postmodern relativism. Still at medical school, one of my first rotations was, ironically, rheumatology: the study of muscles and joints and the diseases that impact them.

In one consultation that I observed, an elderly couple came in with severe rheumatoid arthritis. There was a fierce intimacy to their agony as they released floods of tears together, synchronized in sickness and in love. The doctor told them, as he had told me a few weeks earlier, that there was little more he could do; everything that materialist science suggested had been done. To my surprise (and horror, at the time), I felt tears running down my own face. I had witnessed the limits of the medicine that my health hopes and career dreams were tied up in.

I ran out of the hospital having a meltdown. I found a phone box and called my mom, by this point a professional psychotherapist. She was there for me in just the way I needed. I went to her house and collapsed in a heap for the first, but sadly not last, time. Multiple paradigms were shifting within me. My sense of being a healthy young man was collapsing. My ideal of becoming a doctor-scientist was fading. My faith in romance saving me was dying. The turmoil I felt within, driven by patterns that couldn't cope with my changing reality, overwhelmed the natural joy within. I sank into full-blown clinical depression. The gilding on the chandeliers of the vast ballroom of life disappeared. What once inspired me now just ached.

My GP prescribed me antidepressants, and I was referred to a unit to be assessed for my pain. They gave me a final diagnosis: fibromyalgia. The severity of my symptoms was rated a 9 out of 10. They told me there was little else that could be done; that my pain was a life sentence; and that I would live a very limited life. During this period I came to the conclusion that I was less interested in treating full-blown psychiatric conditions and more excited about supporting people through the challenges of life. Perhaps I could use philosophy—wisdom that can change our paradigms—to help myself, and then others, thrive. I felt a flicker of hope as I finally accepted that a life outside of medicine might be a better fit for me. I made the decision to let go of the safe career I had been focused on—with guaranteed income, recognition, and respect—to explore the unknown.

∞

Painfully, I relinquished the need for approval—from my dad, my grandmother, my peers, anyone—to start out on a new path. Having fallen completely head-over-heels in love with the history and philosophy of ideas, I applied to PhD programs in the field—focused on the concept of "intuition"—at American schools where cross-disciplinary thinking was encouraged. While I waited to hear about the PhD programs I had applied to, I needed to earn a living.

My father told me about a role in advertising agencies called "account planning". He described it as the application of philosophy and psychology to real-life commercial problems. It sounded enjoyable and interesting so I dove into the media world of the mid-nineties. My hunt to forge a reliable pathway towards human thriving was about take a very useful, albeit twisted, detour into the domain of desire. All my nascent ideas about shifting paradigms were about to be tested in the real world with advertising campaigns that would impact tens of millions of people (whether for good or ill is eminently debatable).

SPIRITUAL ATHEISM PRINCIPLES:

- Be conscious of the paradigms through which we see and study the world. Deconstruct these paradigms, and the truth claims made within them, using our critical thinking. This reveals that all paradigms of thought are historical, political, and partial as opposed to absolutely timeless, neutral, and impartial.
- Realize that knowledge can be, and usually is, used to gain control and power over others—so challenge, compassionately, the paradigms, politics, and power plays that are being enacted and leveraged when people promote religious rules, 'scientific' solutions, and 'spiritual' products.
- Be aware that scientific truths are as much 'constructed' within a specific historical paradigm as they are 'discovered' in nature. This is because all scientific theories interpret the data of primary properties within conscious, secondary qualities. These interpretations change over time based on both new data (often from more advanced measuring tools) and new paradigms of thought (that are always evolving and developing in culture.)
- Move beyond 'postmodern' negation and deconstruction to build firm philosophical foundations with which we can make positive choices—rather than merely criticizing the ideas, beliefs, and choices of others.
- Embrace the necessity to step beyond data, which is always about the past, in order to make empowering and powerful choices that solve problems in the present and that help us forge a better future.

CHAPTER 7
CAPITALISM AND CONSUMERISM: THE DESIRING LIFE

I was recruited by a global ad agency to work on Nike and various other 'youth' brands. As serendipity would have it, the agency I worked in had been developing a methodology to help brands, like their clients Apple, create paradigm shifts in consumer culture.

Within weeks of starting the job, I was actually being paid to help cause epistemological breaks. I was asked to focus most of my energy on understanding and growing the gaming market. Our client, Sony PlayStation, wanted to change the episteme of video gaming, taking it out of boys' bedrooms and into everyday life. Today more women play than men.[105] This was not an accident. This future was forged by brand leadership.

Innovation enabled by the investment of capital in risky ideas and inventions, like video games consoles, has shaped our lives in myriad ways. Over the last hundred or so years, products and services that were once the preserve of a small elite have been progressively democratized, and made accessible to all. Wool sweaters, colorful dyed clothing, portrait paintings, cameras, cars, airplane flights, computers, cellular phones: inventions by enterprises funded by private capital have created new and wonderful things that have made our lives easier, richer, and more enjoyable.

It is all but impossible to imagine what life would look like without the ingenuity, prosperity, and openness that are the most positive hallmarks of capitalism as a form of social and economic organization. Little wonder that the number of private-sector corporations that a country has predicts its degree of political freedom. Capitalism and democracy can go hand in hand.[106]

At the ad agency, I was an intrinsic part of that world. I relished making an impact with creative ideas instead of just studying them. But I would eventually realize that, excitement and vanity aside, most marketing exists for one thing and one thing only: to sell more products at higher prices. Few of those products are genuinely valuable to society. The equation is simple. The higher the margin and the more units of a product sold, the more money a company makes. The more money it makes, the more it pays back to its shareholders, the bigger the bonuses for its execs and the more it can spend on more marketing. It's a win-win—for those in the business. For cogs in the machine of capitalism, it's often a different story.

I was a cog in the machine with my first paid job as a burger flipper at McDonald's. At the time, in the late eighties, McDonald's was the largest business in the world. Inside the galaxy of the golden arches I experienced first hand the less-than-glamorous hallmarks of advanced capitalism: low pay compared to profits made, repetitive and uncreative tasks, and poor working conditions. This paradigm, which may feel okay at head office, is much less glossy at the coal-face. It increases profit for the shareholders, but doesn't do much to empower individuals in the labor force.

As an ad agency exec I was charged with creating the desire that has someone go into a store and buy a hamburger or games console. The ad agency had hired me to leverage psychological, philosophical, and biological insights to develop advertisements that trigger cravings for consumption. Conventional consumer capitalism (for there are other, more nourishing, forms of capitalism) works because it leverages desire within what we can call the "deficit" paradigm.

The deficit paradigm has it that we all have deficits in our psyches that can be relieved by buying material goods and services (and the symbolic value of a sexy brand). The doozy is that these deficits usually stem from the disappointments experienced in our early years around which our patterns form to protect us. The specific job of an account planner in an agency is to learn how to trigger the deficit within—the feeling that we are not cool / sexy / attractive / successful / normal / happy / sane—and then offer a way to relieve the fear, albeit temporarily, through consumption. I was trained to offer salvation from suffering within through consumption of stuff.

The unconscious mind, full of shadows and demons, thinks: If I just get the right car, the right job title, the right house in the right neighborhood, the right cell phone, and the right honeymoon experience, *then* I will be happy. Control and Protect Mode thinks that the right phablet, or filling up on high-fructose foods, just might be able to purify us and save us (from the death of god). I bought into this fantasy right along with most. I thought having the right stuff would finally make me loved and wanted. I was wrong.

Consumption can never quite give us what we really need. It hooks us into tiny moments of transcendence as we break through the limits of everyday life through shopping. But, just like with hedonistic drugs, we have to keep consuming to experience happiness. The (often ecstatic) moments of purchase cover up our existential angst. But as soon as we put away the new clothes or the sneakers get a bit dirty, our sense of lack comes back. Brand stories promise an end to our pain and a healing of our trauma, but often are limited to an ersatz rush of pleasurable brain chemicals. When they wear off, we are left not just with the pain underneath, but also cravings for more consumption.

The darkest side of the ad industry is that commercials often exacerbate cravings that may never have taken root if left alone. For example, ads for antiperspirant that tap into feelings of embarrassment about biologically-necessary wet patches under our arms encourage social anxieties that may never have existed without the commercials. The logic of consumer capitalism sees this as an "unmet need" and develops a chemical product which might well hurt both people and planet, to relieve it. Most of us, if not all of us, are full of many desires, or "pain points", that can easily morph into full-blown addictions if they are triggered by ads.

The entire nature of addiction is the quest to quench the flames of heartache inside us with things outside of us. This is, of course, impossible. Even socially-acceptable addictions like working too hard, beating the competition, checking the news every few minutes and running ultra-marathons take their toll on our wellbeing. Until I learned to generate my own sense of inner peace within, I was dependent on sex, work, food, money, running, prizes, booze, and potions to feel good. These addictions are the habitual protective patterns of Control and Protect Mode on speed.

All addiction is a "category mistake", a term coined by philosopher Gilbert Ryle.[107] We confuse the category "things within us that make us whole"—like love, purpose, meaning, connection, and intimacy—with the category "things outside us that feel good for a moment." We keep buying and consuming (or ingesting or practicing) the external in the hope that it will provide what we yearn for most internally. But it never can. I remember the moment that I grokked this fully. I was in a posh airport lounge in Switzerland. It was early evening and I had just finished running a long workshop for a client. I was exhausted. I drifted into the duty-free store. What seemed like a smart solution to my low mood was to buy something fancy, because I was worth it. The high feeling lasted for a few minutes and then dissipated into nothing by the time I landed back at London Heathrow. I don't even remember what I bought. When we become addicted to material things, we have to work more hours so we can pay for our desires.

Our current form of capitalism, dominated by Control and Protect Mode, requires the creation and fulfillment of lack at scale. Before the modern era, artisans created products and merchants imported goods at a human scale. This system of craft, trade, and exchange was underpinned by close relationships and connections between communities. With the birth of industrial manufacturing, driven by the technological fruits of the scientific method, the old paradigm was no longer sufficient.

Once those with capital invest in costly machinery, they need people to buy the goods; otherwise, supply outstrips demand and prices plummet. Deficit marketing, which hijacks the biological machinery of desire, is capitalism's way of ensuring a continuous growth in demand that keeps prices and profits high. The genius of advanced capitalism is that it maintains demand even when markets are saturated—by innovating a steady stream of newer, sexier models for us to desire.

All of this activity is there for one reason: to generate profits for shareholders who have a seemingly insatiable desire for more wealth. In Control and Protect Mode, money is often equated with safety and power. But no amount of money is ever enough if we don't feel safe and powerful within. While consumer capitalism promises us redemption through choice, it ends up enslaving everyone—labor and capital—in a cycle of production and consumption.

The connection between capitalism and slavery is anything but new. The classic capitalist industries of sugar (Tate Modern anyone?) and cotton, which boomed with the desire for candy and clothing in the big imperial cities, created enormous wealth for a few people. The profits were huge because the industry found a way not to pay the people producing the goods: slavery. More slaves stolen from Africa and shipped across the "Middle Passage" to the colonies meant cheaper raw materials to feed the factories in Pennsylvania and Manchester. The slave trade was one of the first "exponential" businesses, long before the term became popular in Silicon Valley, because there was no limit to profits as long as more slaves and customers could be found, which they always could. Slavery was also one of the first global enterprises, free from any regulation for centuries.[108]

Capitalism inspired expansionist nations to colonize the world. Empires boosted national pride while providing cheap raw materials to be magicked into profit. Colonization was also a great solution to the need to create new consumers. Colonial subjects, dominated by laws created thousands of miles away in Brussels or London, had little choice but to buy from their imperial masters. Even if they wanted to buy locally, taxes made non-imperial products exorbitantly expensive.

This is why the symbol of freedom that Mahatma Gandhi chose for India's independence was the *charkha*, or spinning wheel. He wanted it to remind his countryfolk that they had always had their own indigenous capacity to produce wonderful clothes. They did not need to disempower themselves and line the pockets of their colonial masters by buying fabrics woven in the factories of Britain. They had what they needed for human-scale trade, which creates prosperous communities, without the need for vast factories—or the desire-manufacturing factories of Adland.

Don't get me wrong. I love the creativity and dynamism of capitalism. A capitalist enterprise like Apple, Google or Tesla is arguably the most innovative force on the planet (to date). Having worked in and around capitalist enterprises for the best part of twenty years, I have seen what an incredible engine of change they can be. The move from the invention of the first mass-market car to getting an Uber ride home with the click of an app took just 100 years.

Because a business is not reliant on government grants or the whims of the 'good and the great', like most public institutions and charities are, it has the freedom to realize its vision of a better world. By solving problems with products and services that people are willing to pay for, businesses can change the world and improve people's lives. Billions have been lifted out of subsistence farming and poverty through business; and have then been empowered to find jobs with more meaning and more money.

The engine of value creation through invention is totally agnostic. Capitalism, and so marketing and advertising, can be used to create and push products that are profoundly valuable or suspiciously harmful, like cheap sugary drinks. In fast-developing Mexico, which has been importing American products and mindsets for decades, a third of all children are now overweight or obese.[109] They have been trained to fulfill their desires with the food and drink brands of the West.

Capitalist marketing and innovation tools can also be used to create and scale products that inspire, empower, and educate—like the Raspberry Pi computer that my son loves to code on. It all depends on whether the leaders making the decisions are alive to the impact of their actions; and are conscious and courageous enough to do what is best for everyone, not just themselves. In other words, the impact a business has all depends on the secondary qualities of its leaders and what paradigm they operate from within: business as a force for purpose or profit. Leaders, who can be at any position in the formal hierarchy of an organization, make doing the right thing their priority whereas managers focus on doing things right.

Management's relentless focus on driving maximum *efficiency*—a panacea for Control and Protect Mode—can block human creativity and connectivity, which can leave us frustrated and shut down. Unfortunately, efficiency is the modern god of managers everywhere, and conscious, connected, and creative leadership is less easy to come by (although that is changing fast). Efficiency, a term that comes from the study of machines and mechanisms, is about creating more outputs (profit) with fewer inputs (costs). This means focusing on the efficient exchange of materials, whether oil, internet bandwidth, or money, and not relationships between feeling, thinking beings.

Executives (and often those lower down the hierarchy, too) are incentivized to maximize efficiency by linking their bonuses to short-term profits and the price of a company's shares. If stuck in Control and Protect Mode, which is what people are paid the big bucks to be in, most do whatever it takes to boost the figures, even if in the long term it hurts the value they offer the world and contributes to the destruction of the planet.

Efficiency is tied to primary qualities that can be measured: performance, production, productivity. It doesn't account for how things feel to the workers, or about the product's long-term impact on the consumer (or planet). Unfeeling clinical efficiency is what has mangers shut down production in one country—even if the factory has been rooted in a culture and community for a century or more—in order to use labor in countries where people come cheaper, and there are fewer inefficient regulations and costly union demands to deal with. Managers are taught to manipulate measurable primary qualities like KPIs and results without enormous amounts of reflection on secondary qualities like empathy and social justice. Working for such rational organizations can cut chunks out of our soul.

Intense efficiency-driven organizations also stifle our creativity and conscious awareness. Innovation is inefficient. Create and Connect Mode is full of new ideas and loves connecting with others, so it 'wastes' resources on innovative experiments; and 'wastes' time and energy on nurturing and empowering leadership. Managers, like scientists, prioritize 'hard' efficiencies even as the organization loses the 'soft' trust, purpose and imagination it needs to keep changing as times change. This is causing intense challenges for most uber-efficient organizations which are now struggling to fit, let alone forge, the future.

We are incentivized to stay in such organizations, and to give our lives over to working ever harder, with the promise of promotions, bonuses, and perhaps fame. Hooked into the system, we agree, whether tacitly or explicitly, to buy into this paradigm. So we can easily become what William Whyte called "organization man" in his classic book. We stay quiet in moments when we want to share our concerns about policies or practices. We go along with corporate strategies that we know might cause pain to people and the planet in order not to rock the boat. Being part of this almost inevitably takes a toll on us, creating more inner angst to be relieved (often by consumption). Unless we speak out, as leaders, today's form of capitalism will keep moving us towards injustice and unhappiness.

Adam Smith suggested in his epic tome *The Wealth of Nations* that Western capitalism should work for society as a whole because people like "the butcher, the brewer, or the baker" put their own material interests ahead of everyone else's.[110] Their desire to grow their businesses and make more profit encourages them to develop better products and services, and everyone benefits. Take all this self-interest together and we get Smith's famous "invisible hand", which, like science, is supposed to drive progress for all.

Smith was the father of modern economics, the scientific study of how people make, use, and pay for stuff. Economists wanted their branch of knowledge to be as reliable and respected as physics had become. They took as their episteme the ideals of mechanistic and materialist science, even though economics deals with flows of money and resources between emotional human beings, not machines. The Holy Grail was to find inalienable laws of economics, just like Newton found the physical laws of motion.

In the middle of the twentieth century it looked like Simon Kuznets had found just such a law, one that seemed to prove the positive impacts of capitalism on our shared wellbeing. Kuznets was a major player in institutionalizing economics at the heart of government policy. He pulled together the (very little) hard data available at the time and crunched them into a theory. It stated that when a nation's gross domestic product (GDP) grows, inequality will rise at first, but it will then start to fall. This means that all economic growth, of any kind, is good because it eventually leads to benefits for everyone, just as Adam Smith had suggested.[111]

We can just leave the butcher, the baker, the multi-national CEO, and the investment banker to feather their own nests, and everyone will do fine. Kuznets warned that his work was mainly speculation based on a little bit of empirical evidence, and "some of it possibly tainted by wishful thinking",[112] but his hypothesis was turned into the kind of eternal law that economics had been seeking. It has been taught to most economics students as Truth for some fifty plus years.

From the work of Smith, Kuznets, and others such as Milton Friedman, and Friedrich Hayek, sprung an ideology called "free-market capitalism", which has been the basis of most government economic policy in Western and Westernizing countries for many years. The ideology holds that companies should be left alone by government as much as possible and all will be well. Another term for this is "laissez-faire" economics, which comes from a French expression for letting things take their own course. The theory is that when they are allowed to do what they want, companies make a ton of money that will eventually trickle down to everyone, even to those who aren't wealthy. This is the heart of what has become known as "trickle-down economics", or Reaganomics, because President Reagan was such a big fan.

The economist Thomas Piketty became a global sensation when he published, in 2014, an extensive study on the evidence about what really happens in free-market, laissez-faire, trickle-down systems.[113] During the so-called "miracle years", when capitalism first takes off in a country, Piketty demonstrated that economic growth does indeed lift many out of poverty. Paid decent wages at last, people are able to afford a home and consumer goods like cars and washing machines for the first time. But it doesn't last. Once the miracle years pass, inherited wealth generates far more profit than any income we can make from our wages as producers.

In other words, those who are already rich make far more money from investing their capital in property, gold, and rare wines (along with other asset classes that can make capital grow, like Bitcoin) than the rest of us can ever make from selling our time during a lifetime of labor. Wealth rises to the top instead of trickling down to the bottom as everyone hoped it would. For example, in Nigeria, the most populous and richest country in Africa, GDP has risen almost 10 percent each year for fifteen or so years. Yet Nigeria also now has more people in extreme poverty than it did in the 1990s.[114]

A similar picture is forming in other fast-developing countries like

India. This is why we are now witnessing record levels of inequality—Pope Francis calls it "the root of social evil"[115]—which is creating massive instability at the heart of our economic and political systems. At the time of writing, just eight people own more wealth than 3.5 billion or so do and CEOs can easily earn 800 times more than their employees.[116] A few years ago the number was closer to fifty, so even the super-rich are becoming more unequal within their own elite group. Such inequality is no good for us.

Inequality erodes trust and increases anxiety, drug abuse, imprisonment, obesity, and illness.[117] It drives excess consumption, too. But it is not just our psyches and our society that suffer. A 2015 report by the International Monetary Fund has shown that if those at the top of a country grow richer, total GDP growth actually declines over the medium term. On the other hand, increasing the income of the bottom chunk of citizens, even just by 1 percent, results in an increase in overall GDP growth.[118] On top of this, unsustainable extraction from the natural world is destroying the ecology that every economy depends on.[119]

Capitalism is entrenched in the materialist episteme and is rarely tempered by the secondary qualities of care and compassion. A modern-day story has emerged to make this paradigm somehow seem normal, eternal, and essential. Inspired by Judeo-Christian ideas of salvation and redemption, it has been dubbed "prosperity gospel". If we are wealthy, then we have worked hard for it, and so are deserving of riches. Put another way, God shows his love for us by making us successful, healthy, rich, and famous. If we are poor or sick, however, it means God has forsaken us and we are to blame. If we end up homeless or on social security, it must mean that we are not worth saving.

This gospel has seeped into all parts of society. The New Age idea of the "law of attraction" featured in the book and film *The Secret*—the idea that you can attract wealth from the universe by thinking in the 'right' way—is part of this gospel. It is one of the most pernicious memes in the personal development space. It is also the essence of the American Dream, now popping up globally in local variants as the British, Indian, or Nigerian Dreams. The idea that prosperity delivers us from damnation locks us into working hard for things we don't really need, condemning us to a form of secular hell.

Supported by memes from science, like Social Darwinism, we are asked to spin faster and faster, producing and consuming, to rise up the food chain. Drugged on cheap(ish) credit, consumer goods, and technologies, we have put up with the rest of the irksome elements of capitalism. Consumer choice has stopped us from feeling the pain of growing inequality. But that is no longer true. As writer Wolfgang Streek puts it, "coping, doping, hoping and shopping" as survival strategies are no longer working.[120] People seem to be done.

Most people have had to accept flat or falling wages (after inflation is taken into account) for thirty years or more.[121] Austerity is cutting through public services like a hot spoon through ice cream. Schools in Kansas are closing because of a lack of funds[122] and there are reports that many care homes in the UK are on the brink of collapse.[123] For the first time in human history, many kids today will not have as much wealth as their parents did. The shock waves of this realization are only just starting to be felt. Little wonder that stress—the black plague of the twenty-first century—is the largest single cost to the US healthcare system. General Motors spends more per car on healthcare than it does on steel.[124]

The crazy thing is that most of us have grown up so embedded within the consumer capitalist paradigm that all this inequality, addiction, and stress seems normal. If not normal, it certainly is made to look inevitable.

After the fall of Communism in the USSR and the success of state-driven capitalism in places like China and Singapore, capitalism has been portrayed as the only system that works. The author Francis Fukuyama famously said that the permanent dominance of capitalism, and the liberal democracy that usually goes with it, is the "end of history": nothing can come after it.[125]

Consumer capitalism, like all paradigms, is historical. It developed over time within a modern, Western episteme. It is premised on a very modern idea of an "individual" that owns things outright rather than sharing them. Capitalism's rise was inspired by the worship in the West of a god separate from humans with a hierarchy of angels, humans, and animals. The idea that all beings are organized in such a hierarchy is radically different from the belief in many indigenous traditions that all elements in the web of life are equal (e.g. Ubuntu).

The philosopher Descartes fully established the idea of the modern Self—discrete, skin-wrapped, and separate from her environment—with his *cogito*: "I think, therefore I am."[126] Soon after, the concept of the unique and individual self—one that has a will, seeks its own truths, and owns its own land—snowballed. We developed an obsession with private property. Imagine the surprise of the Native Americans when colonists started to put up fences and walls and declare that a certain bit of dirt, a shared source of sustenance, was owned by one person. This right to own land privately is the bedrock of Anglo-Saxon society. Private property lay at the heart of the Founding Fathers' vision of an independent United States.

In the nineteenth century, theorists built Western economics within the paradigm of individuality. The idea of *homo economicus* or "economic man" emerged: a separate individual that makes rational choices as a producer and consumer.[127] The twentieth century then gave birth to the idea of the individual having a private unconscious (that a psychoanalyst could analyze). This was followed by the hyper-individualistic reality of the Thatcher and Reagan years. The twenty-first century has started off with a bang as we broadcast every *individual* thought and image through Instagram or Snapchat.

∞

The individual Self reigns triumphant over all modernity. Nowhere is this more evident than in the ad industry. Agencies are designed to trigger wounded individual selves with commercials. After a dizzying two-and-a-half year learning curve, in which I began to appreciate the power of creative thinking to solve problems at scale, I wanted out. My father reminded me of my commitment to making a difference and doing good in the world. I thought about whether this was the time for starting a PhD program. It was tempting, as it has been many times since, but I didn't know if I'd be doing it because I loved knowledge or because I wanted the kudos. Plus, I still wanted to put ideas to work in the real world.

It was early 1999 and the dot-com extravaganza was coming into full swing. I had never been into technology up to that point. However, a colleague sent me a link to an online pamphlet called *The Cluetrain Manifesto*. Although it was clearly not quite as radical as Marx and Engels' *The Communist Manifesto*, I read it with interest. It discussed, in a language I could understand, how the internet was changing business and marketing forever. The digital revolution was making old ways of doing business—like having a crappy product and then spending a lot of money to 'polish the turd' with a big ad campaign—untenable.

A notion began to take root in me: could technology, with its capacity to create networks of passionate people, be used to connect us all up and empower us to be better together? Could it disrupt old and entrenched forms of power-knowledge that had ruled the world for so long? I became excited by the promises of the psychological and social emancipation that could come about with digital.

Without any previous interest in entrepreneurship, within a few weeks of signing *The Cluetrain Manifesto* online, I started a company with two colleagues from the agency.

I was about to plunge headfirst into the many trials, and occasional triumphs, of fast-growing companies.

SPIRITUAL ATHEISM PRINCIPLES:

- Be aware of how our desires and cravings for protection and pleasure impact our health and happiness—and watch out for others manipulating our protective patterns to fuel addictions that increase their profitability.
- Appreciate that capitalism is a uniquely creative engine of change that allows our collective needs to be met in innovative ways. Yet be fully aware that our current version of capitalism, that is underpinned by a materialist paradigm, is also driving inequality and injustice for many—which diminishes everyone eventually.
- Realize that the individualism of the West — seen in advanced consumer capitalism, free-market economics, and the desire for private ownership and personal gain—is historical and not essential. It has emerged within a materialist paradigm that enslaves us as much as it empowers us.
- Seek productive efficiencies and effective outcomes in our projects whilst tempering the desire for efficiency, control, and profit with compassion, connectivity, and creativity. These heart-led qualities are those we need to innovate sustainably and to lead transformations.

CHAPTER 8

TECHNOLOGY AND ENTREPRENEURSHIP: BREAKTHROUGHS AND BURNOUT

I used to associate entrepreneurship with the sharp end of capitalism and the worst excesses of 1980s "greed is good" culture. I assumed entrepreneurs were only in it for the money. For me, though, as well as many fellow start-up junkies I have met along my way, entrepreneurship has less to do with making money and more to do with being fully empowered. It is thrilling to know that we can wake up each day with an idea, and by the time we go to sleep, have put the idea into action without asking for anyone's permission.

In my first start-up, we were three kids under thirty with a big, but slightly unclear, dream. One of our cofounders left soon after the start, but before long we went from the two of us in a ramshackle room to a team of twenty. A few months in, we visited San Francisco and Silicon Valley, attending parties where the digital Kool-Aid mixers and drinkers came to meet. The air of hubris and hope was exhilarating: like a rave with a business model (though the latter seemed optional during the first tech bubble). It felt like everyone wanted to use tech to bring into being the utopia that ravers had dreamed of but never delivered, too busy obliterating our egos in a bass speaker to build a sustainable enterprise. I was young with very little to lose.

The initial concept of the consultancy we set up was to use human insight and creative strategy to help organizations harness the Digital Age to do amazing things for the world. At the ad agency, the psychological and philosophical tools of paradigm-shifting had been limited to use in brand strategy. Now, we begun to use these tools to help clients create digital ways of doing business, innovate new business models, and to reinvigorate their company cultures. We genuinely wanted to seek the best outcome for the world at large.

For a while, life was super-sweet. I was full of chutzpah, if still lacking in *chochma*, the Hebrew word for wisdom. Rather than dancing in fields by night and sticking it to the Man by day, we were building things with technology that we thought, perhaps naively, could permanently disrupt the status quo and bring about an emancipating revolution. We were ablaze with the possibilities of the network economy, particularly how it can move power from the rich central establishment to the fringe.

The internet and the wave of technologies driving what has become known as the Fourth Industrial Revolution—artificial intelligence (AI), robotics, 3D printing, biotech and much more—*can* change the world for the better. Digital technology can democratize industries by getting rid of the middlemen who used to hold a lot of power. This allows a great number of people to enjoy things that only the elite could access in the past. Ebay has democratized exclusive auction houses like Sotheby's, so that now everyone can buy and sell old stuff. Uber has democratized chauffeur-driven car services. Kiva has democratized getting loans for small businesses.

Whether we want to share ideas, money, our apartment, data, love, or anything else, we can do it together through technology, peer to peer as opposed to expert to consumer. The internet allows us to organize ourselves without hierarchies and to draw on the wisdom of many people—the crowd—to create solutions to our problems in ways nobody could have dreamed only a few decades ago. Digital technology is rewiring the world, inviting us to become more networked and connected to make full use of it.

In fact, the evolution of digital code and social technologies might well be nature's way of healing the emotional and social alienation that technology itself created. Like the dock leaf that grows near the nettle, ready with an antidote to the pain, digital technology has the power to help us heal the psychological, social, and ecological wounds inflicted by the technologies and work conditions that characterized the Industrial Age. This within our grasp, perhaps for the first time in human history, is the tangible possibility of a just and equal society for all.

But technology and disruptive innovation—the term that is used to describe epistemological breaks that 'free' us from old business systems—is an agnostic tool. It can lead to liberation, or it can thrust us into more suffering. The breakthrough innovation process that we offered at our consultancy can be used to solve systemic problems and alleviate suffering, or it can aid in the creation of billion dollar products that lead to rampant addiction. Sadly, the default paradigm in the modern world is to use the power of technology and innovation to make the capitalist machinery go round at an ever-increasing velocity. We ended up playing our part in this.

The "optimization" of everything—the need to make it Better! Faster! Cheaper!—is rooted in the same episteme that gave birth to modern science and capitalism: everything is a machine or a mechanism that can be made to work better and produce more output, productivity, and profit. This is apparent when technologists use powerful algorithms (rules running on computerized machines) to achieve levels of prestige, profit, and power that previously only kings and popes could hope for.

It is also apparent in how much new technology, from smart phones and social media to apps and business software, is all about helping Control and Protect Mode get what it thinks it wants: more money, more efficiency, more recognition. While there is a lot of cash pouring into projects that do things like help wealthy San Franciscans find parking spaces for their sexy Tesla vehicles, there is a lot less being invested in, say, innovations that help the huge numbers of homeless in the same city.

Much new technology hooks into the brain's dopamine system. Meditation apps as well as video games leverage our desire for anticipation and reward to get us to use them more often to get more thrills. Tech companies have armies of talented people whose entire focus is to compel us to swipe our smart phones more often. Each time we do, they make money. Armed with crazy profits, many tech companies find ways to minimize the tax they have to pay for transport systems that get their employees to work, or universities that teach their future staff how to write code.

Talented people are often attracted to the tech space because it can be a vehicle for empowerment. But their genius is co-opted by Control and Protect Mode to further spin the wheels of consumer capitalism. It's a tragedy for us all. As one of Facebook's early engineers put it, "the best minds of my generation are thinking about how to make people click ads. That sucks."[128]

Even the foundational companies of the sharing economy, such as Airbnb and Uber, started out as genuinely empowering business ideas with a humane ambition. But without a purpose rooted in something other than materialism—and an unflinching moral compass so that leaders can deliver their purpose in a creative tension with the need to make profit—the relentless logic of turbo-charged capitalism makes entrepreneurs focus on the money and not the positive impact.

The innovations that most investors want to back are usually those that have very high returns as opposed to the potential to have genuine positive impacts on the world. Founders are pushed to deliver 100x or 1000x the initial investment (a 100x return is when you invest a million and get one hundred million back), which drives them deeper into Control and Protect Mode.

The VCs need to get this kind of return in order to return the promised profits to their own investors and offset the losses from failed projects. The pressure to turn capital into exponentially more capital distorts everything that a funded business does, from the way the founders treat their staff to the quality of the service that users get. They have to generate more margin, take more money from the people being 'empowered' by the service, reduce necessary but undesirable costs like great customer service and employee benefits, and, to top it all, try to automate everything, and get rid of labor entirely.

Even though everyone likes to applaud tech companies as the paragons of innovation, many of them use industrial-age mindsets to increase profits from digital-age products.

My partner and I began our business with a lofty purpose to help tech start-ups help humanity, but before long we strayed from our initial path. Traditional businesses started to approach us, asking for our help to transform their products and services to fit the digital age. Our purpose as leaders was not yet fully developed and our moral compass was obscured by our protective patterning. So we used our breakthrough innovation toolkit to develop products and services that nobody needed, like new alcoholic drinks and candies.

We were caught up in the spirit of the times, sure that a twenty-first century start-up should grow as fast, and as large, as possible through whatever means necessary. The greater the momentum, the greater the valuation of the business and the bigger the amount of kudos one got.

With ambition and quick real-world success, within a year of the founding of our company we had a VC interested in funding us to open a network of offices across the world. Months into negotiations, the day to sign the contract finally arrived. I was about to fly to New York to run a workshop. I called my business partner and told him that my intuition said "No". He agreed and we didn't sign.

A few weeks later the investors in the VC fund were indicted for fraud. All their companies went down like dominoes. We would have gone with them if we had made our decision purely based on logic. This was an early experience of the important role of intuition in leadership. However, we were now hundreds of thousand dollars in debt. We had spent months focused on the deal rather than on landing more projects. Around that time, the flow of funded start-ups started to dry up as the tech bubble burst. We ended the year 2000 with five or six major projects about to begin. By January, all of them were canceled. By February, we were a few days away from the bank pulling the plug.

So we created a new product, an anthropological study to explore the future of technology in the home. The few of us left in the business hit the phones to find customers. In the course of a week, we spoke to hundreds of large companies, trying to persuade someone, anyone, to put some money in. We met four times each day in the large meeting room to inspire each other to keep dialing and smiling—and we made it.

We sold a study, pulling ourselves out of the abyss. This study, and more we ran like it, gave me a precious opportunity to work with my father on things we both loved. He was by then an expert in consumer psychology and a lecturer at Oxford University. I seized the opportunity to reconnect with him by working together. Those years were the halcyon days of our relationship.

Over time, our company became known for being pretty good at the alchemy of anthropology and innovation. Things got easier. But the entrepreneurial near-death struggle had changed me deep within. When we started up, I was young, naive, and had zero status to lose. It was all excitement, fun, and possibility. A couple of years later, with high overheads and a fear of public failure, I had more skin in the game. I lost a lot of my playfulness and become very serious.

Every day I pushed myself and my colleagues, driven by my desire to pitch against big name management consultancies and win work. Having started the business after only a couple of years in the labor force, I had never been given a single day of leadership development. Without being aware of it, underlying my ambition was Nietzsche's "will to power". This pure, untrammeled outflow of Control and Protect Mode animates many entrepreneurs as they try to "crush their competition", as Silicon Valley titan Marc Andreessen describes it (as a compliment). It is social and economic Darwinism on an epic scale. Entrepreneurs fight for more power, more control of the narrative, and more order to take the place of inefficiency.

Like their predecessors who created the first factories, many start-ups today play out a narrative of enlightenment rationality triumphing over the inherent chaos of nature. To modern, data-driven, performance-obsessed companies, the dream of a perfectly rational, efficient world is seductive. The techno-optimism of today holds that all our problems—

including our climate change and population growth problems—will be solved with data and tech. Some, called "transhumanists", believe in the inevitability of an "event horizon" in which we will merge with machines and become invincible.

In my experience, such a drive to master nature, the market, and the world is, in part, a protective mechanism to overcome the disappointments of childhood. Mine certainly was. The guy applauded and placed on the cover of *Forbes* magazine gets to show his dad that he wasn't a fuck-up after all. The gal who was denied luxuries as a kid makes millions to make up for a shitty childhood.

In a materialist episteme it is very easy for an entrepreneur's sense of worth as a human being to become attached to the primary properties of their material-world metrics: the number of app downloads, the headcount of the team, the growth rate year-on-year, and the valuation of the business with each investment. It has become commonplace to hear people brag about just how busy they are; how needed they are by the world. The secondary qualities of team trust, employee wellbeing, user flourishing, and their own inner peace and purpose so easily get lost as they are not the primary concern of Control and Protect Mode.

My first trip on the entrepreneurial merry-go-round was driven by all manner of conflicting desires, most stemming from emptiness in my inner world. I think we built a fast-growing company not because it was the best way to fulfill our purpose, but because it unconsciously seemed like the best way for us to get the respect we desired so much. Yet the 'successes'—from invitations to Downing Street to airline mileage gold clubs—were simply smokescreens to cover up lack and loss within me.

I wanted to change the world, but I also wanted to build a business to get me the recognition (from my dad?) that I craved so much. Over time, the desires of Control and Protect Mode overwhelmed the hopes of Create and Connect Mode. I wanted to prove myself and this begun to twist things. The coveting of recognition is such a strong motivational force in so many of us that Plato, who called *thumos*, thought it one of the three elemental parts of the soul. *Thumos* is the ambition to assert the full magnitude of the individual self.[129]

The constant pressure made our growth stressful and exhausting for everyone. Tension and exhaustion pushed me further into Control and Protect Mode. As I hustled, I took every mistake people made personally. They could never be good enough for me, just as I couldn't be good enough for myself. The psychiatrist Frantz Fanon wrote that oppression hurts both parties. As a controlling manager whose style was not tempered by compassion and empathy, I found this to be true. Our employees disliked me, which set me up for even more pain given my historic desire to be liked.

It is the job of leaders to develop skills in emotional connection, wisdom, and storytelling so we can take people on the journey of transformation. This means learning how to hold space for people to change; and providing them with the safety they need to learn and grow. It also means shielding people from fear and stress so they can thrive. I had no clue about any of this and was unable to support my team emotionally. I transmitted my fear to them through my shadowy patterns. I was emotionally labile not stable so was unable to let go of these old habits even though I wanted to.

The business had grown so far, so fast, that the center could not hold. My entrepreneurial bubble burst, though not for the obvious reasons. Technically, we had 'made it'. We were a business success story. But without the internal strength I needed to deal with the frenzy of pitching, growth, and delivery, something had to give. It was me. I snapped. Just as I had done years before when I left medical school in a panic, I called my mom and proceeded to meltdown in front of her over a long afternoon.

Apparently, high-speed and high-growth entrepreneurs experience more stress, post-traumatic stress disorder (PTSD), and mood disorders than employees. Either in childhood or in business, or both, many have been traumatized, which locks them into old habits and defensive patterns. So busy staying focused on external metrics (their company valuation, their user stats) that they often have trouble focusing on their own core human needs; they do not eat, sleep, or exercise nearly as well as others.[130] Locked into the habits that made them successful, they can find it very hard to change.

While the tech world pushes to solve other people's 'pain points' with faster and smarter algorithms, the entrepreneurs themselves are beset by personal problems that are resistant to machine thinking and lines of code. This is because we are biological organisms, imprinted by the experiences of our early years that influence everything we feel, think, and do later on. When machines get overused, worn, and rusty, they can be fixed quickly. A human being torn apart by speed and need cannot. We take much longer to heal.

My experience of entrepreneurial burnout has convinced me that it is not simply exhaustion or tiredness, which a few weeks of rest or a meditation retreat can fix. Burnout is a whole-system response to unsustainable and painful emotions, thoughts, and actions. I believe that problems such as depression, anxiety, and roller-coaster mood swings that often arise with pernicious stress are neon signs indicating that something is wrong inside us, and usually with the environment in which we have chosen to live and work within. These signs tell us that either what we are doing, or the way we are doing it, is not working for us, deep down. They signal that we need to make fundamental changes. If we avoid this inner data, eventually our body decides to show us who is boss and shut us down. This is what happened to me. I simply had no choice but to stop.

I went on leave for a month to decompress and see if I could decode the burnout. I didn't know if I would ever set foot in my own company again. While I was trying to claw my way back from the edge, our accountant and advisor teed up a sale of the company to one of our rivals. The figure being mooted was in the millions. But I was cooked. With intense psychological pain and a massive flare-up of fibromyalgia plaguing every waking minute, I knew I couldn't work a single day more in my own business, let alone a few years in someone else's, tied in with "golden handcuffs" (working for a period of time to continue corporate expansion before you receive the big bucks).

This was not just about my health. My ethical and moral fabric had been torn apart by the work we did. I had reached another bifurcation point. I could override my intuition, take the money—a large enough sum that I'd never have to earn money again—and successfully exit, which is what was expected of me. Or I could listen to the signals within myself and walk away.

We only get the benefits of transformation once we let go of the emotions, assumptions, and habits that are blocking our growth. We can't make an exciting new LEGO model until we break apart the old one—and perhaps swap out a few of the old pieces. This can be exceptionally painful, as my sons who adore LEGO have found out. The last thing most of us want to do is to let go of the habits that have gotten us safely through life and protected us from threats for so long. The more our habits have driven our success, even if we know they also sabotage lasting peace and purpose, the harder they are to give up. However, there is no way to game this system. We cannot have the transformation we long for without first letting go of the thing that keeps us locked in place. I let go of the 'empire' and walked through another sliding door.

∞

The pain I was in actually helped me to let go of the promise of fame and fortune, which was what my wounded self desired so much. It was not rational to walk away from never having to work again at twenty-nine. Yet something far wiser than my smart, yet limited, mind made me do it. To this day, when I talk about why I made this choice it mystifies many people. As a culture we are so wedded to the American Dream—and its Silicon Valley version—that this decision seems nonsensical and illogical. But as the sixteenth-century mathematician and Catholic theologian Blaise Pascal said, "The heart has its reasons that reason knows nothing of." My heart was done. The two questions were, "Why?" and "What next?"

I began to contemplate these questions in earnest. I wanted to understand what was calling me away from the company I had sweated so much for. I started to realize that I had strayed too far from my original ambition to be a psychiatrist, a healer of the soul. The part of me that knew this, that I have since named the Connector—the drive to thrive that animates Create and Connect Mode—also knew that I was not a fit for creating products and marketing activities that push people away from love and connection.

Within the glaring light of an expanding awareness, I saw that I had developed a business that was impressive (if you like that kind of thing), but not a fit for who I really was. It served what my personality desired not what my character longed for. I saw that I had become an instrument of techno-capitalism, using my skills to amplify suffering rather than reduce it. The wiser part of me had brought me to my knees to give me a message: this isn't a fit. It is not working for you or the world.

It was time to finally listen to that wisdom.

SPIRITUAL ATHEISM PRINCIPLES:

- Be open to using technology to connect people in new ways; to democratize products and services that empower people; and to liberate us all from old forms of disenfranchising and centralized power.
- Use technology to solve problems that really matter at scale. Avoid using it to spread addictions and inequalities at scale. Build business models that are driven by compassion, connection, and purpose as much as profit, efficiency, and scale.
- Realize that entrepreneurs can help change the world in innovative ways and that self-reliant entrepreneurship can be deeply empowering for us personally. Always be aware that our entrepreneurial ambitions and actions can be driven by our protective patterns. Such motivations will eventually generate more problems in the systems we work within—as well as drive us to exhaustion and burnout.
- Temper our drive for speed, power, and economic growth with leadership that is empathic, enlightened, and empowering—so we do not contribute to more suffering in the systems we are part of.

CHAPTER 9

WISDOM AND ENLIGHTENMENT: BECOMING A SPIRITUAL ATHEIST

There I was, having just turned thirty, a supposed business success… and I was a wreck. I decided that I needed to do whatever it would take to heal myself once and for all. That meant dealing with the seemingly endless shame and pain of thinking myself to be a fat, ugly, unlovable guy; the social anxiety I felt as I walked into every party or meeting; the damaged relationship templates that tanked my capacity as a leader and lover; and the gnawing physical agony in my muscles. I wanted to make sure I would never have a breakdown forced upon me again, nor be at the mercy of unconscious forces that could jeopardize my relationships, my work, and my health.

I had two guides toward the light at the end of the tunnel: anguish and yearning. They usually are available to us all to move us forward toward our own transformation and so, freedom. For me, the pain was full-blown fibromyalgia (including fatigue and irritable bowel syndrome) and the chronic depression, and anxiety that had been troubling me since my youth. The yearning was to find my way to a life philosophy, and a reliable set of tools and practices, that could provide me with an emotional safe haven and a lodestone of meaning to guide me onward.

Conventional atheism had taken me far, enabling me to escape from the outdated rules of religion, become more scientific in my outlook and recognize the desire for power-knowledge that hides behind so many claims to truth. However, something was clearly still missing, I reasoned, because otherwise I would not be in the mess I was in. I recalled one of the life-changing insights of my time studying philosophy: epistemological rupture or breakthroughs happen when we examine our assumptions and ask ourselves whether they're still helping us thrive.

By systematically questioning everything I thought I knew, I realized that I had fallen for the materialist paradigm—as it manifests in science, technology, and business—without fully understanding the central assumptions it rests upon. Plato called such assumptions "noble lies". The foundational noble lie at the heart of materialism is that we are separate entities from the material world around us. This leads us to feel like we are lonely, lack some things and are fearful of others. On the separation between I as a scientist and It as an object, the rational knowledge, technologies, and businesses that help us live such long, yet often unhappy and unfulfilled lives, have been built.

Materialism has us see the world through a lens that has been fully disenchanted from faith and magical thinking. Materialism seeks to dismiss spirituality as weird and Woo Woo while elevating the rational as the only truth in town. This anti-wisdom stance, requires us to downgrade our subjective, emotional experiences in favor of dispassionate, rational objectivity. We must switch off our empathy and compassion in order to be 'scientific', 'business-like', and 'man up'.

The logical conclusion of this materialist worldview is that the universe is empty of meaning, consciousness and love. It is made up of inert matter that has, by chance, produced life. Interior qualities like joy and purpose cannot be measured in chemical mass or amounts of currency, so they are seen as not real. Untempered by 'illusory' secondary qualities, rationality has prioritized efficiency and productivity above all else. But materialism clearly does not have all the answers. Materialism cannot ensure hungry mouths are fed in the booming economies of California and Nigeria, let alone assuage the anxiety and depression that are running rampant in every modern society.

No matter how much religion I had rejected and science I respected, I was never fully willing to give up the idea that there may be purpose, meaning, and love inherent in the building blocks of the universe. But, like many atheists, I had always been turned off by spirituality wrapped up in New Age packaging. The aesthetics did nothing for me. The superstitions about 'chem-trails' and the like, which I had first encountered as a teenager at the squat parties of Camden Town in the late eighties, were a turnoff. It all seemed too close to the mumbo-jumbo side of the religion I had chosen to walk away from.

So I decided to follow the motto of the Royal Society, the British science institution: *nullius in verba*, or "Take nobody's word for it". Siddhārtha Gautama, aka the historical Buddha, said something similar in the *Kalama Sutta* (or sutra): "Do not go with what you have acquired from repeated hearing, nor upon tradition, nor upon rumor, nor upon scripture."[131] So I ignored the New Age packaging and dived into many different ways to explore my inner world to try them out for myself. Soon I was reading 'uncool' books with lotus blossoms on their front cover, and attending workshops marketed with badly designed yin-yang symbols. Hackles raised, I nevertheless gave up my reservations and plowed in.

I let go of my resistance to the lurid associations of Mesmerism and learnt how to use hypnotherapy to enter non-analytical, non-rational states. I begun to meditate every day. I tried 'hot' forms of spiritual practice, like breathwork and ecstatic dance; and 'cool' practices like the Chinese art of *qi gong*. I was seeking a reliable route to connected and ecstatic experiences that did not involve any potions: I wanted to find Nietzschean festivals of atonement and sacred games that could give me refuge from my own pain and fear without the distractions of hedonism. I became a fully committed "psychonaut": a traveler into the inner realms of my own consciousness. I was no longer hooked on *wanderlust*, seeking the Other as an escape from myself in extreme travel. I was following, finally, the first philosophy principle to "know thyself" (and what we are really capable of).

Once I found a way to stop my mind from thinking, analyzing, and chattering away for a few seconds, and then minutes, at a time I experienced something so seminal that it would change my life for ever. I felt, deep in my entire bodymind, that I was, in a way that is hard to explain in words, connected with the rest of reality. I no longer felt alone or separate; nor fearful and lacking. I felt myself to be a fundamental part of the whole we call "the universe". I went from seeing the world as many to seeing it as One. This was spiritual enlightenment. This was liberation.

If you look within, and find ways that work for you to enter the flowing, connective consciousness that William James talked about, I am certain that you will discover that you are not limited or separate. You will instead experience yourself as limitless and liberated: an elemental part of life itself. You will overflow with fullness. You will find a refuge within that you can always return to, and within which you can never be emotionally hurt again. In this refuge, no fear, worry or craving can touch you.

As we learn how to go deeper within, with more intense forms of meditation, ecstatic practices and shamanic processes, all separateness between us and the material world melts away. We see just how small the modern, individual 'I' is compared to the enormity of the universe. We may reach an end point: an event horizon, where we experience pure awareness without any sense of Self. We are a witness to what is happening, but we are empty of individualistic needs and concerns. When this happens the separate 'I' in us "dies", leaving a sense of presence that is way bigger than 'me'. We have no mind, or all mind; take your pick. This is the genuine *mysterium tremendum et fascinans*. And it is freely available to us all in every moment.

If we engage with the mystical realization of unity we go through multiple "ego deaths": we 'die' as separate individuals stuck with old patterns and are 'reborn' free and on fire. This can happen multiple times a day. But the last thing our egoic 'I' wants to do, as it works so hard to impose order on the chaos and keep us safe, is to die. It thinks that if it does disappear, it will be the end of us. So it fights any wisdom philosophies and practices that might 'blow it out' (the literal meaning of the term *nirvana*). Control and Protect Mode is there to keep us surviving at all costs. So it hangs on tooth and nail to the limited consciousness of the fearful and power-hungry 'I' rather than slip into the expansive awareness of being one with the universe. It resists ego-death with ever-stronger patterns and ever-smarter stories. We become more cynical, smart and knowing . . . but lose more connection, love, and flowing.

I call the animating force behind Control and Protect Mode the Protector. The Protector is a metaphor that I use to enable us to engage with this part of us all that resists transformation in an effort to stick with the (mostly illusory) safety of the status quo. The Protector is energized by the drive to survive. It is designed to keep repeating patterns that once worked to protect us rather than risk embracing new ways of thinking and doing that might help us love, lead, and thrive... but could also open us up to criticism and vulnerability.

The tragicomedy is that this part of us, crucial as it is to survive crossing a busy street or stepping on a snake, holds on to pain and patterns that sabotage our plans: you know, plans like having a truly intimate relationship with another human being, trusting our team, or having a fully purposeful career. The protective patterns that enable us to become separate and defended individuals then hold us back from accessing the peace and purpose we yearn for most. The result is suffering surrounded by intense cravings for stuff (profit, power, position) and aversions to pain (criticism, impotence, irrelevance).

When we are in rational and reasonable Control and Protect Mode, the 'I' of everyday consciousness appears like an unassailable 'fact'. So solid does it appear that Descartes mused that only this Self, the self that has awoken to the power of reason, can be the foundation of human knowledge. As Descartes observed, 'I' may doubt my body exists—in fact, 'I' may doubt that any matter exists outside my consciousness—but 'I' cannot doubt that I exist when I am thinking.[132]

When this separation between observer and observed became embedded within the core episteme of the modern world, we were cast adrift from our own essence as united with the whole. We became marooned on islands of isolation and alienation. Yet we only need look at Ubuntu in Africa to realize that the concept of a totally separate, rational individual with private needs and private property does not exist in the same way in every culture. In fact, with Ubuntu, people are not born as a self-contained Cartesian subject. They acquire their sense of 'I' through *relationships* with other human beings (and organisms).

When we actively choose to get out of our heads, and into our bodies through meditation or ecstatic experience, the separate 'I' of modernity turns out to be way more ephemeral than it first appears. If we shift our attention away from the separatist logic of Control and Protect Mode, towards the unitive feelings of Create and Connect Mode, the 'I' starts to take a back seat. In this moment, the Connector within us takes over and allows the Protector, full of patterns about being right and in control, to relax.

Together, the great wisdom traditions—such as Taoism, Sufism, Kabbalah, some forms of Buddhism, Hindu Vedanta, Christian or Gnostic mysticism, and the local indigenous practices found across Africa, America, and the Pacific—contain a treasure trove of ideas and techniques about how to get into Create and Connect Mode even when we are feeling afraid, tired, and upset. Most of these traditions share a crucial common principle: find a way to experience who you really are within connective consciousness, and you will be liberated from suffering, confusion, and doubt. Until this happens, you will be condemned to a life of meaningless nihilism or materialist narcissism. There are no exceptions.

Each wisdom tradition arose to teach us that we cannot flourish until we break out of "separation consciousness" and free ourselves from the fearful emotions, negative thoughts, and selfish behaviors it brings. They exist to teach us how to live in harmony with nature, our own inner world, and each other. Over time they have developed a 'science'—a rigorous and organized body of knowledge—of the secondary qualities of our consciousness. They have done, inter-subjectively, what science could not do objectively: create a reliable map for how to find lasting peace, love and joy. This map helps us to consistently experience oneness, understand the experience, and then use it to thrive.

The everyday practices of the wisdom traditions developed to help us learn how to shift out of Control and Protect Mode and into Create and Connect Mode at will, in an instant. They exist to reassure the Protector so that it stops dominating our reality and allows the Connector to get into the driving seat. With commitment to one or more wisdom practices, we can begin to experience moments of connective consciousness every day; and expand how long we are in this state so that ease and flow become our default way of being in the world.

When we engage the Connector and enter connective consciousness, in place of ideas about what we need to do next to get ahead, in place of concepts like 'better' or 'worse', there is a pellucid, piercing sense of awareness utterly unlike separation consciousness. In place of the terrors of ageing, loss, rejection, loneliness, despair, and such like, we enjoy something like *satchitananda*: our being becomes continuous with the cosmos, which leads to a sense of the joy of being alive. A Tibetan Buddhist teacher within the Dzogchen tradition describes this as a state "in which one experiences bliss like the warmth of a fire, luminosity like the dawn, and nonconceptuality like an ocean unmoved by waves."[133]

Connective consciousness sees continuity between ourselves and our world. We experience connectivity in the place of separation. We are no longer afraid, alone, and disconnected. We are all one. We witness the world in and around us, but we do not identify with what we observe. Thoughts simply arise out of, and disappear back into, the ocean of oneness. As our 'I' dissolves, we witness a truth beyond all price: that we are, were, and always will be unified with the universe. This is the ultimate truth of all mystical paths. For me it was the only truth deeper than the pluralism, but also nihilism, of postmodernism. With science useful but partial and ever-evolving, as well as subject to criticism as a form of power-knowledge, oneness is the only bedrock I have found upon which we can build a philosophy for life.

The Indian traditions describe the truth of oneness, in the great collection of teachings called the *Upanishads*, as *tat tvam asi*: "thou art that". You are the beach, the pebbles, the sky, and the sand; and, in some hard to articulate way, me and us all. It may be unreasonable and irrational, but nevertheless, it feels like the most obvious truth when we are in connective consciousness. If we practice ways to let go of our analytical and defensive Protector, safely and with sincere intent, we can all find a way off our isles of modern individuality and into 'enlightened' states of connective consciousness. Every human being has this ability. As the *Upanishads* say, the experience of the Connector is "the hidden Self in everyone".[134]

The incredible experience of coming home to our own nature as one with the oneness does not happen unless we find reliable ways to repeatedly loosen the grip of separation consciousness—and even with the tools, it takes much discipline to use them regularly. The challenge for many moderns is that wisdom tools and practices have been shunted aside to make way for either religious power or rational progress (as well as commercial profit).

Over millennia, the liquid spirit of connective consciousness seems to have been transmuted into the solid scripture of organized religion. Intuition heard within was turned into God's demands (or labeled as demonic possession). Wisdom teachers were transformed into religious prophets and priests. Everyday ecstasy became divine rapture that only a few were lucky enough to be given (by God). Perhaps the priests and their aristocratic brethren told us to avoid direct experiences of oneness because such empowerment threatened to upend the status quo.

Witches in (New) England and Medicine Men in the new colonies of European empire were condemned as bogeymen and women by the

Church. Mystics, who could guide us to enlightenment, and shamans who were stewards of wisdom techniques, slowly died out in the West. Then, science begun to attack everything that religion had not already destroyed. Rationalists and atheists, began to laugh at anyone claiming a relationship with something other than matter. Separatist Control and Protect Mode spent centuries crushing united Create and Connect Mode. Mysticism became a dirty word.

Reason rooted out religion and replaced ideals of love with ideologies of progress. Love, whether *eros* or *agape*, cannot exist in the materialist paradigm other than as a by-product of brain chemicals designed for procreation. So the spiritual baby of connection was cast into the gutter with the religious bathwater. Militant, cynical, and ironic atheism now dominates the public domain. Whereas in the past people were able to live with both science and spirituality, as Newton, Bacon, and even Darwin did, materialist rationality tried to get rid of everything but reason.

Fixated on the scientific gaze outwards, we stopped gazing into the mysteries of our own consciousness. We hacked through magic and myth with machetes of reason and all that was left when we were done were the partial truths of objective science: everything is separate and all is disenchanted. Reason condemned all states of consciousness other than the rational and analytic (and masculine) as lunacy, quackery and superstition.

A few Western thinkers tried to show us that mysticism and reason do not have to be at war. William Blake, Ralph Waldo Emerson (who read the Hindu *Vedas* daily), and Alan Watts dared to challenge the dominance of the rational mind. The German Arthur Schopenhauer studied closely the mystical Indian texts, suggesting that connective consciousness is a source of insight that the rational mind *cannot* access. Schopenhauer saw the mystical as being able to augment and improve the perceptiveness of our reason, not block it. Writing in 1818 he said of the *Upanishads* that they are "the greatest privilege which this still young century may claim" and they were his greatest solace.[135] But these voices have been in the minority.

With genuine liquid spirituality fading from the public domain, reason and the primary properties of matter have been prioritized. This has led us to focus on acquiring more money, more houses, more published papers, more positions of power, more app downloads, and more organizational headcount rather than promoting the 'secondary' qualities of peace and unity. We have more affluence than ever, but we also have anxiety at record levels. Without liquid spirit and connective consciousness to guide our leadership choices, we have developed an obsession with easy-to-measure primary properties like KPIs and GDP at the expense of secondary qualities like community, compassion, and, yes, love.

It took me many years to both find the practices that were a fit for me and to put aside my cynicism, which I had developed to protect me from what I did not understand, in order to engage whole-heartedly with my own inner reality. As I fell deeper into the work, walking time and time again through what the Zen Buddhist tradition calls the "gateless gate", I understood that I had always been connected with everything. I was, like you are right now, already enlightened. I just didn't realize it for years. There is no gate of enlightenment to go through. We just need to wake up from the slumber of separation.

Over time I tried to understand, as best I could with my reasoning mind, what I was experiencing in my heart and body. It was within this personal crucible that my insights into spiritual atheism as a *bios* first started. I dusted off my copy of the *Zohar* and began to delve into it, as well as many other mystical works. I went to the source, reading the philosophical texts, in translation of course, that are our collective birthright.

Accumulated over many centuries of trial and error, these wisdom texts contain the inner "esoteric" teachings of religion without all the "exoteric" trappings of dogma, revealed scripture, rules, hierarchies, and so on. They contain wisdom—sets of principles to guide us but never rules that must be obeyed—designed to help us integrate all aspects of our shadow into our lives so that we can live peacefully and purposefully, even in the face of constant chaos, challenge, and threat. Rules benefit the rulers. Principles benefit the people. But unlike rules, principles cannot be simply obeyed without energy or effort. They must be interpreted afresh by each person who engages with them. There are no easy ways out. No-one from the past, nor even the present, can tell us how to live our own unique lives. We have to engage with the principles and bring them to life in our own way in relationship with the external world we find ourselves in.

The first step on the path to a rigorous spiritual atheism is to make sense of the principle of oneness. The oneness is called many things: the Beloved in Sufism, the Way in the *Tao Te Ching*, both *Brahman* (the absolute) and *Atman* (the individual soul) in Vedic texts, Buddha-nature in Mahayana Buddhism, and the Endless Light, or *Ein Sof*, in Jewish Kabbalah. Whilst each has specific meanings and nuances unique to its own tradition, I believe each of these describe something shared and perennial: that the ground of all being in the cosmos is interconnected and infinite. Even though matter appears as diverse and divided within separation consciousness, in connective consciousness everything appears to be one. Oneness is the absolute reality and the most important human truth.

If you are still cynical, then listen to arguably the greatest scientist that has ever lived, Albert Einstein: "A human being is part of a whole, called by us the 'Universe' – a part limited in time and space. He experiences himself, his thoughts, and feelings, as something separated from the rest… This delusion is a kind of prison for us… Our task must be to free ourselves from this prison by widening our circles of compassion to embrace all living creatures and the whole of nature in its beauty." He believed that the "finest emotion of which we are capable is the mystic emotion," which he saw as the source of all science and art.

I think of the mystical concept of the Beloved, Brahman, and Buddha-nature as metaphors that have emerged in different cultures to explain the same human experience. Each term tries to state, within the conceptual language of its cultural context, that reality is *non-dual*: everything is one, not two or more. Enlightenment is the realization that every thing that exists, including our Selves, are part of one great chain of being. When we experience deep meditative or ecstatic states (we might imagine that the former 'freezes' separation consciousness into quiescence, the latter 'burns' it away in a frenzy), we realize that the ground of everything is not made up of multiple separate things. Reality is neither this thing nor that thing—*neti neti* in the wisdom path of Advaita Vedanta—but all things. The primordial substance is both matter and mind. It is both ideal and material. And we are intrinsically part of it.

This mind-boggling idea is described wonderfully by the Buddhist concept of *pratityasamutpada*, or "dependent origination", which is brought to life beautifully in the *Flower Garland Sutra*. Reality is presented as a net used by the king of the Hindu gods, Indra. The net, which is draped over his palace on Mount Meru, goes on infinitely (he is the king of the gods, after all) and, hanging at each cross-point, is a jewel. If you look closely at one of the jewels, in its polished surface you can see all the other jewels reflected. Each jewel relies on the brightness and integrity of the others for its own luminosity. Each jewel contains an image of every other jewel, just as any part of a hologram contains all the information of the entire image. Every cell within us reflects the billions of galaxies in the cosmos.

There are many others ways to conceive of the non-duality and the non-dual universe. Some prefer a metaphor of emptiness, rather than fullness. They experience non-duality as the void, or *sunyata*, in Buddhist philosophy. If you are a humanist, you can think of it as brotherhood and sisterhood. Science fiction writer Philip K. Dick, of *Minority Report* fame, called the non-dual universe V.A.L.I.S.: Vast Active Living Intelligence System.[136] I think of it as an infinite orchestra playing an endless symphony, always seeking more growth, more evolution, and more complexity in the music. There are no separate individuals in the orchestra, even if we all play a different instrument. If one instrument plays a flat note, other parts of the orchestra adapt. When a new tune starts to arise, as it always will, we can either say "Yes", and serve the expansion of the tune; or we can say "No!" to it and try to fight reality. The symphony is the Tao. It is everything in the universe harmonizing in constant co-creation. The universe is not a noun, but a verb of constant co-creative becoming.

It is important to remember that all words and concepts, no matter how useful or specific, are there to guide us to experience this oneness, this non-duality, *for ourselves*. But they are not the truth in themselves. They are just words. Language separates us from what it is describing as much as it connects us. It bewitches as much as it liberates. So we must use language, concepts, and ideas as scaffolding to help us get it and grok it. And then let go of language as partial and existing in mind. In other words, "the *Tao* that can be named is not the *Tao*" as the *Tao Te Ching* begins; it is just a useful concept we use to describe experience so people are inspired to find it for themselves. The words in this book are not the answer. They are merely here to inspire you to find answers for yourself.

Whatever term we use for the experience of non-duality and oneness, there is never a need for a god with spiritual atheism. There is no agent to worship. There are no white beards, angel wings, succubi, elves, or anything else remotely anthropomorphic. These are familiar human-scale ideas that perhaps attempt to turn an experience that defies reason—the experience of being pure liquid love—into something that the mind can grasp, the concrete concept of a god (or a son of god).

With spiritual atheism, there is no personal deity with needs, nor a divine lawgiver who rewards the good and punishes the bad. There is nobody to pray to (to ask for forgiveness, blessings, or cash). There is no dogma to buy into and no doctrine to conform to. There are no priests with privileged access to the truth. There are no rules to obey to help us feel good and worthy, and no divine revelations from any god. There are also no miracles—aside from the daily miracles of photosynthesis, abiogenesis (life on earth), and human creativity.

God is definitively still dead. In fact, God has always been dead because any god is an attempt to turn liquid spirit into a fossilized entity. This is a fail. Spirit, consciousness, is alive; and so is our universe. Some of the early Greek philosophers, like Pythagoras and Plato, believed that the aliveness of the universe was obvious and given. However, the universe was turned into inert matter to be studied through the scientific method with the rise of reason. Yet life-forms like ourselves are not static, but are being continuously regenerated. In your bodymind, every molecule is broken down and recreated again thousands upon thousands of times an hour, even as your experience of being persists. Following the mathematician and inventive philosopher Alfred North Whitehead, we can be freed from materialism's obsession with inert primary properties by seeing the universe as an alive organism.[137]

We need not be religious to access this aliveness, this living oneness. There is no need to become a hippy either. There is no need to have *Om* tattooed on our skin and no need to give up all our worldly possessions (although I can totally understand why we might want to do either). There is no need to believe in conspiracies (which may or may not be true). Spiritual atheism and New Age aesthetics are not the same thing. You can dress like a hippy and be rapaciously ego-driven. You can dress like a hipster and be totally love-driven. And vice-versa. Aesthetic choices are not the same as metaphysical ones. It is the metaphysics that count, not the clothes.

As a spiritual atheist, I reject superstition, magical thinking, scripture, priestly power, stale rituals, and all god-like figures, as any other atheist would. I know them to be an often dangerous and sometimes deadly nonsense. I also don't need to engage in any cults or communes (although co-living and co-working are very appealing). At the same time, I recognize the need to awaken ourselves from the slumber of materialist separation and discover the reality that we are connected. The key to spiritual atheism is to realize that we are not trying to deny matter or undermine science. We are simply attempting to recalibrate the balance between mind and matter to allow us to thrive in a world that has both primary and secondary qualities, that appears both dead and alive depending on which lens we look through.

To experience consciousness and matter in harmony is critical, and it is at the core of spiritual atheism. Many modern-day spiritual gurus teach that consciousness (or spirit) is more important than matter. This view sees the material world as a compelling experience that is ultimately an illusion that leads us to suffer, since we crave some material things and want to run away from others. They teach people to reject the material world and renounce all worldly goods. The logical end point to this is to become a monk or spiritual mendicant, taking the path of the ascetic (although many gurus somehow manage to hold onto a predilection for stuff, like fleets of Rolls Royces and gaggles of acolytes).

On the other hand, atheists and scientists tend to be materialists who believe that matter is primary and that consciousness, and spiritual experiences, are the compelling delusions. This can lead to prioritizing material gain, tangible proofs, and real-world impact over everything else. It can also lead to hedonism. Both of these positions seem to deny the most fundamental thing about our lived experience: we are material and mind *at the same time*. Choosing either idealism or materialism denies one part of our essential being. If we see the world through the lens of scientific rationality alone, all we will see is separate atoms, leptons, and cells. If we see the world through the lens of mystical intuition alone, all we will see is consciousness, ideas, and the mind.

We can learn to see the world in both ways, at one and the same time. We do not need to choose either science or spirituality. We can have both. Scientific insights and spiritual intuitions can both be right. One has mastery over primary properties like size, speed, and density. One has mastery of secondary qualities like love, purpose, and happiness. As long as we are not irrationally dogmatic about science or spirituality, making them into a religion with prophets (whether idols like Charles Darwin or Jesus), and scriptures (*The Origin of the Species* or the Bible), we can have it all. However, if we privilege one over the other then we lose essential tools and thinking from one of the domains that we need to thrive in this crazy, beautiful world.

The split between primary and secondary qualities is not essential in nature. A cat or bat does not distinguish between the two. Only we humans do. The split is a man-made construct that has led to both the great successes and failings of religion and science. We can fuse together the two within us and heal the split, the schism, at the center of our selves and our world. We can be *both* spiritual *and* scientific.

One of the earliest philosophers in the West, the Greek Heraclitus, gives us help to shift into the seemingly paradoxical wisdom of such both/and thinking. Heraclitus states, in one of the fragments of his work that remains, “that which differs with itself is in agreement: harmony consists of opposing tension, like that of the bow and the lyre.”[138] He used the word *palintonos* to describe this harmony of seeming opposites. When we learn how to feel and think “palintonically”, we see only one universe that appears as consciousness inside us; and material particles that can be measured by that consciousness outside us. Our awakened bodyminds are the one place where we can reunite scientific object and conscious subject.

Spiritual atheism offers us the tantalizing opportunity to master *both* our material *and* conscious aspects and, in so doing, be able to live fully, love wholeheartedly and lead transformationally. As long as we don’t believe in a totalizing paradigm which denies all other ways of knowing, we can have both spirituality and science; the cake and the munching of it. There is no need for intellectual guilt, as we are not betraying rationality. We are trusting objectivity and reason to tell us about the natural world while honoring contemplation and meditation, and shamanic and ecstatic states, as the most reliable guides to our inner world.

Spiritual and scientific congruence can be seen with the two modes/brain networks I have been referring to throughout this book. I believe these two modes are the everyday manifestations of our dual-aspect nature. Control and Protect Mode sees the world as separate lumps of material to be measured and mastered. Create and Connect Mode sees the world as alive, connected and creative. To thrive we must keep them in balance and consciously choose the right mode for the moment, rather than just react. I believe them to be roughly equal to the “animal soul” (closed and controlling) and the “human soul” (open and creative) that feature in an important Kabbalistic text called *Tanya*.[139] The two modes can also be seen in the Taoist concept of the "human mind" and the "mind of Tao".[140]

The great challenge to people of reason is that we cannot push through to the mystical with the reasoning mind alone. Trained in the ways of Western rationalism, I had for years approached it with my intellect. I had read mystical texts and analyzed them with my mind rather than allowing them to be *felt* in my bodymind. I did not know, until I experienced oneness regularly, that the metaphorical 'organ' through which we experience unity is not our head but our heart.

Simply put, we cannot experience the expansive sense of the Connector through our thinking Protector. We need to get out of our head and into our entire bodymind. We must find practical and experiential ways to leave Control and Protect Mode and enter Create and Connect, and that means opening up our hearts and allowing our minds to be free. As one of the early Sufi mystics tells us, in an incredible Persian poem about finding oneness within called *Conference of the Birds*: "Give up the intellect for love and see, in one brief moment, all eternity".[141]

It is entirely reasonable, rational even, to believe that states of love and connection are just a trick of the mind; a few nerves misfiring. We can blame it on madness or chemicals. You can have that opinion if you want. But no scientist on the planet can tell you with any certainty whether it is or it isn't. Western science cannot give us firm facts about our interior experiences. It was never meant to. It can only tell us about primary properties, like blood flow in the brain.

Therefore no scientist will ever be able to *prove* to you that experiences of connective consciousness—of enlightenment—are real or an illusion. You can only discover the truth of oneness for yourself. Given that hundreds of thousands of people have reported experiences of connective consciousness, over thousands of years, this is a compelling reason to believe that we all can get there too. Connective consciousness is empirical fact from the school of life, even if we cannot replicate it easily in a lab to 'prove' it. Consider, that is Control and Protect Mode that wants proof. Create and Connect Mode is curious about what the experience might be like. Control and Protect Mode wants to grasp the mechanism. Create and Connect Mode is simply inspired by the mystery.

Spiritual atheism is a form of "dual-aspect monism" that holds that in the really real world, primary and secondary qualities are *one*. Whether we *measure* it in Control and Protect Mode or *experience* it in Create and Connect Mode, reality is only ever one thing: the non-dual universe. In this vision, science and spirituality are not two non-overlapping "magisteria" dealing with very different and disconnected realms of reality (as some have suggested[142]); they are two aspects of the same underlying, non-dual reality. The materialist lens of indestructible matter and the idealist lens of pure consciousness see the same thing in different ways. Matter is immanent shape and form. Consciousness is transcendent awareness. As it states in the Buddhist *Heart Sutra*, emptiness is form and form is emptiness. Because they are two aspects of the same thing, all remains one.

The Early Modern Jewish proto-atheist philosopher Baruch Spinoza got here first when he suggested that Descartes' "extending stuff" (the primary properties of physical matter) and "thinking stuff" (the secondary qualities of conscious experience) are but two different expressions of the same single substance. Scientists call this substance nature or matter, and mystics call it consciousness or spirit. Spinoza realized that no matter what we call it, *Deus sive Natura* (god or nature), it is all one thing.

The scientific concept of the Möbius strip, which you can see pictured on the cover of this book, is a good metaphor to help our minds visualize the mystery that allows something to be two and one at the same time.

It sits right at the intersection of science and wisdom. You can make a Möbius by cutting out a strip of paper, giving it a twist, and gluing the two ends together. Once it is connected, run your finger over the strip. You will see that although there are two clear sides—consciousness and matter—there is actually only one side, since your finger can keep on going without interruption. Each side is forever connected, forever one, although they are seemingly separate. There is only one strip, one universe. But there is also a very real illusion that there are two separate sides. Both of the sides count. The strip is like a mathematical version of the ancient Chinese symbol of the *taijitu*: the yin and yang sign. The yang and yin represent the two aspects of all being within the one, unified and integrated Tao.

Neither a material nor a conscious lens is better or worse, privileged or disowned. It is not about retreating into idealism, nor about losing ourselves in matter. It is about being in balance, in a creative tension between the two, able to consciously choose which lens to use to solve a specific problem. Is it more fitting to the moment to be in Control or Create, Protect or Connect?

Spiritual atheism is informed by science, but not limited to it for sustenance. It is inspired by spiritual wisdom, but has no need to deny anything that is provable in the material world by smart science. If you choose spiritual atheism, the double-bind that holds so many of us in its vice-like jaws will collapse under the weight of its own contradictions. You will no longer have to choose a single arbiter of truth. You can have both the joy and connection you can *experience* with spiritual oneness and the *cognitive* certainty and control you get with hard science. You can enjoy both reason and mysticism as equally rigorous, yet different, ways to understand our universe.

For a spiritual atheist, the mind-body problem dissolves. Mind and body are two aspects of the same Möbius-strip-like reality. We *measure* what we call "body" when we weigh it or put it in a scanner. We *experience* mind (or consciousness) when we meditate, make love or dance. The hard problem of consciousness also gets dissolved (if not scientifically solved): rather than look at consciousness as some bizarre epiphenomenon that emerges from physical reality in ways that can't be explained, we realize that all matter must have some kind of interiority within it. This doesn't mean a rock thinks like we do, but that it has the building blocks of an interior experience that could scale up into consciousness.

The idea that all matter has consciousness within it has been around for a very long time but for the last century or so it has been frowned on as mystical nonsense. However, as materialism has failed to explain consciousness, it is having a modest resurgence. Philosophers call it "panpsychism", although I believe "panconsciousness" is more accurate. Even rationalists, like philosopher Galen Strawson, can see that if everything that exists in the world must show up in matter, then consciousness must also be physical in some way.[143] How can consciousness magically 'emerge' from matter if it isn't there already in some form?

The neuroscientist and psychiatrist Giulio Tononi has proposed a testable scientific theory for panconsciousness called "integrated information theory": as matter becomes complex, the information within it becomes more integrated, and it becomes more able to do more advanced information processing; like thinking and being aware of itself. In Tononi's view, even a very simple information-processing system—say a manual thermostat used to switch on central heating—has at least some kind of minimalist proto-consciousness, because it integrates a teeny bit of information.[144] Only human beings have human-style consciousness and self-awareness because we are embodied in human-style complex biological material that integrates and processes a lot of information.

Ideas like those put forward by Tononi might open up science to a massive paradigm shift in which connective consciousness is integrated into materialist science, and which could lead to new knowledge, tools, and technologies for human and planetary thriving. Scientific studies of phenomena like meditation, altered states of consciousness, reincarnation, psychedelics, and near-death experiences present well-documented 'anomalies' that do not fit in the current materialist paradigm.[145] For example, a controversial series of studies at the prestigious Cornell University, which involved over 1,000 research subjects, suggest that people might be able to know things before they happen (a phenomenon called precognition).[146]

Imants Barušs, a Professor of Psychology, has co-written a book, published by the august American Psychological Association, detailing many scientifically studied phenomena that can only be explained if we break out of materialism and willingly enter into a "post-materialist" paradigm.[147] The anomalies that keep arising are forcing consciousness and psychological scientists today to have a stark choice: stay true to the scientific method (and the spirit of science) by studying these phenomena without the influence of materialist dogma; or remain wedded to an outdated paradigm that requires willfully ignoring the evidence and giving up all pretense to scientific objectivity.

A manifesto to push forward a post-materialist science can be found online.[148] Rest assured, we do not need to enter a supernatural world of Woo Woo and magical thinking to be part of this. We can still seek a naturalist way of understanding such phenomena as long as we are prepared to expand our notions of what our awe-inspiring quantum and relativistic nature/deus is capable of. I seek natural explanations without being limited to the materialistic paradigm, a position called "expansive naturalism".[149]

Although we don't want to fall into the materialist trap of needing to know the exact mechanism for how mind and matter interconnect—for this is the hallmark of Control and Protect Mode wanting proof in the form of primary properties—I do find it useful to get a sense of how this universe of consciousness and matter might be structured. I wrote my final dissertation on this in the HPS department. A few years before I was at university the first ever brain imaging studies on mystical states had been carried out. These have since spawned a whole field called "neurotheology". Two of the pioneers of this work, Eugene D'Aquili and Andrew Newberg, suggested that there are two ways a human brain can function: a normal mode for everyday safety and survival, what I now call Control and Protect Mode. And there is a second, rarer mode, which I call Create and Connect Mode, which, when pushed to the extreme, allows us to experience mystical states.[150]

It seems clear that the primary properties of the brain will change when we experience secondary qualities of connective consciousness. Emerging research on people on psychedelics report that they experience more of the inherent interconnectivity of life and a blissful sense of "oneness".[151] As they slip into connective consciousness, diverse parts of their brain, that don't usually communicate with each other, start to do so.[152] The brain seems to become less ordered in such states; it becomes more "entropic" and interconnected. This seems to open up 'trippy' creative ideas and insights that can't be accessed in normal states. Studies have shown that such brain changes stick.

Long-term meditators show pronounced increases in the number of neurons connecting different parts of their brains (they also develop much less age-related wear and tear).[153] The rich body of work from neurotheology and psychedelic studies suggest that *all* our brains have hardware that allows us to experience ourselves as either separate from the rest of the world or as an intrinsic, connected part of it. We can *all* access both separation consciousness and connective consciousness. We can all be spiritual atheists.

One physical place within which the two aspects of our non-dual universe might converge powerfully is in our brain's neurons.[154] Whereas dualist Descartes believed that matter and consciousness interacted in the pineal gland in the brain, to him the seat of the soul,[155] world-famous physicist and philosopher Sir Roger Penrose and the iconoclastic anesthetist Stuart Hameroff who hosts a scientific conference, *The Science Of Consciousness* (at which I have presented) have suggested that the dual aspects of monist reality might be "entangled" in the microtubules in the brain.

Their hypothesis, called orchestrated objective reduction (or Orch-OR), sees consciousness not being 'caused' by neurons firing in mechanical ways, but by quantum processes within neurons. Consciousness is not produced by nerve activity but by the "acausal cause" of quantum effects (and the phenomenon of decoherence when particles go from an entangled state to a classical mechanical state). Consciousness would, in this view, no longer be an epiphenomenon or illusion, but intrinsic to all matter.[156] Fascinating research into the quantum processes behind photosynthesis and smell has shown that quantum decoherence, once thought to only happen in very cold and clinical laboratory conditions, can happen in the warm and wet biology of human beings.

EEG rhythms, whose origins have never been explained by science, may derive from vibrations in these microtubules. This means that all the characteristics of Delta, Beta, Gamma, and Theta waves, which are associated with various states of consciousness—dreaming, sleep, creativity, logic and the like—may originate in quantum decoherence within brain neurons.

It has been estimated that, if our brains are indeed quantum mechanical, each neuron might be able to compute 10^{14} bits per second of information, massively increasing the brain's computing power beyond the few bits of information that can be processed through mechanistic nerve firing. This means that we could be both mechanistic and quantum mechanical beings, blending Newtonian physics and the 'weirdness' of quantum mechanics. Subjective consciousness would then connect to the most basic dynamics of the material universe; and would then arise in the brain but not be entirely reliant on it.

The data from quantum mechanics are extremely reliable. The theory is elemental to much of our everyday technology: computers, LEDs, lasers, digital cameras or smart phones. First discovered in the early part of the twentieth century, its wild complexity and counter-instinctive nature is bedazzling. One of its originators, Nils Bohr, apparently said that "if you can fathom quantum mechanics without getting dizzy, you don't get it."

Fully dizzified, I can grasp that the empirical data within quantum mechanics can be interpreted in many different, equally valid ways. This in itself is profoundly interesting as it shows how subjective opinion within our consciousness is needed to make sense of objective facts within the study of the elementary particles of the universe. This means that it is unlikely that materialistic science will ever be able to determine which interpretation is totally correct, because quantum mechanics is a fusion of the hard facts of matter and ever-changing concepts in consciousness. Quantum mechanics does not seem to be able to separate primary qualities from secondary.

Each interpretation of the quantum mechanics data tells a different story about what our universe is like at its core. In the conventional story, called the Copenhagen interpretation, the scientist, the observer of experiments regarding particles, exists outside of reality. However, the observer becomes part of the equation as soon as he or she begins observing particles. In the act of observation, the scientist collapses the wave function, a kind of smearing of matter known by the French as a "density of presence", and a particle goes from being concurrently everywhere and nowhere—in a state of potentiality called "superposition"—to becoming fixed in one place. It goes from existing in a state of "complementarity", as *both* a particle *and* wave, to having a definite state.

A second compelling story, by leading physicists David Bohm and Louis De Broglie, says that we can determine where a particle is at all times without the conscious choice of the scientist… as long as we accept that particles have no geographical limits at all. The entire atheist/materialist worldview is premised on observable, measurable local connections between things. Locality means that objects can only impact other objects if they touch each other, either directly or with some kind of field like electricity or magnetism.

The Bohmian interpretation of quantum mechanics states that reality must be "non-local". Particles are all connected and so can exert on each other what Einstein called "spooky action at a distance'.[157] This would mean the universe is fundamentally interconnected. Non-local connectivity might allow us to understand how strange synchronicities, out-of-body experiences, meditative intuitions as well as the well-documented capacity of particles to become "entangled" all occur.

Later in his life, David Bohm came up with a way of metaphysically understanding how this might occur with his idea of an Implicate Order, where everything is connected together in some way and all is possible, which 'unfolds' into an Explicate Order, the tangible, actualized, 'real world' that we study with materialist measurement. Potentialities from the Possible World become actualities in the Actual World. This *bona fide* scientific thinking, that emerged from his pilot wave theory, might provide us with the kind of expansive naturalism we need to understand uncanny events—and so re-enchant our lives without religion. Put another way, *both* matter *and* consciousness approach of spiritual atheism could help explain the weirdness of quantum mechanics which is both other-worldly and very, very this-worldly.

The pioneering physicist Christopher Fuchs says: "If you have it in your heart — and not everyone does — that the real message of quantum mechanics is that the world is loose at the joints, that there really is contingency in the world, that there really can be novelty in the world, then the world is about possibilities all the time, and quantum mechanics ties them together." This 'loose-at-the-jointness' could be what allows insights and ideas to come into the observable, Actual World from the Possible World where everything is tied together in a web called, by the wisdom traditions, the ground of all being. This may happen through resonances: 'strange attractors' that guide a system to self-organise towards a more complex, creative and, perhaps, fitted state.

William James, the pioneering psychologist and challenger of orthodox scientific materialism, suggested over a hundred years ago a way of understanding how such quantum interconnectedness might show up in everyday human consciousness. This has become known as the transmission or filter model.[158] Over millenopenia, Buddhist contemplative science has come up with a similar theory of human consciousness.[159] Such a framework might help us comprehend how we have intuitions, insights, and ideas that seem to come from beyond the Cartesian 'I', something materialist theories fail to do.

In such a framework, the brain is elemental to consciousness, and shapes it, but does not produce it mechanistically. Consciousness pervades the entire world, including the brain. It is one of the two aspects of the non-dual reality that is everywhere. The brain then 'renders' consciousness into the experiences and thoughts we have in any given moment. In this view, we cannot have human-style conscious awareness without a brain; but the brain is not sufficient for consciousness. Much like a radio does not *create* the program you are listening to but turns radio waves into coherent sound using electronics within, the brain may access non-local information from connective consciousness and turn it into our experiences.

Experiences of oneness, flow-states, dreams, visions, and intuition would then be what occurs when the brain changes how it filters the enormity of pure connective consciousness. In this moment we might get access to Jung's collective unconscious. Aldous Huxley, an ardent materialist before he took psychedelics to explore his own consciousness, also proposed such a filter model, using the analogy of a "reducing valve". When we meditate, move ecstatically, or take a shamanic medicine plant, the "doors of perception" are opened, the valve stops reducing so much data, and we see the world as it truly is: infinite (and intense.)[160]

The recent studies in which scientists have scanned the brains of people taking LSD and psilocybin corroborate such a model: the unconstrained mental experience associated with psychedelics is linked to less activity in parts of the brain that might filter or limit the full experience of connective consciousness.[161] The entropic state that follows leads to a less definitive order or pattern being imposed on the billions of bits and bytes of data coming into our brain. We get the whole kahuna burger of reality with #nofilter.

I think it likely that, as well as rendering non-local information from the oneness, the Implicate Order, the brain also accesses local information from our memories, as materialists might propose. It then integrates the two streams of data together into our consciousness. The relative mix between the two sources of information would then determine what mode we are in and what kinds of thoughts we can have (like a DJ mixing between tunes A and B on the decks). If we rely heavily on Control and Protect Mode, we are limited to existing patterns, rules, and habits encoded into neurons. In Create and Connect Mode we are opened up to connective consciousness and thus to genuinely fresh ideas, empathic insights, and moral intuitions.

This dual-aspect insight into human consciousness is why I don't believe AI will ever be genuinely creative (you can find a debate I was part of on this topic on the BBC World Service). Many technologists are certain that machine learning will be able to replicate human thought. I believe we will get to a genuine form of artificial *intelligence* which will be able to give us a run for our money when it comes to the calculating, linear thinking of Control and Protect Mode. But I don't believe that computers will be able to engage in the non-linear, imaginative, and empathic consciousness of Create and Connect Mode. Therefore there will never be artificial human *wisdom*: creative, compassionate, conscious. Machines can do algorithmic, rule-based learning; but they cannot do rule-breaking creativity.

Ironically, a post-materialist, utterly interconnected, scientific paradigm could have developed right from the start of the Scientific Revolution. Hundreds of years before Bacon, Descartes, Newton, and Galileo came along, Islamic men of learning were practicing science as part of the belief that everything in the world is *tawhid*: unified and connected to everything else. One of the most important of these was Ibn al-Haytham, who wrote a masterful book on optics in 1021, a good 500 years before Isaac Newton did.[162]As a Muslim scientist, he dug deep into nature to understand more about the one, unified, reality he called *Allah,* and not to dominate a disconnected, separate physical reality.

The Renaissance man Johann Wolfgang von Goethe also saw the potential for such an "empathic" way of doing science. He was saddened by a materialist paradigm that disconnected the observer from the observed, saying: "It is a calamity that the use of experiment has severed nature from man."[163] Goethe challenged Isaac Newton in a public war of words to decide the kind of science that would become the norm. They were both studying color but, unlike Newton, Goethe did not want to merely *explain* color as a primary quality of light, but to *understand* how the physical nature of color interacts with our consciousness. Clearly, Newton won the battle over which paradigm science would evolve within—but Sir Isaac himself was an avid alchemist and not a materialist. He saw his scientific work as a side-show compared to his systematic study of religious texts to find the hidden truth of the spiritual/material universe.[164] This 'fact' was repressed for centuries by materialists.

The lens through which we see the world shapes the knowledge we discover/co-create. Our *metaphysical* paradigm shapes how we use knowledge: to connect or divide, to heal, or alienate. We can choose, like Bohm and Spinoza, to see matter and consciousness as complementary ways of engaging in one universe. We can trust in a science that seeks empathy and wholeness instead of just separation; and a skeptical and rigorous spirituality that avoids superstition and magical thinking.

The years ahead may see science move beyond the limits of materialist metaphysics to help us account for the lived experience of so many millions of people who have awakened into connective consciousness. However, we must be prepared for the reality that the scientific method, which is a historical process that evolved to study measurable matter only, may never *fully* explain consciousness, connective or otherwise. This may even be the case with a post-materialist science.

No matter the scale of our rational scientific genius, there may always be a *mystery* within the nature of conscious life; certainly for our heads if not our hearts. We can relax into not having the final answers in the mind by realizing we always have them waiting for us in our hearts: the answer is always something to do with more (self) love and more connection.

∞

Although I was accessing connective consciousness daily, and the start I was still plagued by psychological pain and protective patterns. It was time to harness both science and spirituality, united together, to deal with my breakdowns, resolve my anxieties and emotional upsets, and discover how to have lasting peace and purpose inside. I wanted to heal my past so I could thrive in my future. I had everything I needed for this transformation within my conscious and material bodymind… as do you.

SPIRITUAL ATHEISM PRINCIPLES:

- Explore a variety of wisdom practices—contemplative/meditative and ecstatic/shamanic—to discover the full richness of our conscious experiences and capabilities. Such practices allow us to break out of separation consciousness (where we feel alone, fearful, and lacking) and into connective consciousness (where we feel loved and supported).
- Commit to one or more wisdom practices, with discipline, to experience ourselves as interconnected parts of one universe. Reality reveals itself to be 'non-dual' (not split into two of more things). We feel ourselves to be one with all that is. Such experiences are often called 'mystical' and are felt within as "love", "truth", or "creativity". Others can point out the way but we must all experience such experiences, and so discover the elemental truth of 'spiritual' enlightenment, directly for ourselves.
- Understand that the enlightening experience of non-duality cannot be deconstructed by 'postmodern' philosophy as it is a felt sense in our

'hearts' rather than a belief system in our 'minds'. This is not the case for our (often religious) explanations of such experiences, which are as much constructed by culture as they are 'discovered' by contemplation.

- Realize that there is no need to engage in magical thinking or New Age aesthetics to live a profoundly 'spiritual' life. Nor do we need to obey any religious rules or pray to any gods. We can 'dialogue', at any time, with our consciousness within (and so the alive universe) to choose what to do next that brings more love, truth, and creativity into the moment.
- See science and wisdom as two complementary, yet equally valid, ways of knowing the world, each with their own domain of excellence and research methods. The scientific traditions create the most reliable and consistent insights about the material world of 'primary properties'. The contemplative traditions create the most reliable and consistent, insights into our conscious inner world of 'secondary qualities'. Therefore we can enjoy 'spiritual' experiences of oneness and connection in our hearts without betraying reason and science in our minds.
- Appreciate that our non-dual universe has two aspects, forever intertwined: matter and consciousness. Seek to integrate both aspects into a coherent understanding of how consciousness and matter show up within us as two different aspects of the same non-dual reality.
- Be open to the possibility that human consciousness is not 'caused' by matter (brain neurones) but is 'rendered' by it. It is likely that consciousness pervades all matter as a complementary aspect of a non-dual reality. Consciousness in human beings is reliant on biological matter to be genuinely self-aware and creative. Therefore Artificial Intelligence, being inorganic, is unlikely to ever be truly conscious: there may not be any "Artificial Wisdom" so we must harness our own.
- Explore a 'post-materialist' scientific paradigm that studies 'non-local' connections between matter that conventional materialism cannot account for. It is unlikely, even in a such a post-materialist paradigm, that any scientific or rational model can be constructed/discovered that accounts for our entire reality because science relies on methodologies and metaphysics that were designed to study one aspect, matter, alone.

CHAPTER 10

HEALING AND TRANSFORMATION: PUTTING SPIRITUAL ATHEISM INTO PRACTICE

Once I had a more or less stable and reliable access to the experience of oneness within me, I began to rapidly explore how to use it to solve my chronic psychological and physiological problems. Whenever I found myself stressed, struggling, or stuck, I dove inside to see what was going on in my conscious, secondary qualities as well as how these feelings and thoughts showed up in primary properties like "fibromyalgia fog", muscle pain, fearful stomach flutters, headaches, and more.

Instead of just reacting with patterns, I focused on finding my way back to connective consciousness so I could have more choice in how I responded to people and 'problems' around me. This opened up space for me to change. If I woke up at night worried, or had just had a fight with a lover or friend, I would focus on discovering what imprint or template had been triggered in me. I spotted the patterns I used to cover up original traumatic fears, pains, and memories that were stuck in my bodymind.

I approached this inner work systemically, with almost scientific rigor. After identifying an emotional wound, I would find ways to *use* connective consciousness to transform it, causing paradigm shifts in my thinking. You can discover a detailed, step-by-step process to do this in my book *Switch On*.

As I practiced reconnecting over and over again to the universe I was already an intrinsic part of, using meditation, ecstatic/shamanic practices, and hypnotherapy, I discovered a core principle of healing: when we experience a live connection to the universe we feel a sense of "love" within. Love is the metaphor we humans use to describe the feeling of oneness and unity. This love then allows us to experience old pain and trauma in a safe way and eventually let go of it. Love within provides us with what attachment theory calls an "internalized secure base" so that we can heal trauma and become more whole.

Rather than seek security in others, which is what happens in co-dependency, we build it within. Because the love is self-generated, it is unlimited and totally unconditional. This kind of love is the only thing I have ever heard of, or experienced myself, that is bigger than our fear and therefore strong enough to transform our protective patterns. If we don't feel this unconditional, universal, *spiritual* love then there is nothing bigger than ourselves into which we can release our pain, disappointments, and troubles. We are stuck with them.

Even if we've not had much biographical trauma—acts of omission and commission like neglect and abuse in our childhood—we will suffer inside as long as we consider ourselves separate from the world. Separation is the ultimate source of all our suffering because it drives lack and so endless and unquenchable desire (the Buddha pointed out in the Four Noble Truths that desire is the root of all angst[165]). Therefore the only way to relieve the suffering is through unity, aka connection/love.

What is more, almost all our emotional baggage comes from not getting love in the way we wanted it. Perhaps the care we received from those who raised us wasn't constant, nourishing, or appropriate. Perhaps it came and went in unpredictable ways, or was overbearing and needy. Few of us grow up receiving the love and safety we want in exactly the way we want it. This generates an unstable attachment to others and to the universe we are part of. We experience various forms of loss and lack; of trauma and wounding.

As adults, these inner wounds then manifest as stress or stuckness, or something more intense like anxiety, depression, or chronic pain. However, if we penetrate to the hidden order of things, we discover that however they manifest, the source is always fear and lack where there should be safety and love. We can only heal such traumas if we repair the issues in the same domain in which the original disappointments occurred. That domain is love/safety/connection. So we cannot become the most creative, collaborative, loving and inspiring version of ourselves without regular access to such love. Nothing else can substitute. This has *nothing at all to do with religious faith*. The feeling of love that arises from the experience of connective consciousness is a reliable and stable 'truth' that can be experienced by all. Love is the ultimate solvent to melt down pain that is holding us back.

When we practice returning to connective consciousness to dissolve pain with it we develop what influential psychologist and Sufi teacher A. H. Almaas calls "basic trust" in the inherent nourishing support of the universe. He likens this to finding a sustainable sense of being held, the secure attachment of John Bowlby that we all want and deserve.[166] We start to trust that, despite the sorrows both everyday and extraordinary—whether the dementia and death of loved ones or the genocide of an entire people—the universe is there to ensure we learn, develop, and become more whole. The universe allows us to adapt and grow consciously by providing a limitless source of love within which supports us to let go of old pain and trauma. As we let go, we receive new ways of thinking and feeling about life. We have breakthroughs. When we embody and embed the breakthroughs, we are transformed. Suffering is reduced and thriving is increased every time we go inside and let go.

By using connection/love as a context to explore difficult content, we can bring up fear and pain memories *safely*. With the universe at our back, we can let go of trauma—usually with a long exhale and sigh of relief—rather than repress the sadness and frustration. Tears may flow, which is an entirely appropriate response, childlike not childish, to really feeling grief, loss, and pain. In order to let go of emotional baggage like this, the stuff that stops us being confident, creative, and compassionate, we have to really *feel* the feelings that we have repressed so they can be relinquished from our biologies.

It is vital that we feel old pain in a way that does not re-traumatize our systems. Ruminating on dark thoughts and intense memories—without feeling safe, secure, and loved—can simply reinforce the fears and the anxieties. Control and Protect Mode becomes activated to defend us from more pain and so we use more patterns, better patterns, stronger patterns to defend ourselves. Bringing back pain memories in the context of limitless love stops this cycle and allows us to let go of things permanently. We can safely bring into full awareness memories that were once disappointing and hurtful. We can then shift our relationship to them emotionally in our bodymind (a process scientists have called "reconsolidation").[167] This process of healing happens deepest and fastest when we feel most safe and loved.

With love at my back, I was able to finally crack open the iron rings of self-protection that I had erected around my heart. When I experienced unity, at-one-ment with the universe, I finally felt safe. I started to systematically release my frustration with life and my resentment over the childhood I didn't get, using whatever pain had been triggered that day as a guide to where to focus my self-healing efforts. The more connection I felt within, the safer I felt and the more I could grieve fully for my losses and my lacks. I cried hot tears of grief and stored up angst for years (usually on my own in the safety of my wisdom practice). But, like in young children, the tears come and go fast when we really feel the pain rather than try to repress it. I allowed myself to be vulnerable because I knew nobody could hurt me emotionally again. I was no longer a defenseless infant. I was a man who owned his own experiences. When I encountered the triggers and terrors of a normal day (we call such moments 'stress' in popular parlance), I used the problem as a way to grow, usually by letting go of something and becoming more trusting. If I can do this, with the amount of sadness and suffering that was stored up in me, I believe that virtually anyone can. It takes time, but it is the only reliable path to inner peace.

As we release the traumas of childhood and the terror that comes from a sense of separation, our patterns start to lessen their hold on us. As we release into peace, we find less and less need to complain, blame, or shame anyone, including ourselves. We are then free to invent new ways of thinking and behaving. This is self-transformation in action and there is no limit to how much we can transform in a day.

All our patterns are designed to protect us from a world that we did not trust in our formative years. Our Protector steps in during moments of doubt, confusion, and discomfort to help us feel safe. We get controlling, angry, or we shut down for a reason: to keep the world at bay. Our patterns, so often self-sabotaging, were originally useful defensive adaptations. When we feel stressed, anxious, or afraid, we lock into Control and Protect Mode and enact habitual patterns that once worked to keep the world out

—but now hurt and hinder more than help as they keep us disconnected, alienated, and alone. Meanwhile, inside our biologies, cortisol-infused stress kills us, quite literally.[168]

Patterns that may have helped us get through life as a child or teenager, are rarely a good fit for adult life. Such patterns are designed by a five-, seven- or twelve-year-old version of ourselves to keep the scary world at bay. This means that our patterns are stuck in the past, freezing us in time as the upset child we once were. But the world is always changing. So to thrive within it we have to develop responses that fit the way the world is today. The fittest, with their primary qualities like speed, strength, and sexual attractiveness, survive to fight another day. The *fitted*—adaptable, responsive, and creative in their secondary qualities like the stories they tell themselves and the feelings they feel at work and at play—thrive from day to day.

We must be able to create new habits in the present or we get stuck doing the same thing over and over again, expecting things to be different and life to be consistently great. Without mastering the process of self-transformation, we get trapped in boxes of our own creation. Our comfort zones, our protective patterns, limit us as much as save us. By providing ourselves with the connection/love we need to feel safe, we can willingly let go of repressed fears and memories that lock in these outdated patterns. Experiencing connection floods our mind and body with positive feelings, and no doubt powerful hormones. We let stress go. We shift out of the tunnel thinking we use as a survival strategy. We're able to think new thoughts. We become flexible, open to newness, and responsive to life. We stop repeating old patterns that sabotage our chances to find peace, purpose, and intimacy and innovate new approaches to life, love, and leadership.

Once old habits are released, space opens up for new behaviors, thoughts, and feelings to be enacted. We can be responsive and receptive as opposed to reactive and resistant. Our nervous system becomes more integrated and better regulated; and our bodymind as a whole becomes more harmonious. When we transform ourselves, we become more ever-more whole, able to use the full spectrum of responses to any given stimulus, no matter how initially stressful. Holy, whole, and heal all come from the same etymological root. There is no wholeness without healing.

By learning how to heal ourselves using both material biology and conscious wisdom, we can transform anything about ourselves. I am not talking about becoming someone inauthentic. I am talking about becoming the person you have always been beneath the protective layers of defensive patterns, cynicism, and self-doubt that distort your true character.

When we switch on—and slip into connective consciousness—we can become our endlessly playful, excited, awestruck, curious, creative, and collaborative selves. We no longer need all the seriousness, stress, anger, and fear. In fact, we find our true character by losing our false personality, the mask made up of patterns that we thought would keep the world at bay but ending up keeping us locked away.

We can only make these changes by harnessing the liberating *em*power-knowledge of 'spirituality', whether we call it that or not. Materialism does not acknowledge that love, meaning, or connection exist, so traditional science cannot work in the domain of love and connection. There can be no profound emotional healing without love/connection, whether we feel this in meditation or in genuine community. This is why so many rational people suffer so much; and why our mechanistic medical model and associated health systems have failed to heal mental anguish or prevent the exponential growth of "diseases of despair".

While psychological science has made some progress in helping people change behaviors and reprogram thoughts, only love, that most spiritual of qualities, can ensure we can overcome the anxieties of a Self that feels alone and separate. Without feeling connection/love, we are left tinkering at the edges of our emotional baggage, as I did when engaged in rational psychotherapy and conventional coaching.

To transform ourselves we need the *feeling* cure, not just the 'talking cure'. Healing has to be done where we feel things, in our body—where we have stored up traumatic memories in our guts and muscles—and not just with the mind. As PTSD pioneer Bessel van der Kolk makes clear, we must paradigm-shift out of the medical model to heal trauma. We must be able to *consciously* change our psychology (beliefs, ideas, and stories) and physiology (breathwork, shaking, movement, touch) to heal ourselves and others.[169] Blaming anguish on broken brain mechanisms leaves no room for any conscious influence over our own happiness and wellbeing. This is utterly disempowering.

For example, many doctors believe that broken serotonin machinery leads to depression. And it is true, that for some people, slowing down how quickly serotonin is reabsorbed by taking anti-depressants can lead to an uplift in mood (at least short-term as it did for me). But it is vital to realize that this explanation, that underpins massive sales of pills, is *unproven* by scientific research.[170] The materialist explanation is convenient for doctors, who can quickly prescribe cheap pills rather than engage in the lengthy process of emotional healing. Drug companies love it because they can make huge profits from ameliorating symptoms rather than dealing with complex webs of emotional roots causes. Even we as patients often like it because we can then blame our blues on damaged cellular machinery rather than be responsible for our own mental states.

Treating mental distress with chemicals that alter the brain chemistry can provide respite from the angst. They can offer us psychological space in which we reset our emotions and reconsider our beliefs. This is how I experienced being on antidepressants for the few months I was on them. But it was only through focusing on transforming my consciousness over many years—how I thought about myself and my life each day—that I changed the neural wiring in my brain and body enough to heal myself from depression, social anxiety, and panic attacks. This could only happen because I understood that I could choose to transform my consciousness (secondary qualities) in order to change my neurobiology and cellular machinery (primary properties).

I believe that far from being an aberration, much depression can be seen as a quite natural response to trauma within; pain that has festered rather than been safely expressed and so healed. Anguish, despair, and distress can alert us to the fact that something is not a fit within our consciousness, just as physical pain tells us that part of our material body is in need of attention. Pain, felt in the same place in our brain no matter which kind it is, is our bodymind's way of telling us that we need to do some healing.

Many non-Western cultures see the useful and adaptive role of mental distress as self-evident. In 2012, I traveled to Kenya to train leaders in a NGO. I used the opportunity to film a "teaser" for a transformational travel TV show I have been developing. I asked the Maasai tribesmen I was hanging out with how they dealt with anxiety and depression. Initially they did not understand what I was talking about, since these conditions are largely defined by (and perhaps confined to) Westernized societies. After the translator had done his best to explain, the warriors I met shared that, for them, worries, whether grief or anger, show that something is no longer a fit and so call for transformation. If someone is going through tough times, they all dance, sing, talk, and share until the issue has been transformed collectively rather than repressed individually.

Reducing a complex problem, where individual psychologies and shared social systems meet, to a mechanistic explanation allows for a simple model for health systems and drug companies; but it cannot be the only solution otherwise we would not be seeing such shocking figures for depression. Alternatively, if we come from a place where matter and mind both count, the dual-aspect approach of spiritual atheism, we get a much more nuanced, and logical, understanding of much despair and depression.

A spiritual atheist sees mind and matter as two aspects of the same reality. So *all* disease (or dis-ease) is both physiological and psychological. Pills, immunizations, surgery, and other interventions in our biology will quickly change the material aspect of our bodymind. And shifts in our consciousness, our thoughts and feelings, will change both how we feel, and in time, some material aspects too. By choosing to think different thoughts, our brain cells will fire differently. So we are then empowered to harness both science (say drugs) and spirituality (say meditation) to heal without ideology getting in the way.

Many research studies back up the insight that our subjective psychologies are involved in manifesting the physical symptoms of illness. This is true even in diseases caused primarily by a material pathogen that enters our material body. One study looking at people with HIV discovered that, for every traumatic *psychological* experience someone has in their earlier life, the risk of death due to AIDS goes up by 17 percent. If someone has three traumatic episodes, the risk of death increases by a staggering 83 percent.[171]

New research into cancer also shows that the bodymind of the individual, the 'soil', has as much of a role in the progression of disease as the cancerous cells, the 'seeds'. In fact, cancer looks likely to be a complex phenomenon that emerges out a unique relationship between cancerous cells, normal cells, and the entire ecosystem of the body.[172] Yet many medics resist this thinking because it makes life more complex. A dual-aspect understanding of all dis-ease makes available to us the latest medical advances and timeless spiritual wisdom (without returning to a reliance on 'faith healing').

Put simply, finding our own pathway to 'enlightenment' becomes the start point, not end point, of the journey of unwinding all our neuroses and healing them, one by one, in the universal solvent of unconditional, unlimited love. The experience of oneness, of non-duality, is called "liberation" for a reason (the Sanskrit word *moksha* means freedom.) We are freed to feel, think, and act in ways that fit the present, as the future rushes towards us, rather than be imprisoned in the past by our own patterning.

Once we master how to feel potent liquid spirit flowing in our veins whenever we feel afraid, small, or separate, we can release anything that we are holding on to that is bringing us down. We can let go of pain that we have carried for so long and stored as memories. We can finally cry about, and grieve fully for, what did or didn't happen to us in our formative years. We can break ourselves out of the comfort zones that we imposed on ourselves and take risks that bring with them new rewards. We can make choices that help our life expand rather than shrink. This is true liberty.

Such exhilarating freedom from constraint comes at a cost though. Parts of us have to die—the old patterns with their associated memories of disappointment and loss—in order for us to be reborn. We have to let go of what the Protector believes (separation) in order to embrace what the Connector sees (unity). So we all have a metaphysical choice: One choice is to believe what our Protector thinks it sees: that everything is separate matter. Separate people are always a threat to survival. Therefore, we need to be ready to battle them or run away from them (fight or flight). We must compete with them for what is rightfully ours, no matter who we hurt in the process. We have to accumulate as much material power as possible to be safe. Healing can only come from changes in our material body: from drugs, surgery, or other physiological interventions.

Or, we can go with what the Connector senses: that everything is connected, and that love, consciousness, and purpose are as real as matter. The Connector acknowledges that, rationally, when we look under a microscope or through a telescope, it appears as though everything is separate. But the Connector knows this to be a *relative* truth to the human mind, not an absolute truth of the human heart. In our heart of hearts we know we are all one and that love is the first principle of healing. It doesn't matter whether we conceptualize connectedness as an entangled quantum field, African Ubuntu, or William James' cosmic consciousness. What matters is that we live this oneness in everyday life and use it to become ever more whole. Mastery of a sense of connection/love is the key to a life of freedom.

As adults, only we can give ourselves the love, safety, and sense of connection we need to release the past and thrive in our future. We cannot pretend to feel that love. We cannot talk about it rationally. We actually have to feel it. A god cannot give it to us. A priest cannot. A cult leader cannot. A scientist cannot. A meditation teacher cannot. A therapist cannot. A guru cannot. A doctor cannot. Even if our parents are alive and willing, they too cannot give us that safety and love anymore, because the parts of us that feel disappointed and hurt wouldn't buy it. Our internalized Protector has to feel the truth of love flooding through our bodyminds to stop the defensive patterns and release the trauma. It has to feel a source of love that will never let us down again.

When we learn how to tap into this source of unlimited love that is lying in wait for each one of us, we realize that the Connector is the shaman and the guru within us. All others can do is point out the pathway until we can listen to the best shaman, the one within: the wisdom and sensations of our own bodymind guiding us to become whole.

When we feel this oneness as connection/love by choice, each time we encounter any form of fear, doubt, or lack within, we know how to *surrender* it from our bodymind and be free of it for good. Life, if we want to live it fully, is about letting go… until we must let go of the last thing of course, which is our life itself. To be truly free we must be free of our fear of death (and our fears of dementia, cancer, poverty, failure, aging, or anything else). Death meditations—taking oneself to the point of saying goodbye to loved ones and to life itself—can facilitate letting go of much fear so we become stronger and more energized to live right now. We can practice, in our imaginations, yielding with our last exhale as we release conscious awareness into death.

Most of us have a lot of energy caught up in suppressing our fears around our own mortality. Meditating on death (and on fears like our kids getting seriously sick or worse) is like going inside our bodyminds with a love-fueled dust-buster to vacuum out cobwebs of terror. Rather than relying on a dead religion to cover up our anxieties of death and destruction, we can leverage our live and liquid 'spiritual' connection to be free. We give up the illusion of control in order to gain the certainty of peace. We stop fighting the world, the cycles of birth and death, breakdown and breakthrough, and *surrender* instead.

From the whirling Sufis of Turkey, getting drunk on love of the Beloved as they spin, to the silent stillness of sitting meditation in Chan or Zen

Buddhism, there are many practices that offer access to connective consciousness so we can heal and become whole. However, one way we *cannot* access ecstatic or shamanic states is by remaining smart, rational, and cynical. We have to get out of this mindset, out of our heads and into our viscera, our heart, hands, and guts. We have to put away the books, and start trying stuff out.

There is also a lot of contemporary innovation in this space. As a facilitator of transformation, I have discovered that the right kind of music, combined with movement, meditation, and metaphors that get the imagination working, can bring people to transformation faster and more effectively than almost anything else. As many indigenous traditions have discovered, from African dance to the Greek Mysteries, movement driven to ecstatic levels with music and myth, can interrupt patterns and help release stress.

If you doubt this, go hear Mahler's 4th Symphony live. Sit near the orchestra and let the bittersweet music guide you into the sublime. Or simply listen to Arvo Pärt's Für Alina, right now on Spotify or YouTube, before you read on. Allow the music to help you let go of some sadness or grief that is holding on, but which is no longer serving your wholeness. Music speaks to us in a language beyond words, its grammar quintessentially emotional and spiritual. Because of this, music can slip below the radar of Control and Protect Mode and gets to work on trauma without asking permission from the intellect. It's even possible to get there with art. Utterly modern painters like Vassily Kandinsky and Mark Rothko were expressly attempting to create spiritual, and maybe even shamanic, experiences with their paintings. If you sit in the Rothko room at the Tate Modern, you may find yourself slipping into connective consciousness and able to release something to find peace.

As well as totally 'organic' practices (like those using music, meditation, and movement), recent scientific studies have shown that there are certain substances that can be a useful gateway into the transformative power of connective consciousness, particularly when we first start out on the journey of awakening. "Entheogens" are substances that generate the feeling of having a god, *theos*, within (as opposed to worshiping a personal god like Yahweh outside of us). One of them, ketamine, is fast becoming a big deal in psychiatry as a rapid way of treating "untreatable" depression.[173] Users report that it provides a one-stop-shop to the experience of oneness.[174] Meanwhile, more than thirty years after the drug MDMA was banned from the rave scene, a number of scientific studies have shown that it can stimulate rapid recovery from severe depression, alcoholism, and addiction.[175] Similar research is coming out on other substances like psilocybin (magic mushrooms) and LSD.[176]

Entheogens turbo-charge feelings of connection/love. With a commitment to genuine transformation, and ideally supported by some kind of guide with enormous levels of personal integrity and without huge egos, natural entheogens, such as the medicine plants ayahuasca and iboga, as well as man-made entheogens like MDMA, ketamine, and LSD, enable us to see the world in a fundamentally different way. They can show us states of consciousness that we can then find our way back to without any substances. They seem able to thrust the brain into a more adaptive, creative, and "plastic" state, which makes paradigm shifts more easy to come by.[177]

This liquidity, and the attendant sense of connection, can act as a "Control-Alt-Delete" reboot for the bodymind. Further, when they are used sensibly and for transformation, entheogens may not be harmful. In a major, though controversial, meta-study covering the experiences of 130,000 people, it was found that psychedelic use rarely caused addiction or long-term psychiatric issues.[178] But if we engage with entheogens in the company of shamanic charlatans, in scary settings or simply for hedonistic reasons, I believe they can do a lot of damage. If we find ourselves in any way addicted to the scene, or reliant on them for access to connection/love, then we have missed the point entirely.

It can be very tempting to the Protector to want to bliss out in the oneness using meditation, yoga, dance, and entheogens without doing the transformational inner work. This even has a name in the self-help industry: "spiritual bypass". We bypass self-transformation and get addicted to mystical moments (or the products that surround them) rather than using them to heal. But no amount of stuff—even meditation courses, yoga classes, and the materialist paraphernalia of commercial spirituality—will ever make up for the inevitable disappointments and upsets of our early years unless we heal those wounds.

Meditation and yoga can help us heal if we have a commitment to conscious awakening in order to become whole. But they are practices to feel and harness oneness, not end-points in themselves. If they are not expanding our wholeness, clarifying our purpose, inspiring our leadership, and deepening our moral code, then they are not working as designed.

However we find our way to connective consciousness, and the paradigm shifts that await us there, it is vital that we spend weeks, months, and yes, years intentionally "integrating" our new insights into our everyday habits of thought and deed. Unless we invest in integration, embodying the new ways of being into our bodymind so they become second nature; and embedding change into our schedules and relationships, transformation will not occur and it will not stick. The moments of epiphany and insight must be painstakingly turned into new ways of speaking, acting, and thinking so they become the default way of operating. Our habits lag behind our epiphanies so this can take longer than we would ideally like.

People who do not invest serious effort in integration usually find themselves flipping rapidly between their conditioned-in patterns and brief moments of ecstatic connective consciousness. This can be confusing for them and bewildering for those around them. They might shut out the world again, dissociating into a blissful bubble; or becoming manic with unintegrated spiritual insight. Plus, after moments of major expansion, the Protector can be unsettled and so make people contract. For every three steps forward they leap with each breakthrough, they can often slide two steps back, as old patterning returns to protect them in moments of tension and tiredness. This is the nature of things until we stabilize through integration. Focusing on integration slows us down so we expand *gradually*, patiently turning awakened consciousness into embodied habits, one act and day at a time.

Integration prevents us from talking the spiritual talk without actually changing how we behave. We are all in a process of constant evolution and we will all still react, and be triggered by things. Nobody is perfect and nobody needs to be. I can still be a fool in moments of stress (just ask my wife). However, unless we use connection/love to increasingly walk the walk of genuine self-healing and personal integrity, we not only stay stuck ourselves but we risk undermining the 'cause' and so turn people away from genuine spirituality. They see our shadow, unowned and unconscious, and this can trigger them to hunker down ever further into protective cynicism and disdain.

As I embodied change into my nervous system and embedded it in my everyday habits, genuine transformation occurred. This shifted my relationship to most things, including my body and sense of Self. As I healed (some) aggressive fires and craving desires within, I transformed my lived experience of my past, full of abusive and pitiful moments, to generate a responsible narrative that empowers me. All those templates

I had inherited and constructed begun to be shape-shifted. Rather than remain stuck above my chin, ignoring my body in a mixture of disgust and shame, I began to communicate with it to find out what it needed. I realized that if I didn't love every part of my body as much as I did a summer festival, a sunset, or a meal with friends, then I didn't really love the universe. With self-transformation I was able to run a marathon; walk naked through Burning Man; and become a regular practitioner of yoga.

I still get flare ups of despair and fibromyalgia from time to time, during periods of extreme tiredness and/or when I stop taking care of myself. When the pain comes, I treat it as a call for more self-love, not more self-loathing. As opposed to just logically knowing that I am not evil, I have become certain in my flesh that I was, am, and will always be a source of love, truth, and creativity in the world. This has allowed me to love, and be loved, by my family, wife, kids, and friends. I share what I have been able to change about myself with you to demonstrate that both emotional and physical suffering can be transformed, to a greater or lesser degree, by accessing connection/love within and integrating the insights into who we (think) we are.

The realization of being loved, wanted and even invited here by the universe is life changing (I whisper such words to my kids as they go to sleep most nights). I cannot state this clearly enough or often enough to cynics. All this and much more besides is available to you if you are prepared to go within, through the patterning, to heal the pain underneath with 'spiritual' love. If you are stuck wanting proof, let it go! The desire for proof is Control and Protect Mode wanting to feel right and in control. The best way forward is to try things out, with commitment and discipline, and see for yourself. Do not underestimate the power of conscious self-transformation to change the parts of yourself that sabotage your thriving!

That is not to say that any of this is plain sailing, even with access to all the wisdom practices and scientific insights on the planet. Returning to our true character (who we have always been) rather than acting out our personality (who we became in order to deal with life) takes enormous attention, restraint, and resolve. Life is challenging. If it wasn't we would have no impetus to grow. There is always more room for growth. But rather than see this as a frustrating chore, or at worst, a nightmare, we can see this as living *the* dream: using each day to learn more about who we are, let go of more, and becoming ever-more liberated. We use every challenge we face to surrender more so that we can love deeper, lead further, and thrive more passionately.

The various breakdowns and fails of our lives can be seen as invitations to never have to experience pain like that again. Clinical depression can be a call to connect with the universe and heal our relationship with life. Social anxiety can be seen as a call to fall in love with ourselves and never need external approval again. Relationship implosions can be calls to give up co-dependency by providing ourselves with the secure and stable attachment we need to responsibly intimate with others. Even something like fibromyalgia can be seen as a call to come fully into our bodyminds and tend to its pain. Every challenge is an invitation from the future to bring more of ourselves into the present; and be free of the past.

Each crisis we have can be seen as what Stanley Grof calls a "spiritual emergency". Grof was one of the first therapists to use LSD in the sixties. He later developed a form of transformational work using *just* the breath, Holotropic Breathwork (in which I have done some training).[179] He suggests that spiritual emergencies are not something to repress or ignore. Crises are invitations for us to transform, even if the problem being presented to us looks, and feels like crap. We are invited to "switch on" and shift from protective separation consciousness into creative connective consciousness, and do the inner work. Old patterns will always fail eventually and precipitate a crisis, a "turning point" in the original Greek. As conscious human beings we get to choose how to deal with each crisis: whether to *react* with Control and Protect or *respond* with Create and Connect.

On the pathway of transformation, we must consciously encourage the old patterns to break apart without allowing ourselves to fall apart. We purposefully "unintegrate" our mindset, let go of things that are longer serving us, and then reintegrate the new. Things must always fall apart a little before they can reform. And the reforming takes a long term commitment to learning and integration. But we can engage in this without fear because we know this process does not lead to our own destruction, but our own rebirth. With each egoic death we rebirth our essence, repairing wounds of separation, disappointment, and disconnection.

This concept is analogous to an ancient Tibetan Buddhist wisdom practice called Chöd, which means "cutting through". The practice is symbolized by a *kartika*, a ritual knife that allows us to cut through the bonds of old protective patterns to be set free. We only get to spot these tethers of our spirit when we are triggered by problems. Machig Labdrön, a sage of the practice, said: "To consider adversity as a friend is the instruction of Chöd."[180]

Rather than defend against unpleasant or unsafe experiences, we learn how to leverage them as slingshots to our growth. We master the life-changing practice of transforming reactive demons into creative daemons that befriend us for life. We keep dancing with our shadow and using connection/love to transform it into light. As Carl Jung wrote in *The Philosophical Tree*, "[o]ne does not become enlightened by imagining figures of light, but by making the darkness conscious." We then integrate our learnings from this constant process of inner work into the ever-more whole, healed person we are always becoming.

Deep healing like this, as we take parts of our shadow that have been disinherited or frozen in time and bring them into the light, will happen in a timeframe as much determined by our bodymind as our will. As spiritual atheists see the universe as a living organism and not a dead algorithm, we should be aware that personal transformation is a dynamic and ceaseless process. We don't get to choose when it occurs. We become "biodynamic": responsive to the newness that it is seeking to emerge from us with each moment.

Our Connector will let us know when we are ready, as a whole system, to release something new. We must be careful not to force transformation on ourselves with the urgency of the Protector. It is easy to re-traumatize ourselves if we recall difficult memories without connection/love as the context. The best way to speed up change is to build more resource—more self-love, self-care, and a sense of safety and connection—within.

The universe seems to want our growth and so gives us the stimuli we need to burn off every pattern and dissolve away every pain. This is far from pleasant a lot of the time. But nobody ever said living a liberated life of self-transformation would be nice and easy! This process of self-transformation is called "purification" by many wisdom traditions. It can take many years to purify all those negative, shameful thoughts and troublesome protective addictions with the liquid light of love (let alone all the trauma we have inherited psychologically and epigenetically). But if we stick with it, we can purify pretty much anything in our mind and body. We can change anything about ourselves that we have acquired as a defensive pattern: anger, bad habits, depressive moods, destructive ways of loving, controlling ways in business, poor leadership skills... anything.

Spiritual atheism teaches us that all problems are raw materials to metabolize into creative possibilities within the liquid love in our heart. *All* our suffering can be transmuted into potential to make a real and lasting difference to others. This is not wishy-washy 'positive thinking', but about gaining complete mastery of how to use our conscious aspect to transform our material aspect as far, and as fast, as it will allow. Contrary to what some might assume, spiritual atheism therefore involves more hard work than most paths. When we encounter a problem, we cannot get away with blaming others or complaining about the world. There is nowhere to hide. Instead, we are invited to 'own' every experience as an opportunity for transformation. Don't die with the transformed version of you still inside!

Now, it might seem that the sweet, switched-on feeling of connection/love might be easier to access while we dance in a luscious meadow, watch the sun rise over a stunning vista, or hold a newborn baby in our arm, it is *always* available to us in *every* living moment, whether on a gray January day or just after a double-shift at work. The intrinsic nature of our consciousness means that we can always feel connection/love wherever we are. So there are never any valid excuses for why we can't heal and transform ourselves any time we choose to. This is a constant, and often inconvenient, truth.

∞

Spiritual atheism sees each of us as an intrinsic part of one universe. We are all in this together. This means that the goal of a spiritual atheist's life, and the transformation that comes on the journey, cannot just be for our own happiness (important though this is). It has to involve improving the lives of others in some way (no matter how big or small it seems). All is oneness, and oneness is for all, not just the 1%. This is the invitation to switch on and step up that lies within all suffering.

Once we have freed ourselves from our own mental and emotional slavery, we have way more energy to focus on loving and leading others as best we can. As soon as our energy is no longer taken up by repressing old memories, avoiding our shadow, and denying our power, we start to have the emotional and cognitive resources to look beyond our own needs and to see problems in our communities that we could impact with energy and effort.

We have to be the change that we want to see. Gandhi's famous phrase can remain a cool bumper sticker or it can become a daily rallying cry deep within us. No matter how enticing it might be to our Protector to feather our own nest, our Connector knows it has a duty to step up as a leader and use our unique skills and talents to help the world thrive—not at some distant point in the future, not once we are in heaven, but in our lifetimes. Karl Marx famously stated that "philosophers have only hitherto interpreted the world, in various ways; the point is to change it."[181] I believe the point of spiritual atheism is not just to study consciousness but to transform it, and with it our material world. Once I had made major strides on my own path to healing, it was time to find how I might use my one short life to help others in some meaningful way. For that I needed to find and follow my purpose.

SPIRITUAL ATHEISM PRINCIPLES:

- Own every problem, upset, and fear as an opportunity to be more free of pain and suffering, to feel more loved, and to become more whole/healed. Every time we are triggered into a protective pattern that no longer serves us we can spot it and transform it into new habits, beliefs, and emotions that enable us to thrive. Therefore every moment, whether pleasant or not, is alive with the possibility of self-transformation because we can go within to reconnect and release.

- Consciously release redundant patterns, traumas, and memories from our bodymind both during crises and proactively. Allow what has been repressed to surface so we can accept, grieve, heal, and relinquish.
- Almost all our protective patterns were generated from within separation consciousness (and are maintained by it). Therefore only connective consciousness can render them obsolete.
- Realize that the 'spiritual' experience of connection/love can reliably provide us with the emotional safety we need to dissolve and release protective patterns that no longer serve us, and the pain that anchors them in, without resistance. It may be the only experience that can transform our deepest traumas and most stubborn addictions.
- Recognize that love—romantic, platonic, and 'spiritual'—exists for growth not for pleasure. Love creates a safe 'crucible' within which we can transform our 'shadow' to become more free.
- Seek to integrate new emotions into our nervous system, new insights into our life narratives, and new behaviors into everyday habits to make transformation permanent (which takes time, patience, and diligence).
- Understand that physiology and psychology are two aspects of one bodymind system. Distress in either can generate disease. Interventions to either aspect can bring us back to health, wellbeing, and harmony.
- Draw upon the most advanced medical solutions blended with timeless wisdom to maintain wellbeing. Always ensure that we use critical thinking to discern what solutions work (and who might gain from them).

CHAPTER 11

PURPOSE & LEADERSHIP: CHANGING THE WORLD WITH SPIRITUAL ATHEISM

The Cook Islands are a Pacific idyll located in the vast blue waters between Hawaii and New Zealand. It was the perfect place to go to decompress from burnout/breakdown. At the end of my stay, with time to spare before I had to go to the airport to catch my flight, I found myself diving into a salt-corroded cinema to catch a movie.

The only feature being screened was *The Pianist*, the tale of a Jewish musician who, against all the odds, survives the German death camps. The movie struck me like a lightning bolt. In one scene, the pianist's father is walking along the streets of Warsaw, just after the Germans have occupied the city in 1939. We think that my grandfather's father and brother died in Warsaw around that time. A German soldier takes great pleasure in knocking off the proud, white-whiskered man's hat, then forcing him to walk in the gutter. Something about this needless moment of domination struck deep into my soul.

Within seconds I was crying tears so hot my face felt burned, even in that sweltering tropical paradise. The tears eventually gave way to an incredible explosion of possibility: I was alive! The Nazis had failed in their grand vision to exterminate us all! My existence on the earth was a gift to be grateful for! In that moment, I knew that I *had* to do something positive with my life.

During my teens and twenties I was too traumatized, anxious and confused to hear the clarion call of my purpose resounding within me. After some time spent healing and transforming myself, I was finally able to hear the ever-present whispers of my calling; and devote my life to activities of impact that my purpose demanded of me.

Every one of us has a purpose, by nature of us being both conscious and physical organisms. Purpose is the bridge between the inner world of our consciousness and the problems and issues in our physical world. Purpose calls an individual to act to heal the material whole, whether through a smile offered to someone having a bad day or by building a global purpose-driven business. Purpose is 'spiritual' love becoming tangible impact in the gnarly moments of everyday life as we solve problems that really matter for those that we care about. Simply, purpose is love, in action. It is the experience of connection turned into creative acts that genuinely help others to become free and flourish more.

If we allow our hearts to break open with the enormity of the suffering of the world, our true purpose will emerge. As our hearts are torn asunder with the intensity of the pain felt by so many about so much, our self-protective patterns are encouraged to crumble still further away. This leaves us raw, ripe, and ready to allow liquid spirit, always coursing through our nervous system, to shine the light of purpose out into the shadows of despair. Purpose is our 'best' way of contributing to the alleviation of suffering of others as determined by what we care most about, our cultural background, our talents and skills, and the social and spiritual pain around us. Each of us must find out how to use our skills and talents to help, empower and inspire the people and places we care about.

Purpose is not about being morally superior nor is it about gaining salvation and a place in heaven. It is simply a natural response to suffering when we feel connected to all. Purpose connects the other-worldly love we feel within (when we experience oneness) with the many this-worldly problems around us. There is nothing remotely religious or New Age about this. Purpose exists because we are all part of an interconnected universe that is constantly supporting expansion, learning, and flourishing.

If the system is alive, and parts of it are in pain, then other parts will shift, transform, and change so they can relieve that pain. This desire for wholeness happens at the level of the cell, at the level of the individual organism, and perhaps at the level of Gaia, our planet. Life seeks to maintain life and heal wounds that might limit it. Once we feel we are all connected, all one, then if anyone is trapped in separation in the system—and is suffering—we want to relieve their suffering. This is what purpose is.

We do not get to decide what our purpose is; but we do get to choose whether and how we act on it (or not). Viktor Frankl, a psychiatrist who endured the death camps of the Holocaust, believed that we are all always free, no matter whether in Auschwitz or Alaska, to find ways to contribute to others in even the most challenging of moments.[182] The way to do this is to apply our purpose to any problem and find opportunities to serve within every challenge. It is how we balance our responsibilities to others and our planet with our right to be free, loved and valued for who we are.

If we are stuck in Protector patterning, we don't have the open heart or open mind necessary to truly serve others. Neediness and addiction (even if it is to saving the world) will get in the way of us being truly purposeful. If we have patterns stemming from our own fear, lack, and loss, we will not—biologically cannot—fully give ourselves over to what the universe is asking us to do to heal the whole. On the other hand, purpose emanates effortlessly from the Connector when we are not defending, protecting, and controlling.

To be 'on purpose' we have to make our gains in inner wisdom count in the external world. We do this by coupling our own enlightenment to the cessation of suffering, and increasing the thriving, of others. Our own enlightenment is the gateway into, not the end point of, a life of purpose. We choose to step out of the spiritual bubble and seek out the places where we can most make a difference. As our hearts becomes more whole, less energy is taken up with repressing painful memories and protecting ourselves from the world. As we purify ourselves, more of our energy can be invested in changing the world around us. Before the light can shine clear and true from us, we must polish the lens and remove the distortions that collect on it. These marks on the lens are our protective patterns and the shadow within. By paying attention to them, we can step into our full power as purpose-driven people.

In the Jewish mystical tradition of Kabbalah, changing (or "repairing", to be exact) the world is called *tikkun ha-olam*. However, we can only focus on this purpose-work if we are already practicing *tikkun ha-nefesh*: healing ourselves so we are better able to be compassionate, loving, and purposeful in the moment.[183] The processes of self-healing and world-change are forever coupled. This idea can also be found in the Christian mystical tradition of Gnosticism, which inspires us to solve problems in nature using the light of liquid spirit, connective consciousness, within each of us.[184]

Spiritual atheism, as a philosophy of life, shows us that changes in our inner world and outer world are not two separate silos, but part of one continuum.

In order to fulfill our purpose in the world, we must become leaders. Leadership is the ultimate frontier for all spiritual atheists (and so why I spend half my time teaching and training leaders). We cannot truly serve the world without stepping into positions of leadership, whether that is within our intimate relationships, family systems, organizations, or the entire global ecosystem. This is because purpose is about contributing to others, serving their wholeness and reducing their suffering.

The focus on suffering is key. Many despots and dictators believe they are working for the greater 'good', and that the changes they are making will benefit the majority even if a minority are homeless/imprisoned/executed. In the name of manifesting "the good", political power and regulation has been responsible for some of the worst violence enacted on humanity (and the planet). Adolf Hitler authentically believed that he was leading the German people away from moral decay and social decline towards the good. He is even said to have believed that his destiny was to become Germany's Joan of Arc.[185] By seeking the good of the Aryan majority his efforts became a terrifying assault on the lives of a large minority (including my family).

The grasping, reasoning mind, driven by unresolved pain and heartache, thinks it knows what is good for everyone. By seeking the reduction of suffering wherever we see it—we all know what suffering looks and feels like—we can ensure that nobody is subjected to oppression as a cost of bettering the lives of others by chasing some rational concept of "the good". It is impossible to ever be sure that what we think is "the good" really is good, and beneficial for all. So it's better for us to stick to reducing suffering, and, if it feels purposeful and intuitive after deep reflection and contemplation, to then focus on increasing thriving.

To ensure we don't damage people in the name of leadership, we must lead with whole and not hurt hearts. An open and loving heart, purified of much fear and loathing, wants to make sure everyone feels safe, seen, and heard. It wants to care, caress, and heal quite naturally. This means becoming ever-more aware of our conscious experience, felt senses, and emotions so that the choices we make serve everyone and not just ourselves. Leaders who are dominated by a Will to Power, no matter how righteous their beliefs, inevitably end up hurting everyone, including themselves. If we go out into the world held hostage by hurt hearts, we will likely use the awesome power of technology, innovation, and entrepreneurship to scale, amplify, and accelerate projects that do not alleviate suffering. The Zyklon B, used in the gas chambers of Auschwitz, was a disruptive innovation born from protective and controlling hearts. It brought industrial scale to a task that was, up to that point, 'inefficiently' carried out by bullets.

In my experience of training thousands of senior leaders, social innovators, and social entrepreneurs all over the world, people who are not guided by genuine 'spiritual' purpose—that emanates naturally from a whole heart but not a hurt one— focus on solving problems that are echoes of their own unresolved wounding; prefer to alleviate symptoms not root causes (which is far easier to measure) because they are driven by the desire to be appreciated and rewarded; and seek to change the world by "attacking" the people that their Protector sees as "wrong", which almost always perpetuates the very problems we want to dissolve.

Only leaders who proactively heal the splinters in their own hearts can bravely lead us into the new world in ways that help others feel safe enough to change their mindsets and behaviors. *Thumos*, when clarified and purified, turns from indignant rage to inspired courage. It is a "spiritedness" that drives us to act, to stand up, and be counted as heart-led activists, but without needing to accrue all the benefits ourselves in the form of revolutionary recognition or wealth. With a whole heart, leaders can challenge impoverished materialism with empathy and integrity rather than with anger and violence.

Nelson Mandela spent a good part of his twenty-seven years in prison working on himself so he could emanate full power as a transformational and conscious leader. He went in as an angry firebrand, full of patterns of rage and victimhood. He came out a leader of change of world-historical proportions. The long years inside allowed him to 'purify' his pain and anger and become a transformational leader who guided his people, white and black, to a relatively peaceful transition in South Africa. He said that "if I had not been to prison, I would not have been able to achieve the most difficult task in life and that is changing yourself."[186]

Through the constant act of self-healing, *tikkun ha-nesfesh*, we discover new capabilities that become essential for our leadership work doing *tikkun ha-olam*. We transform shadow into skillful means (and resolve). Our purpose projects (and purposeful relationships) keep throwing up more personal challenges to transcend so we can develop new strengths in areas where once we lacked. The cycle is eternal. The more we transform, the more power we have to support other people to transform too.

For example, without interminable days of feeling like a worthless piece of shit, I would not have the compassion I need to guide people who are struggling on their own path to transformation. If I had not had daily physical pain from fibromyalgia, I may never had gotten out of my head long enough to heal myself let alone teach this to other "heady" people too. If I had not left a money-making business to start a new one more aligned with my real and healed values, I may not have the sensitivity needed to help others align their own projects and companies around purpose. If I had not transformed my management style after failing so horribly to lead my first team, I would not be able to guide senior execs, most a lot older than me, toward more conscious forms of leadership. I share these with you to demonstrate that all of the trials and tribulations of life are worth it *if* we can metabolize them into ways to contribute to the world purposefully as leaders.

Being on purpose, taking action as leaders to bring more connection/love into the world, is anything but convenient. It demands sacrifice. In the months and years after I exited my agency, I gave up most, if not all, of my old lifestyle choices in order to focus on unfolding my purpose. As well as refusing to take a reasonable entrepreneurial exit, I went on to refuse project after project that could have made me lots of money but would not have helped the world. I gave up the kudos of my friends and family and even the ability to say what I did for a living in one simple sentence. I still refuse a lot of opportunities if they feel off purpose, a choice made all the more fun by having to support two small kids.

I have lost clients, TV shows, book deals, and press columns because I emphatically declare that my work is guided by purpose aka love. It seems anathema to many in the public domain to be openly love-inspired. This has been painful to my Protector (i.e. my ego), but it has also helped me burnish away any last cravings for recognition. My true north has become my purposeful connection to spirit, rather than the usual metrics of 'success'. Purpose has become the anchor for all of my leadership decisions. It ensures that I don't get pulled into the Protector's patterns—me! mine! more!—that lead to more suffering for myself and others. Well over a decade after I first discovered my purpose, it sings my tune each day ("teach the truth!" I hear calling right now). It also tells me when I veer off path: when I seek fame and fortune in the place of being of genuine service.

I tell you this so you can be prepared for the *quid pro quo* of purpose: limitless fulfillment, freedom and meaning, but also many challenges as we bring it to life in a system that is set up to pull us away from our loving truth. Once found, our purpose will usually demand that we change some or all of our political, consumer, career, and business choices to align with it. Purpose discovery is non-reversible. Once we understand our calling to serve others, any time we spend *not* honoring the call of purpose will bring existential agony. Nothing is as painful to us, nothing can spark such torment, as knowing that we are off purpose once we experience the flow and joy of being on purpose. As has been said: hell is meeting the purposeful person you could have been.

When we have yet to find the truth of who we are, we can drown out the call of our purpose with drugs, exotic holidays, sex, work, exercise, extreme sports, and anything else that we use to stay within our comfort zones. I did for years. Once we switch on though, we can no longer avoid our calling and experience anything other than suffering.

By developing basic trust, we can relax into knowing that the universe will give us experiences that help us to live a purposeful life. But it does not mean we will be constantly happy or that our experiences will be pleasurable all the time. Thriving means we are growing at the very edge of our capacities, which is usually thrilling but often unenjoyable. As the Greeks made clear, *eudaemonia* (thriving) and hedonic happiness (pleasure) are not the same.[187]

In order to get the "purpose dividend" of meaning we must be ready to pay the "purpose premium", which might mean giving up respect, security, and wealth. Purpose helps us find peace with the myriad disappointments of life, and guarantees us growth, meaning, and profound levels of fulfillment. But it may not involve us being rich, recognized, or respected. Purpose asks us to break free from the delusions of the "prosperity gospel" within advanced capitalism and to develop intense equanimity about the Return On Investment from our work. The universe wants us to be stretched to our full capacity by our purpose as we serve more and contribute more; but it is agnostic about whether we are on the front cover of *Forbes* or retire to Florida because of it.

Like with all things, the Protector can hijack even our most purposeful intentions in order to do its job of keeping us safe and surviving. It can have us start comparing our purpose to see if it is bigger or better than another person's, which is impossible as each is unique to the individual *and we all have one*! Our purpose cannot be better or worse than anyone else's. It is just what each of us can do to ease the pain of others *today*. Purpose has no need for ambitious scale or big numbers; it is content to improve the life of a single person, no matter in what small way, each day.

The Protector can have us focus all our time on our mission projects, where we feel useful and valued, whilst having us leave behind purpose-widows and purpose-orphans because the pleasures of real-world 'success' see more desirable than constant challenges within our intimate relationships. The Protector can even have us find ways to turn wisdom practices, designed to help us *practice* living and contributing from connective consciousness, into ways to get pleasure.

Yoga as a Western lifestyle activity is often limited to getting the tight butt and nice vibes that the Protector desires. Yet the great sage Patanjali tells us in the *Yoga Sutras* that if we practice yoga properly, it will lead us to change our lives and the world.[188] He says that we will give up many of our possessions and start to practice *ahimsa*, or nonviolence: the core of Gandhi's purpose-work to bring social justice to all Indians. Likewise, mindfulness and meditation can be used as a gateway into conscious awakening, self-healing, and a life of transformational leadership. Or we can allow the Protector to promote it, and profit from it, as a way to get more stuff done and be more efficient.

Purpose in business is hijacked all the time by Control and Protect Mode. Business purpose can inspire an entire organization to contribute their full selves to solve problems that matter in the world. But often it is used to push teams to go the extra mile without ensuring that the company does things ethically. Having an abiding purpose as a business inevitably leads to massive 'inconvenience': we have to align our business models, digital marketing strategies, hiring and firing policies, and everything else with purpose (aka connective consciousness). This means pretty much everything in the business will need to be relooked at through an awakened lens. But the Protector wants to have the benefits of purpose without changing anything about how business is done. This leads to "purpose-washing". Without an awakened, purified, and healed heart, the logic of separation-fueled capitalism will co-opt purpose as a tools to fulfill the cravings for power and profit.

I am no purist or ascetic, and I live very much in this world. But there is no getting around the sacrifice that spiritual atheism requires as we transform ourselves so we can play our part in transforming the world. Genuine spirituality is not necessarily about feeling nice, pleasant, or even happy. It demands that everything in our material world be realigned around the transcendent truth of connection/love. It is not about having a Buddha statue in the corner of our home or lighting incense, although these may all be part of a genuine wisdom practice. It is about making tough choices every day about what we say, buy, think, and do in order to serve connection/love.

This means we need to reassure our Protector at every turn so it does not hijack our purpose work to become rich or rewarded. Many of the great wisdom traditions have developed great hacks to stop our Protector hijacking our purpose. Mahayana Buddhism developed a way to avoid the trap of spiritual bypass and keep us focused on service to others.

This practice invites spiritual atheists to make a vow to never disappear into their own experience of spiritual bliss until they have brought about the release from suffering of all sentient beings. The pledge is called the Bodhisattva vow.[189] We commit our personal development and inner work of transformation to other beings.

The Vedic tradition has developed a way to avoid our Protector seeking rewards and recognition from our purpose work: devotion. Devotion is one of the core teachings of the Indian enlightenment classic the *Bhagavad Gita,* a text so good that Gandhi called it his "handbook to life".[190] This devotional way of living, called *bhakti yoga,* is about feeling insane amounts of love in our hearts when we create and deliver our purpose projects so that we focus on that and not on the rewards. The *Bhagavad Gita* suggests that when we do things with devotion, we take action but it is actionless in the sense that there is no Protector thinking it is in control and wanting to be paid for its good works. Our Connector guides us with what to do next without the need to get hooked on what we will get back. We become unattached to the fruits of our labor.

When I crave great book reviews or bigger numbers at my workshops (which I can get hooked into from time to time), I jolt out of connective consciousness and land back into desire and separation. This limits my capacity to serve book readers or workshop attendees with my whole heart; and also leads me to feel inadequate. But if I *devote* my writing and teaching work back to the universe it is flowing from, I become relaxed about the metrics. I become passionately committed to my love-fueled intentions, but am not attached to how many people like my work. I wrote this book as an act of devotion; no matter how it is received, it came from the best of my love. That is enough. Devotion keeps my heart open and my sight true and prevents my work from being distracted by the Protector's need for kudos and rewards. I know I am merely a channel for love to come from the whole to the part; one of billions of stewards of our collective wisdom.

The Connector within inspires us to make choices that reduce suffering and increase thriving in ourselves and others. Every outcome of every decision we must make—like those at the start of this book—is dependent on whether we make choices with a sense of connection or protection. Given that we are not in a life or death situation most of the time, making the majority of our choices within Control and Protect Mode (based on survival) may not help us to flourish with inner peace and a sense of purpose. The more we make everyday decisions from within Create and Connect Mode, the more we feel connected and are creative!

As an intelligent living system, the universe provides the wisdom we need to make great choices and to bring more love and less pain into daily life. We just have to stay open to the Connector's guidance, usually called "intuition". Intuition can be verbal, visual, or just a deep sense of what to do next. But we cannot hear its low, slow whispers above the clamor of 'shoulds' and 'musts' that arise when we feel fearful and defended. Intuition is the voice of the Connector leading us to make decisions that will reduce suffering and increase thriving for everyone. Instinct, the voice of the Protector, barks at us what we need to do to survive. By refining our capacity to discern love-fueled intuition from fear-driven instinct, we get clarity on how to make more purposeful choices.

Quakers have a powerful wisdom practice that seems to help differentiate between intuitive responses and instinctual reactions. When they gather, they sit in silence until someone "quakes" with intuition, which they interpret as the authentic 'voice of god'.[191] The many global businesses started by Quakers used to use this circle of quietude and intuition to make better, and more ethical, choices. We can all use this practice to choose what to do next throughout the day. When I quieten down my mind, and feel into my body as a whole, my Connector will usually inform me what to do next. If it doesn't, I try to hold off making a decision until I get a clear felt sense in my emotional and physiological bodymind giving me a read.

We cannot second-guess genuine intuition; but we can refine it by repeatedly testing it out with both wisdom and critical reason to see if it is protective patterning or genuine insight. This is where much of our attention must go if we want to make choice informed by both science (the details of which we often don't fully understand) and our own wisdom in harmony. Much as we may want to, in the complexity of modern life, we cannot make every decision in our life and in leadership with reason and evidence alone (even if they were the only guide to truth, as rationalists believe.) Data, whether it's about the stock market or our carbon footprint, is always about the past and so is always incomplete when it comes to forging the future. By parsing empirical data within our intuitive bodymind, even if what we come up with scares or confuses our reasoning mind, we make better choices. Research studies have even provided evidence that those who harness their intuition as well as using hard data get the best results.[192] This is because they have access to both elements of their biological being—matter and consciousness—not just the former.

We also get help from the Connector, when we make choices that are *not* aligned with our purpose. When I am off purpose, acting in an inappropriately protective or controlling way, my felt senses starts to fire up strange and unpleasant feelings. The closest term I can use to describe it is 'shame'. Pioneering neurobiologist Dan Siegel believes shame is the feeling we have when there is a rupture in connection.[193] This makes sense if we see purpose and intuition as flowing from connective consciousness.

By not acting in alignment with this force, we break the connection. The result is often an icky feeling like we are letting ourselves (and our universe) down. I see the unease as a signal to cease and desist what I am doing and reflect. I pay attention to my actions and thoughts; and then seek to transform any patterns that are playing out so I can return to the flow of purpose. With hindsight, the 'negative' feelings I was having about my first business was growing shame that our business model had morphed out of alignment with my purpose.

If we are locked into the materialist paradigm, we can have no purpose and no intuition. Materialist atheists don't believe we have a purpose beyond passing on our genes. Materialism sees no meaning in nature because it does not believe that subjective experiences like pain or pleasure, fear and love, and limitation and liberation really exist. In fact, hardcore materialists (like the New Atheists) hold that we are in an utterly meaningless universe. It's all one big accident. So there is no transcendent truth to root our purpose in and give life meaning or value. Everything is local, random, and relative.

The irony is that a rigorous *materialist* study of over 1,500 people, that took place over fifteen years, concluded scientifically that having a purpose in life can prevent us from experiencing Alzheimer's, dementia, and cognitive decline.[194] This is empirical fact. Yet the materialist episteme has no good explanation for how a sense of purpose in our consciousness, which is itself an illusion to materialists, can make our bodies healthier, less inflamed, less at risk of stroke, and quicker to bounce back from illness—all proven by science. Spiritual atheists however can embrace purpose and intuition because we see mind influencing matter and matter influencing mind. They are two aspects of one underlying reality.

Our purposeful ideas, insights, and intuitions are *not* religious rules.

They are not magical thinking, superstitions, or conspiracy theories. They are a felt sense emanating from a bodymind that is connected and engaged in life, attentive to shifts in the systems we touch. I believe that the intuitions and ideas that come to us in connective consciousness contain non-local information. This is sacrilege to materialists but there are plenty of open-minded scientists, like David Bohm, who have attempted to make sense of this.

The renowned quantum physicist Wolfgang Pauli worked with Carl Jung to develop a dual-aspect theory of matter and consciousness that could account for the synchronicities we encounter in life and which seem to guide to make certain choices.[195] In my experience, such "meaningful correspondences" show up to confirm we are on the right path; or to shove us onto a more purposeful one if we are not. They seem to happen more frequently the more inner work we do: we release old patterns that block our awareness of synchronicities showing up in the moment.

Non-locality is also at play, it appears, when we have a new idea or epiphany. Materialists reduce all activity in the world to inert matter. In this view, imaginative art and purposeful innovations come from existing data/memories that are recombined in unexpected ways. This means there can be no genuine newness or novelty in the world, simply endless permutations of existing elements.

Yet most artists, musicians, writers, and innovators I have met or researched have a very real felt sense that their creations are being "channeled" through them rather than coming from their intellects. The great composer J. S. Bach said: "I play the notes as they are written, but it is God who makes the music." Legendary post-structuralist and anthropologist Claude Levi-Strauss said: "I don't have the feeling that I write my books… I have the feeling that my books get written through me."[196]

We often experience such ideas and epiphanies as an "uprush" from subliminal consciousness, according to research done by Frederic W. H. Myers.[197] I have experienced such uprushes on countless occasions; as well as guided many others to have them too. They are an empirical fact that you are likely to have experienced many times yourself but which conventional mechanistic science cannot explain. The pioneering systems biologist Stuart Kauffman has come up with a theory to account for them that quantum mechanics can support. He suggest that there is a "partial lawlessness" in the material universe which opens up cracks through which transformational ideas and insights can burst forth.[198] In his view, the laws/rules of physics are not "causally closed". This is what allows newness to emerge in systems. When we "channel" art and ideas we are acting as a conduit for newness to come into being. We unfold content from Bohm's Possible World to shape the Actual World.

It appears that human beings are the *only* organisms that can *consciously* tap into connective consciousness to accelerate problem-solving in the material world (although animals from dolphins to crows can creatively solve problems too). From such an understanding, *the* purpose of human life emerges: we are here to serve whatever is seeking to emerge from the Possible World into the Actual World—which reduces suffering and increases thriving— with our entire bodymind.

To live, love, and lead fully means consciously co-creating with the universe itself in a constant dance. We tap into the whole and channel heart-led ideas into the world. The ideas and intuitions we need, lie pregnant in every interaction in our participatory universe, as long as we can flip out of Control and Protect and into Create and Connect. We can engage with connective consciousness at any time and ask it for 'guidance' on how to best support the unfolding so that harmony is the outcome. The idea that nature is whole, a oneness, that a human being is part of—and can align with by choice—is the core teaching of many of the wisdom traditions, whether we are looking at Western Stoicism or Eastern Taoism. As William James suggested, genuine spirituality is about sensing that "there is an unseen order and the supreme good lies in harmoniously adjusting to that order."[199]

Another way of saying this is that we "dialogue" with the universe we are an intrinsic part of so that we keep moving towards harmony with every choice. We can constantly dialogue with ourselves, others, and the planet to discern what will reduce suffering and what will increase thriving in the moment we are in. Martin Buber, a Jewish philosopher, thought that every time we speak with the universe, another person, or parts of ourselves in genuine dialogue, we feel connective consciousness "surge between us".[200]

If we engage in dialogue with the Possible World, through meditation and ecstatic/shamanic practices, we will usually come to understand how to serve whatever is seeking to emerge. This helps us lead the transformations that are most needed in ourselves and our specific communities to reduce suffering. This is nothing to do with prayer to a personal god. It is the individual engaging in a co-creative relationship with the universe.

The choices that we are called to make by our purpose and intuition are not moral in the sense of the shame-and-blame morality of the Judeo-Christian religious traditions. Where religion sees 'evil', spiritual atheism sees 'evil' acts as defensive patterns that are inappropriately seeking protection not connection. Where religion sees 'good', spiritual atheism sees people acting in alignment with their healed hearts to serve the reduction of suffering of others. Neither are intrinsically good or bad, but they will result in different levels of harmony.

By understanding our biological and spiritual selves, we can shift the paradigm of morality from good/bad to fit/fail, appropriate/mismatch, or harmony/discord. This, in turn, breeds a sense of compassion for all who transgress boundaries because we understand that they are not bad but that their Protector is doing whatever it can to keep them safe, using old rules and habits that are no longer helping. We are also more open to supporting such people to transform pain and patterning within, and to bring them back to connection/love.

This is way more profound then it might look because it goes some way toward solving the greatest paradox of modernity: the need to choose either transcendent religious morals or fall into postmodern relativism. Before the Enlightenment, morality was defined by scripture and the interpretation of the rules found within it by a pope, rabbi, or imam. But once we entered the Age of Reason, religious rules were declared null and void. Nietzsche, amongst others, showed us that our ideas about morality evolved within history and were not timeless and essential commandments from god.[201] He believed that this liberated us from the conventions of the moral majority and so we could finally become free: true masters of our own destiny. But this left secular society without hard-and-fast rules for 'good' behavior. Without a transcendent moral truth grounded in god and his words, we were left with ethical quagmires that underpin much of our contemporary political and social challenges.

Many rational philosophers tried to make a reliable, rule-based system of values work using reason and no religion. Immanuel Kant believed that he had developed a morality that was objectively true, rationally unimpeachable, and therefore relevant to every human being. Kant thought that if everyone acted on this "categorical imperative" with their full faculties of reason, then rationality would triumph over irrationality and the world would be harmonious.[202] Jeremy Bentham sought to *measure* the value of an act and so be able to mathematically define what was objectively "good" and what was "bad". The resultant metric, "utility", was the sum of all the pleasure minus the sum of all the pain.[203] The choices, policies, and strategies that create the most utility can then be prioritized rationally, an idea that still holds sway in many corridors of government and commerce.

These projects failed precisely because reason and science removed values—that is to say, *conscious* opinions about what is better or worse—from knowledge. Because science aims to be objective and therefore valueless, there is no logical way to go from what science says *is* the case in nature to a moral law telling us what *ought* to be without subjective opinion, which is unscientific and irrational. Nobody can ever tell anyone else that circumcising their child is categorically good or bad based on research studies because no scientist can ever get in the mind of an infant (or parent) and decide whether the benefits outweigh the costs for all. Utilitarians (like doctors and economists) usually have more power-knowledge than those who have less of a voice in society which means utilitarian rationality is not such a great leap forward from religious rules. Which scientist or politician gets to play god and tell everyone what is more instrumentally useful or more rational for everyone else? Who will be hurt by their choices?

Anthropologists like Geertz and the post-colonial thinkers like Fanon and Freire have shown us the dangers of believing that any one idea of what is good—historically, this has usually meant a Western, white, male, and educated idea of the good—is universal. Each culture has a different paradigm of morality that makes sense within its own set of assumptions. Frankfurt School critical thinkers and Foucault demonstrated that anyone claiming to know what is good for others will usually be, whether unconsciously or not, attempting to maintain their own power and position. But this then opens the door towards moral relativism, where there is no right or wrong. To a relativist, the value of every choice must be considered relative to its own paradigm, even if it is violent or abhorrent to others. We must let the crooked CEO, the venal dictator, and the genital-mutilating father do their thing if it fits with their culture values and meaning-systems. Postmodernism fails because it says anything goes.

Both Kant's and Bentham's rational solutions to the moral disenchantment of the world failed because they both rely on subjective secondary qualities whilst trying not to. Rather than embrace the science of subjective experience—the contemplative traditions—they tried to stick with just the rational science of matter. Control and Protect Mode attempted to get rid of Create and Connect Mode which is what accesses the intuitions and felt sense we need to weigh things up and gauge what fits and what doesn't.

Spiritual atheism offers us a way to resolve this. With spiritual atheism—rigorous science woven together with equally rigorous wisdom—we look to scientific research to give us the best available knowledge about the things we can see and measure… whilst being comfortable with the stark reality that our 'spiritual' intuitions are ultimately the *only* guides to matters of conscience, whether immunizations for kids or investments for adults. Because we understand the inherent value of both objective 'facts' and constantly refined subjective intuitions, we get to embrace the rational ideals of Kant—that there might be some moral *principles* that we might all share—whilst acknowledging that what we intuit, dynamically and in the moment to be right may not be so next year or in a different context.

This reality puts a huge onus on us as individuals, and as leaders, to be able to be clear on what is the intuitive and wise voice of our Connector and what is the panicky, fearful voice of our Protector as it tries to defend us, usually inappropriately, by being self-centered. It becomes the primary duty of each citizen to do the inner work needed to be able to discern what they are being called to do by connective consciousness; and how to get out of Control and Protect Mode long enough to act consciously. As such, each individual has to 'own', refine, and develop their own consciousness.

There is no way out of this duty because neither religion nor reason can give us rules to fit all occasions. We have to discover what is the most appropriate thing to do with each decision as we unfold our purpose in dynamic interplay with the world itself. Rules, whether scientific, political or religious, always become obsolete the moment they are created. Principles always stay alive because they must be interpreted anew by each individual as they live into each unique moment.

If we citizens do *not* do our own inner work then we need the State to enforce lots of rules and regulations designed to ensure we play nice. Governments must step in with law and order to overcome what Thomas Hobbes called, in *Leviathan,* "our continual fear and danger of violent death, and the life of man, solitary, poor, nasty, brutish, and short."[204] This political reasoning has been the justification for strong government, authoritarian leaders, and heavy-handed policing for centuries.

Like most of the rationality that comes from separation consciousness, it is partly true: if we stay in Control and Protect Mode, we will try to dominate one another with power, knowledge, wealth, and property. If we only compete and cannot collaborate and co-create, we will hurt one another. Then we do need laws to protect everyone's rights. However, if we are taught how to enter Create and Connect Mode, as the wisdom traditions teach us, we can all learn how to make *appropriate* choices together without restrictive and often outdated laws mandating it.

This is why big government is a sign that our consciousness has become under-developed. Thomas Paine, a British philosopher who emigrated to Philadelphia just as the American War of Independence kicked off, said in his revolution-inspiring book *Common Sense*: "Government, like dress, is the badge of lost innocence ... For were the impulses of conscience clear, uniform and irresistibly obeyed, man would need no other lawgiver." In other words, we only need lots of regulation if we aren't switched on.

Conscious, intuitive and purpose-driven citizenship has never been more important than it is today because we are about to be tested to the limit with unprecedented crises. The Digital Age is like no other. Global risks like climate change, depression, obesity, species extinctions, terrorism, and pollution are a threat to every human (and organism) alive. Meanwhile digital technologies of the Fourth Industrial Revolution—like AI, automation, and the blockchain—are about to transform everything. Nobody can predict exactly what life will be like in a decade, let alone three or four. But we can be sure that it is going to be different, and almost certainly an intense ride for everyone.

People around the globe are waking up to the reality that the current system is failing to provide them with the meaning (or even the money) they need to thrive. Globalization and technology, which can enable global networks of people to work together with common purpose, have been hijacked by Control and Protect Mode as a way to reduce costs, manipulate money, and increase profits. Globalization has focused solely on primary material properties, such as efficiencies and ROI, at the expense of secondary qualities, like forging networks of purposeful ideas and people. People feel that they are losing what really matters to them—community, meaning, and a decent quality of life—and they are deeply troubled by it.

There is understandable fear that technology will replace us, just as cheaper overseas workers have replaced so many in the last three decades. When we add the changes to our lives wrought by factors like severe weather, overpopulation, and resource conflicts, we can be sure that loss—

of reputation, income, pride, quality of live, meaning, and community—will be present in every system we touch for the foreseeable future. This loss, and fear of loss, will likely trigger many people into protection.

In the vacuum caused by the loss of meaning driven by materialist atheism and science, religion-fueled politics is expanding (it is also behind the disenchanted despair that has human beings shooting people and blowing them up, everywhere from Las Vegas to London). One of the reasons that both evangelical Christianity and political Islam have gained such ground in the last few decades is because they seek to return something other than reason, something other than material, back into the core of the body politic.

Sayyid Qutb, a very influential Islamic philosopher and jihadist, was a major critic of Western modernity. He stated that the European psyche was split asunder by the Age of Enlightenment, divided between religion and reason. This led to the degeneration and degradation of Western society.[205] He preached that the oneness inherent in Islam, *tawhid*, is the solution to the chasm at the core of European consciousness. The evangelical fundamentalist and former Chief Strategist for Donald Trump, Steve Bannon, thinks something similar, but from the Christian perspective. Such voices are inspiring many of those in existential despair. But faith-based activists like Qutb and Bannon want to re-ground secular society in organized religion. But because religious belief systems are scriptural and dogmatic, a return to some kind of pre-modern Christian or Islamic piety will involve violence on those who do not belong to these creeds (including those from other sects within their own religion).

Unless we place an authentic heart-led spirituality into public discourse, it is likely that fundamentalists will continue to bring religious dogma back into the world, to the detriment of many. As citizens and leaders, we *must* sign up to an alternative meaning system to religion. Spiritual atheism gives us a way to do this because it presents connection/love—which seeks to alleviate any pain felt in every heart—as a transcendent truth whilst avoiding religious rules and scriptures.

Every person can experience connective consciousness and the caring and compassion that emanates from it naturally if we make this *bios* central to personal and leadership development. This means making the wisdom technologies and practices needed to drop out of separation consciousness and into connective consciousness freely available—as they once were, without any Woo Woo.

The Digital Age, with all its threats to life as we know it, demands that we step up as transformational leaders who can help our communities feel safe enough—in our over-populated, globalized, and digitized world—to share resources and care for each other without protectionism getting in the way. We can honor people's love of their nation, political party, and religion while showing them the enormous possibilities inherent in a digital future *if* we connect and create with each other. Without compassionate and connected leaders that understand how to guide us through change—particularly, how to secure us so that we don't revert back to old patterns like racism and nationalism to feel safe and in control—things are going to get a lot tougher.

We leaders must fearlessly bring the full power of liquid spirit into the actions we take that impact others. This means well and truly stepping out of the spiritual closet and allowing love to flow into our work, our organizations, our communities, and out into the natural world that we are an elemental part of. This need for leaders to purposefully bring more 'spiritual' imagination, intuition, and connection/love into their projects and decisions is a fundamental challenge for our secular society because the separation between Church and State was enshrined at the core of

Western democracies for good reason: to ensure that religious dogma had no way to dominate political life.

Yet proponents of New Atheism, rationalism, positivism, and scientism—which all originate in the fetishization of primary properties and the suppression of secondary qualities—have chased the heartfelt out of the political domain as well as the dogma. But there can be no lasting environmental sustainability, social justice, or political equality until there is less lack and loss within. We won't change what we consume or produce, until we tame the Protector writ both small and large.

Most of our social problems, from individual depression to massive social inequality, are rooted in separation consciousness. So any lasting solution to them must engage with our heart's deepest fears and feelings to overcome this feeling. As prescient ecologist Lynn White Jr. wrote back in 1967, before we realized just how big a crisis there really is today across our economies and environments: "Since the roots of our trouble are so largely religious, the remedy must also be essentially religious, whether we call it that or not."[206] This means that we must bring 'spiritual' connection/love into the center of our education systems, political systems, businesses, and economic models if we want people to recycle more, eat less sugar, exercise more, steal less, be more honest, pay more tax, have more integrity, stop fracking, commit less suicide, make less flashy products, do more empowering marketing, take fewer pills, claim less welfare, and generally do the right thing.

With connection/love at our backs, we can tame and reconfigure capitalism rather than seek to destroy it (which is probably both impossible and misguided). The form of capitalism we have today is simply an expression of billions of fearful Protectors seeking material gain and pleasure as proxies for safety and love. If we shift how people feel each day they show up to produce and consume—empowering people to experience themselves as loved and connected—capitalism can be animated by the Connector not the Protector.

This would be Connected Capitalism, where we leverage Create and Connect Mode to forge social and commercial innovations that lift billions out of material and psychological suffering. We harness profitable business models, technology and innovation thinking as vehicles to scale heart-led purpose. We use capitalism to democratize products and services that genuinely solve problems that matter: poverty, despair, ill-health, social isolation, and chronic diseases. We stop using technology to simply drive efficiencies and profits, and leverage it to solve the great challenges of the Digital Age: how to make life work for 9 billion or so people before we burn ourselves up with relentless addiction, and burn up the planet's finite resources with relentless production.

Rather than always attempting to pocket all the proceeds of business, Connected Capitalism looks to share the rewards as well as the risks. Business entities and technologies like social enterprises, cooperatives, mutuals, crowdfunding, wikis, AI, and the blockchain all have the power to facilitate such a massive recalibration of capitalism. Connected Capitalism can be laissez-faire without it damaging trust and equality in our society because the individual (venture) capitalist, investor, entrepreneur, and leader makes decisions based on their deepest purpose as well as the drive for efficiency by using big data. We can scale through collaboration rather than just through control. Profit can be made; but we invest most of it in employee empowerment and user-centered innovations rather than return all of it to investors and share-holders. Accumulation of wealth and power is not the sole goal of this economic system.

The reason why I run a social enterprise is precisely because it is such a palintonic harmony between purpose and profit. It uses the powerful creative engines of business to deliver purpose—without relying on grants and donations to do our good works. The social enterprise, or some variant of it, is the archetypal entity of Connected Capitalism. Primary properties and secondary qualities are brought together within it so that harmony in the tangible material world occurs.

With fully awakened consciousness we can understand and temper the destructive logic of disconnected capitalism, the turbo-charged "will to power" of Western technology and the stultifying nature of most marketing, media, and communications. We can, instead, leverage their enormous force to empower and enlighten. To do this we must wake up to the Protector-driven patterns, scientific and religious fundamentalism, and economic structures that are locking us in ever-decreasing circles. Rather than revolt against them we can reinvent them, from the inside out, as leaders leveraging caring and compassion in the place of domination and separation.

In a delicious irony, the esteemed academic Pierre Hadot has suggested that such a connection between inner and outer transformation is what philosophy was *always* about for the Greeks; those we hold up to be paragons of pure disembodied and disenchanted reason. His research has led him to believe that our famous Greek ancestors were not philosophizing about the world for intellectual glory, political power, or simply to educate the scions of society. Philosophy for them was a lifelong commitment to using a series of expressly *spiritual* practices to become responsive, agile and adaptive; able to constantly and vigilantly reorient themselves to whatever was happening in the world to bring about personal and societal harmony.[207]

In Hadot's view, Plato was not a philosopher in the way we understand it now. He was a wisdom teacher *w*ho invited people to seek traces of the oneness in all things so they could act wisely in the moment. Plato suggests in his *Republic* that only such true philosophers, lovers of wisdom who no longer want to rule with Control and Protect Mode but instead seek the truth with Create and Connect Mode, should be given the power to lead society.[208] In other words, only those who have transcended the Protector's constant need to compete, grab, and defend should lead us through the trials and tests of the Digital Age.

As leaders inspired by spiritual atheism, we can *all* bring about tangible transformation in the material world inspired by our huge, healed hearts. We appreciate that everyone is responsible for themselves and that nobody should expect handouts, while also knowing that everyone needs compassion (and some form of coaching and empowerment) in order to overcome their problems, especially when they are going through a tough time. By becoming masters at connection/love, we can reach everyone, no matter their ideology, and help them to transform emotional despair into collective hope, as Nelson Mandela, Mahatma Gandhi, and Martin Luther King Jr. all did so powerfully. These men were all expressly *spiritual* leaders leveraging connective consciousness to transform the material world.

We can *all* become leaders like this, palintonically balancing hubris and humility and profit and purpose in service of the whole. Connective consciousness gives us the patience, moral strength, and creative wherewithal to keep going as leaders as we take on gnarly challenges. Nothing else can provide us with limitless energy, courage, and motivation to keep going through the tough times (and keep others in the game too), rather than sinking into self-centeredness, frustration, and despair.

While it might seem easier to remain cynical about the power of connective consciousness to make tangible change in social systems (and even its validity), it is much more inspiring to realize what Gandhi, Mandela, and Luther King Jr all believed in one way of another: love is the most important leadership principle. Love is the start and end point.

It's free, and freely available, to you right now. We can choose to devote our lives, as the Bodhisattva does, to the removal of suffering through purpose-driven projects and transformational leadership. We do this not because of what we can get, but because of how much we can give.

∞

This, then, is an invitation—expressly made to you—to accelerate the transformation of your inner world so you can bring more love/connection/purpose into your family life, community, enterprises, and systems as a transformational leader. Elemental to this is to heal any remaining schism between reason and spirit within you to become whole, able to seamlessly blend intuition and data together when making choices.

You are the one you have been waiting for. You are god and guru, coach and creator, expert and shaman. You can harness the best of reason and emotion, mind and matter, the mystical and the rational, to live, love, and lead fully in this intense, challenging, and amazing Digital Age. Step out of the shadows and stand up for what you *feel* and *intuit* as much as what you believe in. Walk out of the spiritual closet, if you are in one, and unashamedly and unapologetically presence connection/love in every boardroom and barroom conversation you find yourself in!

Spiritual atheism is ultimately about unashamedly and publicly bringing unalloyed love into every personal, relationship, business, commercial, and political decision: how we love, how we heal, who we vote for, what enterprise we work for, and what supermarkets we buy from. It is about explicitly leading projects and people rooted in an abiding sense of connection to the whole, whether you see that as the Brahman, Buddha-nature, or Brotherhood (or anything in between). It is about harnessing the power of a secular, science-inspired spirituality to transform everything in its path without violence or force, healing one's own heart along the way to ensure little distorts or perverts our purpose (for long, at least).

Spiritual atheists are always ready to give up the habits, beliefs and moods that stop us from fitting with the world and our own purpose within. We align ourselves with nature: ours and that of the material world around us. The Taoists call such a person a *Zhenren*, a True Man. The Chinese ideogram for this word brings to life someone who is always in continuous transformation, continuous beta, whilst always staying rooted in purpose. The power of the True Man comes from them always transforming themselves to stay fitted to the world as it changes, rather than from staying the same and trying conserving old power and control. Their power flows precisely because they have no fixed protective patterning keeping them in their comfort zones.

The Stoics called such a person a Sage. Becoming one is the aim of all philosophizing. Nietzsche called this person an *Ubermensch* or Superman. In Christian mysticism, the realized spiritual atheist is the *Anthropos*, or Whole Man, who fuses masculine and feminine, material and conscious, science and spirituality within. They unify the polarities of the world within themselves. Such a person is totally human and grounded in this world yet is, at the same time, as expansive as the entire universe. Such a sage/superwoman is poised at the edge of chaos, channeling possibilities from the Possible World into actualities in the Actual World at breakfast, lunch and supper. We co-create in the moment, without force or effort, whatever is seeking to emerge that reduces suffering and increases thriving.

We have prepared ourselves, internally, to be a crucible for transformation. We are always ready to surrender the past to embrace the future, according to the way of (our) nature. We have a bias for "owning" problems, ours and those we share as a species, so we can transform them and move the human race forward. This does not mean that we are perfect and without flaws. Far from it. It is simply that we know how to consistently, and with alacrity, transform our foibles, 'bad' habits, limiting assumptions and self-sabotaging behaviors to reach a more fitted, flowing and creative state. We are alive and awake to what is possible in the moment. And, as Nietzsche said, "[o]nce you are awake, you shall remain awake eternally."

The transcendence of our limitations and the transformation of our irritations are intrinsic to our natures as conscious living human organisms in an alive, dynamic universe. Once we wake up to this nature, the benefits of the mystical can leap into each moment within flashes of intuition and insight as we start a meeting, drive home from work, listen to our lover share a tough day, or defuse a fight between siblings. With them, we can transform anything in our life or world that is not working anymore (if it ever did).

With spiritual atheism, lived practically by everyday supermen and superwomen, the war between religion and science can be declared over. We can then focus on 'winning' the peace. Together we can join forces to shift our social, economic, and family systems so that 9 billion plus people can thrive on this one small planet. When we choose to reunite our inherently creative, liquid, and loving consciousness with the power of reason, science, and technology, we can lead transformations anywhere and everywhere in the material world. Then, and only then, will everything that our hearts yearn for most be possible.

SPIRITUAL ATHEISM PRINCIPLES:

- Seek life, leadership, and enterprise purpose—the bridges between our inner experiences of love/connection and tangible problems that matter in the material world—so we can serve others each day with our words and deeds. Purpose-driven living, loving, and leading provides limitless meaning and fulfillment but much inconvenience, consistent challenges and endless opportunities for personal growth.

- Realize that the key leadership qualities we need to drive change—confidence, compassion, and conscious creativity—flow from us effortlessly when our protective patterns are not activated. Therefore a continuous and committed path of self-transformation is a prerequisite for fulfilling our potential as transformational leaders.
- See that all our social, economic, and environmental challenges are driven, at their core, by the illusions of separation consciousness and the drive to control and protect. Therefore all transformational solutions must be driven, at their core, by connective consciousness and the drive to create and connect.
- Accept that 'spiritual' connection/love is only absolute truth that can open up a socially-shared morality and ensure that political change is not hijacked by self-serving protection and control. So unashamedly make leadership, political, and business choices based on wisdom, compassion, and intuition as much as reason, profit, and data.
- Harness purpose, love, and conscious creativity to lead transformations aimed at recalibrating our business, social, and political systems. Always err towards a focus on the reduction of suffering for all to guard against us hurt some people (and the planet) in order to help a specific group move towards our opinion of what 'the good' is.

If you have questions about the ideas in the book in terms of life and love, please post them on our Facebook group, *Switch On Thrive Tribe.* You can post questions about leadership on our Transformational Leadership Community on LinkedIn. Do stay in touch on other social channels:

Twitter: www.twitter.com/nickjankel
Instagram: www.instagram.com/switchon_now/
Youtube: www.youtube.com/c/switchonnickjankel

GET INVOLVED

As a purpose-driven social enterprise we are always seeking support from others to bring to life the transformations envisioned within this book. Here are some ways you might want to contribute:

1. **Write a** review on Amazon **and tell others who you think will enjoy this book**. Spreading the word helps to make change happen.
2. Share your insights and ideas on Spiritual Atheism on the Switch On Facebook community.
3. Download free meditations, toolkits, leadership resources and more at www.switchonnow.com/inspiration
4. Support our non-profit programs working with young people so they can deal with bullying, addictions, and abuse, and dedicate their lives to purposeful work.
5. Support our non-profit leadership programs for politicians and social change-agents so they can fulfill their purpose.
6. Support the development of our school curriculum for brain-based and wisdom-wired learning.
7. Join us on one of our personal development or leadership development programs; or use one of our peer-powered toolkits.

More at **www.switchonnow.com**.

FREE READER OFFER

As a truly valued reader, we are offering you a free download of the core principles for living a thriving life within:

THE SPIRITUAL ATHEISM MANIFESTO

You'll get your free PDF when you sign up to our mailing list at **www.switchonnow.com/sa**
If you sign up, you will also receive invites to read future books in advance of publication.

GLOSSARY OF PHILOSOPHICAL TERMS

Actual World: The realm of certainties and measurable facts once potentialities have been converted into reality from the Possible World.

Ahimsa: A Sanskrit principle of non-violence to all living things; the idea that all beings should be treated with compassion and respect.

Anthropology: The study of human societies and cultures, both past and present.

Archetype: The ideal form of a character or concept. Archetypes are present within the collective unconscious, and we can all tap into them. Associated with Carl Jung.

Atheism: The belief that God or gods do not exist.

Beloved: A Sufi term for the universe when in intimate relationship to it.

Bias: see "cognitive bias".

Biodynamic: An act or process that is always responsive to the live, dynamic nature of biological systems to seek wholeness and harmony.

Bios: A way of life; a life philosophy that can lead to a thriving life.

Bodhisattva: A person who has taken a vow, on becoming enlightened, to commit their life to alleviating the suffering of people, creatures, and the planet.

Bodymind: A term for the single combined entity that is our mind/consciousness and our matter/body. It refuses to allow the Cartesian mind-body dualism, which privileges the mind, and that pervades so much Western thought.

Brahman: A term used in Advaita Vedanta for the concept of the ultimate reality that is transcendent and immanent. When we have realization of oneness it becomes clear that our internal self, or *atman,* is the same as, and continuous with, Brahman.

Breakthrough: The transformation of our ideas and beliefs in our consciousness that we embed and embody in tangible changes in our behavior and the world around us.

Breathwork: The active use of breath, in either a meditative or ecstatic manner, to drive transformation.

Buddha: The name of Siddhārtha Gautama, the historical Buddha.

Buddha-nature: A complex and changing term relating to a luminous reality present in every being that allows all to experience the realization of oneness/enlightenment/non-duality.

Capitalism: An economic system in which a society is organized so that capital, including resources, property, and wealth, is owned by individuals and private companies, and decisions are made for the benefit of those who own the capital.

Careerism: The prioritization of career advancement, no matter what the work entails and how much it creates suffering in people or the planet.

Causation: An occurrence in which one event or variable directly causes another; not to be confused with *correlation.*

Cognitive bias: A mental tendency to deviate from purely rational perceptions, beliefs, and judgements.

Collective unconscious: A shared unconscious mind that contains ancestral memory, myths, and metaphors. Associated with Carl Jung.

Colonialism: The belief that other people's lands, resources, and bodies can be taken, controlled, and exploited by another power or State.

Confirmation bias: A cognitive bias in which people seek evidence that confirms what they already believe to be true, rather than remaining objective and skeptical.

Connected capitalism: An economic system in which a society is organized so that capital, including resources, property, and wealth, is invested into projects that reduce suffering and increase thriving for the whole; purpose is slightly more important than profit; and profits are shared between individuals/private companies and the group.

Connection/love: Feeling connected to all people and things, an experience often described by human language as love.

Connective consciousness: A state of awareness in which we feel connected to the universe and can access information and ideas that are not confined to our brain or body. This is not an everyday or 'normal' state of consciousness for most people. It is similar to William James' *cosmic consciousness.*

Connector (see also Create and Connect Mode): The part of us that ensures we grow, learn, and thrive by connecting with ourselves, each other, and the universe. The Connector is a manifestation of a drive to thrive that seeks to creatively break through challenges, expand wisdom and heal.

Conscious: An emerging term in the spiritual world that is used to describe the act of seeking to approach a given situation with love, truth, and creativity. To be conscious we must be aware of our personal pain and conditioning and seek to transform our outdated patterns. Being conscious is usually dependent on having had sustained experiences of enlightenment that have been integrated into everyday ways of feeling, thinking, and acting.

Consciousness: The experiences that we have within our mind and body and the qualities that come from such awareness; the experiences of being aware of one's existence, surroundings and mortality.

Conscious leadership: The leadership of teams, projects, and organizations in a way that prioritizes the reduction of suffering and the promotion of thriving for everyone touched by our activities.

Consumer: A person seen in terms of their interest in, and capacity to buy, products and services in a market.

Consumption: The using up of a resource, product, or service.

Control and Protect Mode (see also Protector): A state of consciousness in which we are focused, often without being fully aware of it, on defending ourselves against threats and dealing with uncertainty to maximize our chances of survival. In this state we rely on efficient, but not always effective, solutions, habits, and thoughts that have worked in the past. These can often include variations of the fight, flight, or freeze response.

Correlation: A connection between two events or variables, not to be confused with *causation.*

Cosmic consciousness: A term used to describe the state of consciousness during unitary or mystical experiences.

Create and Connect Mode (see also Connector): A state of consciousness in which we are focused on growing, learning, loving, leading, and thriving by connecting with ourselves, each other, and the universe. In this state we can access imaginative thoughts, ideas, insights, and intuitions to create effective, if not always efficient, solutions to new and emerging challenges.

Critical theory/thinking: A term used to describe the analysis of the shortcomings of a particular theory, system or statement; and how they have been used to control, dominate, or disempower. Often associated with the Frankfurt School.

Democratize: To make something that was previously reserved for the few accessible, cost-effective, or enjoyable to all.

Dialogue: To engage in a co-creative conversation during which we explore and discover new ideas, intuitions, and insights together.

Disruptive innovation: The creation of policies, products, or processes that challenge the existing rules of an industry, market, society, or culture, create new principles and new value for existing or new groups.

Dogma: Beliefs, ideas and rules that are defined as the Truth, to the exclusion of all else, by people in power and in positions of authority, such as priests and philosophers.

Double-bind: A situation in which a person is presented with two seemingly irreconcilable beliefs or courses of action.

Dual-aspect monism: The view that the mental and the physical are two aspects of, or perspectives on, the same underlying substance.

Dualistic: The belief that there are two (or more) things in reality that often stand in opposition to each other, e.g. matter vs. mind; subject vs. object; sacred vs. profane.

Ecstasy/ecstatic: Relating to experiences where we are outside of our normal consciousness; they often include the sense that we have transcended our sense of being a limited, separate self.

Efficiency: The concept of obtaining the largest measurable outcome from a resource, such as money, time, or energy; the quality of avoiding wastage and driving productivity and profit.

Empirical: A way to describe information or knowledge that is based on observations and direct experience rather than theory.

Enlightenment: A realization by which we understand that we are unified with the universe, connected to it and so no longer separate, alienated, and alone.

Epiphenomenon: A by-product of brain activity; a mental state that is caused by physical changes in matter but has no causal influence itself.

Episteme: A framework or lens through which we see the world and make sense of our ideas and observations.

Epistemological rupture: A change in our framework or lens that results in new thoughts, feelings, and actions.

Essential: A quality of being timeless and inherent in the world.

Entheogen: A substance, usually a plant or psychedelic medicine, that creates or enhances a feeling of connection or love within.

Ethnography: The systemic, scientific study of individual and group culture within anthropology.

Eudaemonia: A Greek term for the concept of thriving or flourishing over time, even if we are not always happy. It is often contrasted to conventional views of happiness as fleeting moments of hedonic pleasure.

Existentialism: A philosophical theory concerned with the authentic, self-discovered experiences of the individual human being. It is predicated on the idea that every person is free to choose their own way and their own experience, and is responsible for the consequences of their choices.

Exit: When an entrepreneur or investors sell all or part of a company, usually through a listing on the stock exchange (an IPO) or through a trade sale.

Expansive naturalism: The belief that only natural, as opposed to supernatural, forces operate in the world and that these forces are not limited to those we can currently measure or explain using the existing materialist paradigm.

Experimental psychology: The study of the human mind through experiments carried out in accordance with the scientific method.

Faith: The belief in things existing that cannot be proven by science or have not been experienced directly, like gods.

Free-market capitalism: An economic system that has minimal government intervention in the form of regulations, incentives, trade barriers, and labor laws, and maximum agency for producers and consumers. This system is premised on the idea that when guided by their own self-interest, producers are the best and most efficient entities to decide what to create, how to create it, and how much to charge for it.

Gnosticism: A syncretic mystical tradition that fused elements of paganism and Christianity.

Gross Domestic Product (GDP): The financial value of all the periods and services exchanged in an economy during a specific time period. This measurement is used to assess the wealth of a country and its growth. It does not include vital contributions like raising a family and volunteering.

Healing: To release pain and suffering within; we dissolve away *imprints* and transform *patterns* so that we are left feeling free, adaptive, and creative.

Hero's journey: An archetypical storyline or narrative structure that involves a hero who goes on an adventure and can only win victory once they have undergone significant changes and transformation of consciousness.

Historical materialism: A viewpoint on the development of humankind that sees history as a progressive conflict and resolution between opposing forces over satisfying material needs. Associated with Karl Marx.

Humanism: A belief system based on the idea that human beings have the power to create their own destiny and improve their own lives, rather than be controlled by dogma, authority, or tradition.

Hypnosis: The induction of a trance-like state.

Hypnotherapy: The use of trance-like states to facilitate change, healing, and transformation.

Idealism: A system of thought based on the belief that only ideas really exist, and all matter is mentally constructed. The mind, and our ideas, are primary.

Ideology: A belief system of ideals and ideas that usually claim to have more truth than others.

Imprint: An event or series of events during our early years that mark us in some way, are memorable, and lead to specific relationship *templates* and *patterns in later life.*

Inner work: The practice of purposefully and consciously examining our inner selves to heal our pain and transform our established patterns, such as emotions, thoughts, and habits.

Innovation: The implementation of creative ideas that generate value and impact.

Integration: The process of embedding new insights from self-healing, self-discovery, and self-transformation into everyday habits, beliefs, and moods; and embedding them in our default orientation to life.

Intersubjectivity: The intertwining of subjective experiences between people. This can be achieved through dialogue, collaboration, or acknowledgment of *interbeing.*

Invisible hand: The idea that individual, often self-serving, actions have unintended benefits to the collective.

Irrational: That which is based on emotion, intuition, superstition, or unreason.

Kabbalah: A long-established and predominately Jewish mystical tradition.

Magical thinking: Believing that something happens as a result of a made-up idea, supernatural force, or something real that has no plausible link to the event.

Materialism: The belief that only matter really exists, and that all mental experience, like consciousness, is dependent on matter and can be reduced to matter. It is related to *physicalism.*

Matter: Physical and material substances.

Mechanistic: Ideas and beliefs that rely on seeing nature as a machine; all phenomena are seen as explainable by reducing them to the machinery of physical processes.

Medical model: A framework of ideas and assumptions about the nature of illness that seeks identifiable physical and material causes, and so physical and material treatments, for all disease.

Medicine plant: A naturally growing herb or plant that is taken intentionally for healing, usually involving ecstatic states. Examples are ayahuasca, psilocybin, peyote, and the *kykeon* of the Greek Mysteries.

Meditation: The use of contemplation and inner awareness as a way to discern truths about ourselves and the world, and to engage in transformation.

Meme: A cultural idea or artifact that spreads through networks of people.

Metaphysics: The part of philosophy that deals with the fundamental nature of reality and explores abstract concepts such as knowing and being.

Modernity: A period of time and a paradigm of thought that is characterized by a sense of individuality, reason, and the rational meeting of individual needs. It encompasses a belief in the power of human beings to improve and reshape their lives with the aid of science, innovation, and technology.

Movement medicine: Dance and ecstatic movements intentionally used for healing and transformation.

Mystical: An experience of unity and connection that is not measurable or explainable using existing tools of science, logic, mathematics, and reason.

Mystic: Someone who has had direct experience of the unity of existence and aspires to live in alignment with that experience.

Naturalism: The belief that only natural, as opposed to supernatural, forces operate in the world.

New Atheism: The belief that not only does god not exist, but that science should be the only arbiter of truth. New Atheists contend that religious faith and superstition should not be tolerated as they are damaging to society.

Nihilism: A worldview premised on the idea that life is meaningless, nothing matters, and no beliefs are true.

Noble lie: An assumption or myth that, though not true, is useful in maintaining harmony within oneself or in society.

Non-duality: The idea that there are not two or more things in reality, but just one (or none). It is usually associated with the realization that everything is one thing, or no thing, but definitely not two or more things like matter vs. mind. Contrasts with *dualistic* beliefs.

Non-local: Referring to action that is at a distance from events; or to information that is not contained in the visible system.

Objective: Not influenced by personal feelings, beliefs, or opinions, and so able to be verified by other observers.

Oneness: A description of the non-dual experience of reality, of nature, where everything, including ourselves, appears to be part of one fabric.

Other (verb): To "other" people means to set them up as different, usually to diminish them and elevate oneself.

Palintonic: A harmonious and creative tension of seeming opposites. Derived from fragments of thought attributed to Greek philosopher Heraclitus.

Panpsychism: The belief that consciousness or subjectivity is ubiquitous in nature and is in all matter in some way.

Pansubjectivism/Panconsciousness: The belief that all matter has the elementary capacity for consciousness or subjective interiority within it.

Pantheism: The belief that everything is god. Often confused with panentheism, which states that everything is *in* god.

Paradigm: see "episteme."

Paradigm shift: see "epistemological rupture".

Participant observation: A technique common in anthropology in which we attempt to understand a culture by both observing it objectively and participating in it subjectively.

Pattern: A habit of feeling, thought, and action which has become an efficient and conditioned response to specific situations.

Philosophy: Literally, the 'love of wisdom', but which has become a professional academic pursuit studying human thought, knowledge, and ideologies.

Physicalism: The belief that everything that exists must be physical.

Pivot: A business term describing a situation in which a company consciously changes strategy in order to avert failure.

Positivism: The belief that science, logic, and rationality unearth reliable and certain knowledge about the world, and that only these methods and lenses can provide authoritative and verifiable facts. Positivists hold that this knowledge allows the human race to make progress.

Possible World: The realm of potentialities, possibilities, and probabilities before they have been converted into measurable reality in the Actual World.

Post-colonial: A description of ideas and beliefs that stem from studying the impact of colonialism on human beings and their environment; usually profoundly critical of colonialist ideas and impacts.

Post-materialist: The belief that there are phenomena in the natural world that are not easily studied by conventional scientific methods, and that cannot be reduced entirely to the movement and modifications of matter.

Postmodernism: The belief that all ideologies must be challenged because they are all products of social, historical, and political factors; ideologies must be challenged to expose who wins and loses with each claim to truth. In particular, this means being skeptical of ideas of progress, absolute truth, and universal morality, reason, and logic.

Power-knowledge: A concept introduced by Michel Foucault stating that knowledge and power are inextricably linked, because people use knowledge to gain and hold on to power; and use knowledge to make their authority seem true, essential, and timeless.

Primary properties or qualities: Qualities of things that appear to be within the thing itself, and not dependent on the subjective consciousness of the observer: e.g. size, speed, mass, density, and so on. Primary qualities may be accurately and repeatedly measured using the scientific method.

Production: The creation of value (defined as worth, usefulness, or importance), usually through the delivery of products and services that are consumed by others.

Prosperity gospel: The belief that wealth and wellbeing are signs of God's love for us, and that religious faith will increase material riches.

Protector (also see Control and Protect Mode): The part of us that defends us against threats and uncertainty to ensure we survive.

Protestant work ethic: An idea made popular by Max Weber, which holds that having a sense of duty to work hard and be materially successful is connected to salvation by God.

Psychoanalysis: The study of the human mind through analysis of the unconscious; a practice for healing the mind through analysis.

Purpose: Love in action. The bridge between our consciousness and the suffering and needs of others.

Qualia: The subjective and conscious experiences of something; what it feels like to see or sense something.

Randomized controlled trial: A way of studying the impact of a drug, treatment, or intervention that attempts to overcome human error and cognitive biases.

Rational: That which is based on scientific knowledge, logic, mathematical calculations, and reason.

Reductionism: The belief that all complex things in nature can be reduced to the movement and modifications of matter, usually atoms, molecules, and sub-atomic particles.

Relativism: The belief that all ideas, including moral ideas about what is good or bad, are relative depending on one's viewpoint or paradigm. Therefore, ideas and truths can only be fully understood and evaluated from within the culture that they develop in. No culture or sub-culture can claim they have the absolute truth that is relevant to all people and across all time.

Religion: The belief in a superhuman or supernatural higher power, usually a personal god or gods; the worship of that power; and the organization that forms to enable and control worship, often through the role of priests.

Res cogitans: Thinking things; consciousnesses.

Res extensa: Extending things; matter.

Romanticism: A movement, originating at the time science grew in power, that sought to highlight the importance of the emotional, creative, and subjective.

Satchitananda: A Sanskrit term for the experience of oneness, of non-duality, that is described as existence, consciousness, and joyful bliss all at the same time.

Scalable: A product, service, or system that can be expanded with minimal limitations and with an exponential growth curve.

Science: Originally meaning "knowledge", it now usually refers to all knowledge about the world derived from using the scientific method.

Scientific method: A way of exploring the natural world to find reliable knowledge about it through repeated empirical observations, measurement, the creation and testing of hypotheses, the public publishing and review of the data and theories, and replication of the results by others.

Scientism: The belief that scientific knowledge is the most important and valuable form of knowledge, and that the scientific method can be applied to every domain of human experience and sphere of the natural world to discover the truth.

Secondary qualities: Qualities of things that appear to be dependent on the subjective consciousness of the observer: e.g. sense of temperature, aroma, smell, taste, sound, and meaning. Secondary qualities do not afford themselves to being measured objectively and scientifically.

Secular: Things that are related to the world and are not bound by any religious dogma, doctrine, or priests.

Separation consciousness: A state of awareness in which we feel disconnected to the material world. This is an everyday and 'normal' state of consciousness for most people.

Shadow: The part of us that contains unconscious aspects about ourselves that we have not integrated into our sense of self, either because we don't like them (usually 'negative' characteristics) or because we don't believe them (usually 'positive' characteristics). Associated with Carl Jung.

Shaman: A person who helps people enter trance states or alternate states of consciousness in order to gain insights needed to keep the individual and group thriving.

Skepticism: A start point at which we doubt the truth of all claims to knowledge, and even whether we can ever know anything with certainty at all. Not to be confused with cynicism, a lack of belief in oneself and humanity.

Socialism: The idea that a society should be organized so that resources, property, and wealth are owned by the community as a whole, and that decisions should be made for the good of the whole.

Spirituality: A sense that there is something more meaningful and connected about the world than just physical mechanisms and matter; a commitment to live according to our deepest values, purpose, and most noble aspirations embodying love, truth, and creativity to serve others.

Spiritual atheism: The belief that God or gods do not exist and no religious scripture or rules are right; that science and reason are the preeminent ways of understanding the material world; yet that there are other experiences that cannot be explained well using science and reason. Core is the experience that everything in the world is profoundly interconnected in some way and that this can be experienced reliably through various wisdom practices. The experiences we have of that connection manifest as love, purpose, truth, intuition, and creativity. They are both life changing and world changing.

Spiritual bypass: The use of spiritual concepts and practices to avoid transforming inner pain but instead to seek pleasure.

Subjective: Influenced by personal feelings, beliefs, and opinions, and so not verifiable by others.

Suffering: The experience of pain, loss, disconnection, and existential agony, usually from a sense of separation, loss, and lack.

Sufism: A long-established and predominately Muslim mystical tradition.

Sunyata: A term in Buddhism that usually relates to the emptiness of all material reality and the void within all. This does not mean there is nothing there, but that reality is no thing.

Superstition: Belief in things that cannot be observed, explained, or proven, often supernatural events such as miracles that seem to have no natural cause.

Surrender: A term for letting go of the individual desire for control and power whilst recognizing the universe always has ultimate control and power.

Tao: The 'way' or 'path' in Chinese and Taoist philosophy; the underlying nature of the universe.

Tat Tvam Asi: A Sanskrit term for the realization of oneness and that you, the individual, are connected to all that is.. Literally means "you are that" or "thou art that".

Template: Ways of relating to people and things that are learned as children, and often copied from caregivers.

The Enlightenment: A period of time during the seventeenth and eighteenth centuries in which modern ideas about the power of reason, logic, science, and progress arose and challenged the authority of religious and aristocratic dogma and power structures.

The Other: People or groups seen as different from, and usually worse than, we are, and which we define ourselves against.

The Reformation: A series of sweeping changes that transformed the Christian religion and forged the Protestant faith.

Thriving: Constantly expanding our potential and living fully no matter whether we experience pleasure or pain as we grow.

Thumos (or *thymos*): A Greek term for spiritedness in human beings. It can manifest as the craving for recognition within venal ambition or the yearning to take a stand to change the world.

Trance, or trance-like state: A state of consciousness that is different from 'normal' consciousness, usually brought about through hypnosis, meditation, contemplation, or an ecstatic experience.

Transformation: The permanent and sustained shifting of an individual belief, habit, or emotion or collective theory, system, or culture in a way that reduces *suffering* and increasing *thriving*. Usually liberates us from the hold the past has over us so we can enjoy the present and create a thriving future.

Transpersonal: A description of ideas and insights that are beyond the limits of biographical history and personal experience.

Trauma: A conscious experience that overwhelms our capacity to process it effectively in the moment, which gets stored in our material bodymind, altering our responses to everyday life.

Trickle-down economics: An economic theory holding that when companies, investors, and entrepreneurs are aided by the government to create value and profit (usually through the reduction of taxes and regulation), wealth will trickle down to all members of society.

Ubuntu: Originating in Africa, Ubuntu is the belief that all human beings exist in a web of interdependencies.

Unconscious: Needs, desires, fear, pain, and memories that we are not aware of in our everyday, waking life.

Unmet needs: Needs, wants, or desired deemed not to be fulfilled in a group of people. In advertising these are often called "pain points", which people will pay to have solved.

Vedanta: A long-established and predominately Hindu mystical tradition based on the Vedas. Also known as Advaita Vedanta.

Wisdom: Insights, ideas, principles, and practices that help human beings to suffer less and thrive more, usually through the experience and leverage of enlightenment to bring more love, truth, and creativity into the world.

Wisdom practice: A practical application of insights, ideas, principles, and practices that help human beings thrive. This is often a form of meditation (e.g. mindfulness or hypnotherapy) or movement (e.g. yoga or chi gong).

Wisdom teacher: Someone who commits their life to teaching others how to live theirs with love, truth, and creativity.

Zero-sum game: A situation that occurs when we are in a system with other people and their loss means our gain, and vice versa.

NOTES

1 "Depression Fact Sheet", World Health Organization, accessed August 1, 2017, http://www.who.int/mediacentre/factsheets/fs369/en/

2 Tom Vanden Brook, "Suicide Kills More US Troops Than ISIL in Middle East", *Newsweek*, December 29, 2016, accessed August 1, 2017, https://www.usatoday.com/story/news/nation/2016/12/29/suicide-kills-more-us-troops-than-isil-middle-east/95961038/

3 "Preventing Suicide: A Global Imperative" World Health Organization, 2014 accessed August 11th, 2017.

4 Sally Weale, "Child Mental Health Crisis 'Worse Than Suspected'", *The Guardian*, April, 29, 2016, accessed August 1, 2017, https://www.theguardian.com/society/2016/apr/29/government-expert-warns-child-mental-health-crisis-worse-than-suspected

5 Carli Lessof et al, "Longitudinal Study of Young People in England Cohort 2: Health and Wellbeing at Wave 2", Department For Education, July 2016.

6 Denis Campbell, "NHS Figures Show "Shocking" Rise in Self-harm Among Young", *The Guardian*, October 23, 2016, accessed August 1, 2017, https://www.theguardian.com/society/2016/oct/23/nhs-figures-show-shocking-rise-self-harm-young-people

7 Anne Case and Angus Dayton, "Mortality and Morbidity in the 21st Century", Brookings Papers on Economic Activity, May 1, 2017, accessed August 1, 2017, https://www.brookings.edu/wp-content/uploads/2017/03/casedeaton_sp17_finaldraft.pdf

8 Opioid Overdoses, Center for Disease Control and Prevention, accessed October 11th 2017, https://www.cdc.gov/drugoverdose/index.html

9 Knowledge Networks and Insight Policy Research, "Loneliness Among Older Adults: A National Survey of Adults 45+", AARP, September 2010.

10 J. Holt-Lundstad et al., "Loneliness and Social Isolation as Risk Factors for Mortality", Perspectives on Psychological Science 10, no. 2 (March 2015): 227–237.

11 Oliver Milman, "Earth Has Lost a Third of Arable Land in Past 40 Years, Scientists Say", *The Guardian*, December 2, 2015, accessed August 1, 2017, https://www.theguardian.com/environment/2015/dec/02/arable-land-soil-food-security-shortage

12 Ian Johnston, "European Smog Could Be 27 Times More Toxic Than Air Pollution in China", *The Independent*, February 10, 2017, accessed August 1, 2017, http://www.independent.co.uk/environment/european-smog-27-times-more-toxic-chinese-air-pollution-china-quality-a7572051.html

13 *The Lancet Commission on Pollution and Health*, October 2017, accessed October 8, 2007, http://www.thelancet.com/commissions/pollution-and-health

14 Jiaquan Xu et al., "Mortality in the United States", (December, 2016) accessed October 11th 2017, https://www.cdc.gov/nchs/data/databriefs/db267.pdf

15 Karl Jaspers, *The Origin and Goal of History* (Westport, CT: Greenwood Press Reprint, 1977).

16 Darcia Narvaez, "Circumcision's Psychological Damage", *Psychology Today*, January 11, 2015, accessed August 1, 2017, https://www.psychologytoday.com/blog/moral-landscapes/201501/circumcision-s-psychological-damage

17 American Academy of Pediatrics, "Circumcision Policy Statement", *Pediatrics* 130, no. 3 (August 2012).

18 R. Otto, *The Idea of the Holy*, 2nd ed., trans. John W. Harvey (New York, NY: Oxford University Press, 1958).

19 Friedrich Wilhelm Nietzsche, *The Gay Science*, ed. Bernard Williams (Cambridge: Cambridge University Press, 2001).

20 Ludwig Feuerbach, *The Essence of Christianity* (Mineola, NY: Dover Publications, 2008).

21 Karl Marx, *Contribution to the Critique of Hegel's Philosophy of Right (1844), accessed on August 11th 2017 at https://www.marxists.org/archive/marx/works/1843/critique-hpr/intro.htm*

22 Max Weber, "Science as A Vocation", in H. H. Gerth and C. Wright Mills (trans. and ed.), *Max Weber: Essays in Sociology*, pp. 129–156, (New York: Oxford University Press, 1946).

23 Charles Taylor, *A Secular Age* (Cambridge, MA: Harvard University Press, 2007).

24 Pew Research Center, "'Nones' On the Rise," www.pewforum.org, October 9, 2012, accessed August 2, 2017, http://www.pewforum.org/2012/10/09/nones-on-the-rise/

25 Damian Thompson, "2067: the end of British Christianity", *The Spectator*, June 15, 2013, accessed August 1, 2017, https://www.spectator.co.uk/2015/06/2067-the-end-of-british-christianity/

26 Epiphenom, "Countries Free of Religion are the Most Advanced, Data Show", Patheos.com, April 14, 2015, accessed August 1, 2017, http://www.patheos.com/blogs/epiphenom/2015/04/countries-free-of-religion-are-the-most-socially-advanced-data-show.html

27 Center for the Global Study of Christiantiy, "Christianity in its Global Context, 1970–2020: Society, Religion, and Mission", accessed August 1, 2017, http://wwwgordonconwell.com/netcommunity/CSGCResources/ChristianityinitsGlobalContext.pdf.

28 Pew Research Center, "The Future of World Religions: Population Growth Projections, 2010–2050", Pew Research Center, April 2, 2015, accessed August 1, 2017, http://www.pewforum.org/2015/04/02/religious-projections-2010-2050/

29 Richard Sosis and Candace Alcorta, "Signaling, Solidarity, and the Sacred: The Evolution of

Religious Behavior", *Evolutionary Anthropology* 12, no. 6 (November 2003): 264–274.

30 Maurice Bloch, "Why Religion is Nothing Special But Is Central", Philosophical Transactions B 363, no. 1499 (June 2008): 2055–2061.

31 Richard Dawkins, *The Selfish Gene* (Oxford: Oxford Landmark Science, 2016).

32 E. T. Gershoff and A. Grogan-Kaylor, "Spanking and Child Outcomes: Old.Controversies and New Meta-Analyses", Journal of Family Psychology 30, no. 4 (June 2016): 453–469.

33 Giovanni Novembre et al., "Empathy for Social Exclusion Involves the Sensory-Discriminative Component of Pain: A Within-Subject fMRI Study", Social Cognitive and Affective Neuroscience 10, no. 2 (February 2015): 153–164.

34 Andrew Scull, Charlotte MacKenzie, and Nicholas Hervey, *Masters of Bedlam: The Transformation of the Mad-Doctoring Trade* (Princeton, NJ: Princeton University Press, 1996).

35 C. Fred Dickason, *Demon Possession & The Christian* (Wheaton, IL: Crossway Books, 1989).

36 Cecilia Tasca et al., "Women And Hysteria In The History Of Mental Health", Clinical Practice and Epidemiology in Mental Health 8 (2012): 10–119.

37 John Launer, "Anna O and the 'Talking Cure'", QJM 98, no. 6 (June 2005): 465–466.

38 Lionel Fanthorpe and Patricia Fanthorpe, *Mysteries and Secrets of Voodoo, Santeria, and Obeah* (Toronto: Dundurn Press, 2008).

39 Gregory A. Kimble and Kurt Schlesinger, *Topics in the History of Psychology*, Volume 2 (Hillsdale, NJ: Lawrence Erlbaum Associates, 1985).

40 Rachel Bachner-Melman and Pesach Lichtenberg, "Freud's Relevance to Hypnosis: A Reevaluation", *American Journal of Clinical Hypnosis* 44, no. 1 (July 2001).

41 Jeremy Holmes, *John Bowlby & Attachment Theory: Makers of Modern Psychotherapy* (London: Routledge, 1993).

42 Jeremy Holmes, *John Bowlby & Attachment Theory: Makers of Modern Psychotherapy* (London: Routledge, 1993).

43 David J Walling, *Attachment in Psychotherapy* (London: Guilford Press, 2015).

44 Jeremy Holmes, *The Search for the Secure Base: Attachment Theory and Psychotherapy* (London: Routledge, 2001).

45 Elsevier, "Trauma's epigenetic fingerprint observed in children of Holocaust survivors", Elsevier.com, September 1, 2016, accessed August 1, 2017, https://www.elsevier.com/about/press-releases/research-and-journals/traumas-epigenetic-fingerprint-observed-in-children-of-holocaust-survivors

46 Bessel van der Kolk, *The Body Keeps the Score: Brain, Mind, and Body in the Healing of Trauma* (New York, NY: Penguin, 2014).

47 Carl Jung, *Symbols of Transformation*, trans. R. F. C. Null (Princeton, NJ: Princeton University Press, 1977).

48 Paulo Freire, *Pedagogy of the Oppressed*, trans. Myra Bergman Ramos (New York, NY: Bloomsbury Academic 2000).

49 Stephen Cave, "On the Dark History of Intelligence As Domination", *Aeon*, February 21,

2017, accessed August 1, 2017, https://aeon.co/essays/on-the-dark-history-of-intelligence-as-domination

50 Franz Fanon, *The Wretched of the Earth*, trans. Richard Philcox (New York: Grove Press, 1963).

51 Clifford Geertz, *The Interpretation of Cultures* (New York, NY: Basic Books Classics, 1977).

52 Desmond Tutu and Mpho Tutu, *Made for Goodness: And Why This Makes All the Difference* (San Francisco, CA: HarperOne, 2011).

53 "Achievements in Public Health, 1900–1999: Control of Infectious Diseases", *MMWR* 48, no. 29 (July 1999): 621–629, accessed August 1, 2017, https://www.cdc.gov/mmwr/preview/mmwrhtml/mm4829a1.htm

54 Charles Darwin, *On the Origin of Species by Means of Natural Selection* (London: John Murray, 1859)

55 Statute Law Revision Act 1888 (vict) s 51–52 c 3.

56 Charles Taylor, *A Secular Age* (Cambridge, MA: Harvard University Press, 2007).

57 Michael Marett-Crosby, *Twenty-Five Astronomical Observations That Changed the World: And How To Make Them Yourself* (New York, NY: Springer, 2013).

58 Siyuan Liu et al., "Neural Correlates of Lyrical Improvisation: An fMRI Study of Freestyle Rap", *Scientific Reports* 2, no. 834 (November 15, 2012), accessed August 1, 2017, https://www.nature.com/articles/srep00834

59 Rex E. Jung et al., "The Structure of Creative Cognition in the Human Brain", *Frontiers in Human Neuroscience*, 7 , no. 330 (July 8, 2013).

60 Rex E. Jung, "Evolution, creativity, intelligence, and madness: 'Here Be Dragons'", Frontiers In Psychology (2014).

61 Ronald A. Cohen, *The Neuropsychology of Attention* (New York: Springer US, 2014).

62 Filip Buyse, The Distinction between Primary Properties and Secondary Qualities in Galileo Galilei's Natural Philosophy (Quebec, 2012), accessed August 1, 2017, https://www.academia.edu/6652802/The_distinction_between_Primary_Properties_and_Secondary_Qualities_in_Galileo_Galileis_Natural_Philosophy

63 John Locke, *An Essay Concerning Human Understanding* (London: Penguin 1998).

64 René Descartes, *Meditations and Other Metaphysical Writings*, trans. Desmond M. Clarke (New York, NY: Penguin, 1998).

65 Francis Bacon, *Novum Organum*, ed. Joseph Devey (New York: P.F. Collier & Son, 1620), available online at http://oll.libertyfund.org/titles/bacon-novum-organum

66 *List of Cognitive Biases*, Wikipedia, accessed August 1, 2017, https://en.wikipedia.org/wiki/List_of_cognitive_biases

67 Open Science Collaboration, Brian A. Nosek et al. "Estimating the Reproducibility of Psychological Science", *Science* 349, no. 6251 (August 28, 2015).

68 Daniel C. Dennett, *Consciousness Explained* (New York, NY: Back Bay Books, 1992).

69 Fabrizio Benedetti, *Placebo Effects* (New York, NY: Oxford University Press, 2014).

70 For a great documentary on the movement watch *High On Hope*, by Piers Sanderson (2009).

71 Barbara Ehrenreich, *Dancing in the Streets: A History of Collective Joy* (New York, NY: Holt Paperbacks, 2007).

72 William James, *The Varieties of Religious Experience* (New York, NY: Penguin Books, 1982).

73 Michael Murphy and Rhea White, *In the Zone: Transcendent Experience in Sports* (London: Penguin Books, 1995).

74 W. F. H. Myers, *Human Personality and Its Survival of Bodily Death: Volume 1* (New York, NY: Dover Publications, 2005.

75 Lynn Bridgers, *Contemporary Varieties of Religious Experience: James's Classic Study in Light of Resiliency, Temperament, and Trauma* (Lanham, MD: Rowan & Littlefield Publishers, 2005).

76 Carl Jung, "The Concept of the Collective Unconscious", *Collected Works Volume 9* (London: Routeledge, 1959).

77 Robert A. Johnson, *Ecstasy: Understanding the Psychology of Joy* (New York, NY: Harper, 2007).

78 Mircea Eliade, *Shamanism: Archaic Techniques of Ecstasy* (Princeton, NJ: Princeton University Press, 2004).

79 Beatriz Caiuby Labate and Clancy Cavnar, *Ayahuasca Shamanism in the Amazon and Beyond (Oxford Ritual Studies)* (New York, NY: Oxford University Press, 2014).

80 Mara Lynn Keller, "The Ritual Path of Initiation into the Eleusinian Mysteries", *Rosicrucian Digest* 2 (2009).

81 Christine Morris and Alan Peatfield, "Experiencing ritual: Shamanic elements in Minoan religion", in M. Wedde (ed.), *Celebrations. Sanctuaries and the vestiges of cult activity* (pp. 35–59), Papers from the Norwegian Institute at Athens 6, The Norwegian Institute at Athens (2004).

82 Simon Reynolds, *Energy Flash: A Journey Through Rave Music and Dance Culture* (Berkeley, CA: Soft Skull Press, 2012).

83 John Buckman, "Social and Medical Aspects of Illicit Use of LSD", *International Journal of Social Psychiatry*, June 1971, http://journals.sagepub.com/doi/abs/10.1177/002076407101700301

84 *Criminal Justice and Public Order Act 1994*, accessed August 1, 2017, https://www.legislation.gov.uk/ukpga/1994/33/section/63

85 Paul Chevigny, *Gigs: Jazz and the Cabaret Laws in New York City* (New York, NY: Routledge, 1991).

86 Shane Frederick and George Loewenstein, "Hedonic Adaptation", in Daniel Kahneman, Edward Diener, and Norbert Schwarz, Norbert, *Well-Being: Foundations of Hedonic Psychology* (New York, NY: Russell Sage Foundation, 1999).

87 Thomas Kuhn, *The Structure of Scientific Revolutions* (Chicago, IL: The University of Chicago, 1970).

88 Rex E. Jung et al., "The Structure of Creative Cognition in the Human Brain", *Frontiers in Human Neuroscience*, July 8, 2013, http://journal.frontiersin.org/article/10.3389/fnhum.2013.00330/full

89 Michel Foucault, *The Order of Things: An Archeology of Human Sciences* (New York, NY: Vintage, 1994).

90 National Institute for Health, "What is Fibromyalgia?" NIH, November 2014, accessed August 1, 2017, https://www.niams.nih.gov/health_info/fibromyalgia/fibromyalgia_ff.asp

91 George Loewenstein, "Hot-Cold Empathy Gaps and Medical Decision Making", *Health Psychology* 24, no. 4 (July 2005): S49–S56.

92 For more on this, see Cathy O'Neil, *Weapons of Math Destruction* (New York, NY: Crown Publishing, 2016).

93 Charles Darwin, *The Expression of Emotion in Man and Animals* (London: John Murray, 1872).

94 Timothy Snyder, "Hitler's World", *New York Review of Books*, September 24, 2015, accessed August 1, 2017, http://www.nybooks.com/articles/2015/09/24/hitlers-world/

95 James Q. Whitman, "Why the Nazis Studied American Race Laws for Inspiration", Aeon, December 13, 2016, accessed August 1, 2017, https://aeon.co/ideas/why-the-nazis-studied-american-race-laws-for-inspiration

96 Edwin Black, *War Against the Weak: Eugenics and America's Campaign to Create a Master Race* (Washington, DC: Dialog Press, 2012).

97 Alexandra Minna Stern, *Eugenic Nation: Faults and Frontiers of Better Breeding in America* (Berkeley, CA: University of California Press, 2005).

98 Lillian Faderman, *The Gay Revolution: The Story of the Struggle* (New York, NY: Simon & Schuster, 2016).

99 Neel Burton, M.D., "When Homosexuality Stopped Being a Mental Disorder", *Psychology Today*, September 18, 2016, accessed August 1, 2017, https://www.psychologytoday.com/blog/hide-and-seek/201509/when-homosexuality-stopped-being-mental-disorder

100 Michel Foucault in Michael Kelly, *Critique and Power: Recasting the Foucault/Habermas Debate* (Cambridge, MA: MIT Press, 1994).

101 Bertrand Russell, *The Scientific Outlook* (Abingdon: Routledge, 2009).

102 Francis Bacon, *Novum Organum: New Organon or True Directions Concerning the Interpretation of Nature* (1620)

103 René Descartes, "Discourse on the Method of Rightly Conducting One's Reason and Seeking Truth in the Sciences", earlymoderntexts.com, last amended November 2007, accessed August 1, 2017, http://www.earlymoderntexts.com/assets/pdfs/descartes1637.pdf

104 David Fuller, "Insisting on the truth in times of chaos", accessed August 1, 2017, https://medium.com/perspectiva-institute/the-man-for-the-times-of-chaos-jordan-peterson-2df43c24672f

105 Internet Advertising Bureau UK, "Gaming Revolution", iabuk.net, September 17, 2014, accessed August 1, 2017, https://iabuk.net/research/library/gaming-revolution

106 John Micklethwaite, *The Company: A Short History of a Revolutionary Idea* (New York, NY: Modern Library, 2005).

107 Gilbert Ryle, *The Concept of Mind* (Chicago, IL: University of Chicago Press, 2000).

108 Blake Smith, "Why the Original Laissez-Faire Economists Loved Slavery", Aoen, June 29, 2016, accessed August 1, 2017, https://aeon.co/essays/why-the-original-laissez-faire-economists-loved-slavery

109 S. Hernandez-Cordero, et al., "Overweight and Obesity in Mexican Children and Adolescents During the Last 25 Years", *Nutrition & Diabetes* 7, no. 3 (March 2017).

110 Adam Smith, *The Wealth of Nations* (New York, NY: Modern Library, 1994).

111 T. Piketty, "The 'Kuznets' Curve, Yesterday and Tomorrow", in A. Banerjee et al., eds., *Understanding Poverty* (New York, NY: Oxford University Press, 2006), 21.

112 S. Kuznets, "Economic Growth and Economic Inequality", *American Economic Review* 45, no. 1 (March 1955): 1–28.

113 Thomas Piketty, *Capital in the Twenty-First Century* (Cambridge, MA: Belknap Press, 2017).

114 BBC News, "Nigerians living in poverty rise to nearly 61%", BBC.com, February 13, 2012, accessed August 1, 2017, http://www.bbc.com/news/world-africa-17015873

115 Emma Green, "The Pope Tweeted That 'Inequality is the Root of Social Evil': Big Deal?" *The Atlantic*, April 29, 2014, accessed August 1, 2017, https://www.theatlantic.com/business/archive/2014/04/the-pope-tweets-the-internet-freaks/361376/

116 Deborah Hardoon, *An Economy for the 99%: It's time to build a human economy that benefits everyone, not just the privileged few (Oxfam, 2017)*, accessed August 1, 2017, http://policy-practice.oxfam.org.uk/publications/an-economy-for-the-99-its-time-to-build-a-human-economy-that-benefits-everyone-620170

117 Richard Wilkenson and Kate Pickett, *The Spirit Level: Why More Equal Societies Almost Always Do Better* (London: Bloomsbury Press, 2011).

118 Era Dabla Norris et al., "Causes and Consequences of Income Inequality: A Global Perspective", International Monetary Fund Staff Discussion Note, June 2015, accessed August 1, 2017, https://www.imf.org/external/pubs/ft/sdn/2015/sdn1513.pdf

119 Adam Tooze, "A General Logic of Crisis", *London Review of Books* 39, no. 1 (January 5, 2017), accessed August 1, 2017, https://www.lrb.co.uk/v39/n01/adam-tooze/a-general-logic-of-crisis

120 Wolfgang Streek, *How Will Capitalism End?* (New York, NY: Verso, 2017).

121 Drew DeSilver, "For Most Workers, Real Wages Have Barely Budged for Decades", Pew Research Center, October 9, 2014, accessed August 1, 2017, http://www.pewresearch.org/fact-tank/2014/10/09/for-most-workers-real-wages-have-barely-budged-for-decades/

122 Steve Benen, "More Kansas Schools Forced to Close", MSNBC.com, April 23, 2015, accessed August 1, 2017, http://www.msnbc.com/rachel-maddow-show/more-kansas-schools-forced-close.

123 "What's it like to live in a care home? Findings from the Healthwatch network", August 10, 2017, accessed Nov 3, 2017, http://www.healthwatch.co.uk/resource/whats-it-live-care-home-findings-healthwatch-network

124 Associated Press, "Report: U.S. Health Care System Is A Liability", NBC News.com, March 12, 2009, accessed August 1, 2017, http://health.nbcnews.com/_news/2009/03/12/2535642-report-us-health-care-system-is-a-liability

125 Francis Fukuyama, *The End of History and the Last Man* (New York, NY: Free Press, 2006).

126 John O. Lyons, *The Invention of the Self: The Hinge of Consciousness in the Eighteenth Century* (Carbondale, IL: Southern Illinois University Press, 1978).

127 Joseph Persky, "Retrospectives: The Ethology of Homo Economicus", *The Journal of Economic Perspectives* 9, no. 2 (Spring 1995).

128 Ashlee Vance, "This Tech Bubble is Different", *Bloomberg Businessweek*, April 14, 2011, accessed August 1, 2017, http://www.bloomberg.com/news/articles/2011-04-14/this-tech-bubble-is-different

129 Ulrich Steinvorth, *Rethinking the Western Understanding of the Self* (Cambridge, Cambridge University Press, 2009).

130 Michael A. Freeman et al., "Are Entrepreneurs 'Touched With Fire'?" Pre-publication Manuscript, April 17, 2015, accessed August 1, 2017, http://www.michaelafreemanmd.com/Research_files/Are%20Entrepreneurs%20Touched%20with%20Fire-summary.pdf

131 Jake H. Davis, *A Mirror Is for Reflection: Understanding Buddhist Ethics* (New York, NY: Oxford University Press, 2017).

132 René Descartes, *Discourse on the Method of Rightly Conducting The Reason And Seeking Truth In The Sciences (*Project Gutenberg, 2008) accessed August 1st 2017, http://www.gutenberg.org/files/59/59-h/59-h.htm

133 Dudjom Lingpa, *Dag snang ye shes drva pa las gnas lugs rang byung gi rgyud rdo rje'i snying po.* Collected Works of H. H. Dudjom Rinpoche (Vimala)

134 Eknath Easwaran, *The Upanishads* (Tomales, CA: Nilgiri Press, 2007).

135 Varadaraja Raman, *Indic Visions: In an Age of Science* (Bloomington, Indiana: Xlibris, 2011).

136 Roger J. Stilling, "Mystical Healing: Reading Philip K. Dick's *VALIS* and *The Divine Invasion* as Metapsychoanalytic Novels", *South Atlantic Review* 56 (May 1991): 91–106.

137 Roland Faber et al. (eds.), *Butler on Whitehead: On the Occasion,* (Lanham, Maryland: Lexington Books; 2012).

138 Katalin Nun, *Volume 2, Tome II: Kierkegaard and the Greek World – Aristotle and Other Greek Authors (Kierkegaard Research: Sources Reception and Resources)*, ed. Jon Stewart (Abingdon: Routledge, 2010).

139 Rabbi Rami Shapiro, trans. *Tanya, the Masterpiece of Hasidic Wisdom* (Nashville, TN: Skylight Paths, 2010).

140 Thomas Cleary, The Taoist Classics (Shambhala Publications, 2003).

141 Dick Davis and Afkham Darbandi, *The Conference of the Birds* (London: Penguin, 2011).

142 Stephen Jay Gould, "Nonoverlapping Magisteria", *Natural History* 106 (March 1997): 16–22.

143 Galen Strawson et al., *Consciousness and Its Place in Nature: Does Physicalism Entail Panpsychism?* (Exeter: Imprint Academic, 2006).

144 Christoph Koch and Giulio Tononi, "A Test for Consciousness", *Scientific American*, June 2011, accessed August 1, 2017, https://www.scientificamerican.com/article/a-test-for-consciousness/

145 *Beyond Physicalism*, eds. Edward Kelly, Adam Crabtree, Paul Marshall (Lanham, MD: Rowman & Littlefield, 2015).

146 Daryl Bem, "Feeling the Future: Experimental Evidence for Anomalous Retroactive Influences on Cognition and Affect", *Journal of Personality and Social Psychology* (2011). doi: 10.1037/a0021524

147 Imants Barušs and Julia Mossbridge, *Transcendent Mind: Rethinking The Science Of Consciousness* (Washington DC: American Psychological Association, 2017).

148 For more information, see "Manifesto for a Post-Materialist Science", Open Sciences, 2014, accessed August 1, 2017, http://opensciences.org/about/manifesto-for-a-post-materialist-science.

149 *Religion and Atheism: Beyond the Divide* eds. Anthony Carroll, Richard Norman (London: Routledge, 2016).

150 Andrew Newberg and Eugene D'Aquili, *The Mystical Mind: Probing the Biology of Religious Experiences* (Minneapolis, MN: Fortress Press, 1999).

151 Michael Schartner et al., "Increased Spontaneous MEG Signal Diversity for Psychoactive Doses of Ketamine, LSD and Psilocybin", *Scientific Reports* 7, no. 46421 (April 19, 2017), accessed August 1, 2017, https://www.nature.com/articles/srep46421

152 Robin L. Carhart-Harris, et al., "Neural Correlates of the LSD Experience Revealed By Multimodal Neuroimaging", PNAS 113, no. 17 (April 26, 2016), accessed August 1, 2017, http://www.pnas.org/content/113/17/4853.full

153 E. Luders et al., "Enhanced Brain Connectivity in Long-Term Meditation Practitioners", *NeuroImage* 57, no. 4 (August 15, 2011): 1308–1316.

154 "Discovery of quantum vibrations in 'microtubules' inside brain neurons supports controversial theory of consciousness", *ScienceDaily*, 16 January 2014, accessed August 1, 2017 at www.sciencedaily.com/releases/2014/01/140116085105.htm

155 René Descartes, *Passions of the Soul*, trans. Stephen Voss (Indianapolis, IN: Hackett Publishing Company, 1989).

156 Stuart Hameroff, Roger Penrose, "Consciousness in the Universe: A Review of the 'Orch OR' Theory", *Physics of Life Reviews* 11, no. 1 (March 2014): 39–78.

157 Bruce Rosenblum, *Quantum Enigma: Physics Encounters Consciousness* (New York, NY: Oxford University Press, 2011).

158 Edward Kelly and Emily Williams Kelly, *Irreducible Mind: Toward a Psychology for the 21st Century* (Lanham, MD: Rowman & Littlefield, 2009), p. 73.

159 B Alan Wallace, *Bridge of Quiescence: Experiencing Tibetan Buddhist Meditation* (Peru, Illinois: Open Court, 1998).

160 Aldous Huxley, *The Doors of Perception* (Thinking Ink Ltd., 2011).

161 Robin L. Carhart-Harris et al., "The Entropic brain: A Theory of Conscious States Informed By Neuroimaging Research With Psychedelic Drugs," *Frontiers in Human Neuroscience* 8, no. 20 (February 3, 2014), accessed August 1, 2017, http://journal.frontiersin.org/article/10.3389/fnhum.2014.00020/full

162 Saleh B. Omar, *Omah Ibn Al-Haytham's Optics: Study of the Origins of Experimental Science* (Beirut: Bibliotheca Islamica, 1977).

163 Ernst Lehrs, *Man or Matter* (Miami, FL: HardPress Publishing, 2010).

164 Michael White, *Isaac Newton: The Last Sorcerer* (New York, NY: Basic Books, 1999).

165 Dalai Lama, *The Four Noble Truths*, trans. Geshe Thupten Jinpa, ed. Dominique Side (London: HarperCollins 2013).

166 A. H. Almaas, *Spacecruiser Inquiry: True Guidance for the Inner Journey* (Boston, MA: Shambhala, 2002).

167 Henrik Kessler et al., "Reconsolidation and Trauma Memory", in Nikolai Axmacher, Björn Rasch, eds., *Cognitive Neuroscience of Memory Consolidation* (New York, NY: Springer, 2017).

168 J. P. Godbout, R. Glaser, "Stress-Induced Immune Dysregulation: Implications for Wound Healing, Infectious Disease and Cancer", *Journal of Neuroimmune Pharmacology* 1, no. 4 (December 2006): 421–427.

169 Bessel van der Kolk, *The Body Keeps the Score: Brain, Mind, and Body in the Healing of Trauma* (New York, NY: Penguin, 2014).

170 Joanna Moncrieff, "Rebuttal: Depression is Not a Brain Disease", *Can J Psychiatry* 52 (2007): 100–101.

171 Leserman J, Petitto JM, Gu H, et al. "Progression to AIDS, a clinical AIDS condition and mortality: psychosocial and physiological predictors", Psychol Med. 2002; 32(6): 1059–1073.

172 Siddhartha Mukherjee, "Cancer's Invasion Equation", *New Yorker*, September 11, 2017.

173 Singh, Ilina, Morgan, C, Curran, V et al, "Ketamine treatment for depression: opportunities for clinical innovation and ethical foresight", *Lancet Psychiatry* (2016).

174 Karl Jansen, *Ketamine: Dreams and Realities* (San Franciso: MAPS, 2004).

175 D. E. Nichols, "Psychedelics," *Pharmacological Review* 68, no. 2 (April 2016): 264–355.

176 P. C. Dolder et al., "LSD Acutely Impairs Fear Recognition and Enhances Emotional Empathy and Sociality", *Neuropsychopharmacology* 41, no. 11 (October 2016): 2638–2646.

177 Robin L. Carhart-Harris, et al., "Serotonin and brain function: a tale of two receptors", *Journal of Psychopharmacology* (July, 2017), accessed August 1, 2017.

178 Terri S. Krebs, T and Påt Ørjan Johansen, "Psychedelics and Mental Health: A Population Study," PLoS ONE, August 19, 2013, accessed August 1, 2017, http://journals.plos.org/plosone/article?id=10.1371/journal.pone.0063972.

179 Stanislav Grof, Christina Grof, *Spiritual Emergency: When Personal Transformation Becomes a Crisis* (New York, NY: TarcherPerigree, 1989).

180 Tsultrim Allione, *Feeding Your Demons: Ancient Wisdom for Resolving Inner Conflict* (New

York, NY: Little, Brown and Company, 2008).

181 Karl Marx and Friedrich Engels, *The German Ideology, including Theses on Feuerbach* (Prometheus Books, 2011).

182 Viktor E. Frankl, *The Will to Meaning: Foundations and Applications of Logotherapy* (New York, NY: Plume, 2014).

183 Estelle Frankel, *Sacred Therapy: Jewish Spiritual Teachings on Emotional Healing and Inner Wholeness* (Boulder, CO: Shambhala, 2005).

184 Elaine Pagels, *The Gnostic Gospels*, (New York, NY: Weidenfeld & Nicolson, 2013).

185 Robert Waite, *Hitler: The Psychopathic God* (New York, NY: Basic Books, 1977).

186 Katie Kindelan, "Nelson Mandela: The Inspiring Words He Told Oprah Winfrey", ABCnews.go.com, December 6, 2013, accessed August 1, 2017, http://abcnews.go.com/blogs/entertainment/2013/12/nelson-mandela-the-inspiring-words-he-told-oprah-winfrey/

187 Susan David, Illona Boniwell, and Amanda Conley Ayers, eds., *Oxford Handbook of Happiness* (New York, NY: Oxford University Press, 2014).

188 Swami Satchidananda, *The Yoga Sutras of Patanjali: Commentary on the Raja Yoga Sutras by Sri Swami Satchidananda* (New York, NY: Integral Yoga Publications, 2012).

189 Geshe Sonam Rinchen, *The Bodhisattva Vow* (Ithaca, NY: Snow Lion, 2000).

190 Mohandas K. Gandhi, *The Bhagavad Gita According to Gandhi* (St. Paul, MN: Wilder Publications, 2012).

191 Edna O. Schack, Molly H. Fisher, Jennifer A. Wilhelm, eds., *Teacher Noticing: Bridging and Broadening Perspectives, Contexts, and Frameworks* (New York, NY: Springer, 2017).

192 Daniel Goleman, "The Focused Leader," *Harvard Business Review*, December 2013, accessed August 1, 2017, https://hbr.org/2013/12/the-focused-leader

193 Daniel J. Siegel, *Pocket Guide to Interpersonal Neurobiology: An Integrative Handbook of the Mind* (New York, NY: W. W. Norton & Company, 2012).

194 P. A. Boyle et al., "Effect of Purpose in Life on the Relation Between Alzheimer Disease Pathologic Changes on Cognitive Function in Advanced Age", Archives of General Psychiatry 69, no. 5 (May 2012): 499–505.

195 Harald Atmanspacher, "Dual-Aspect Monism à la Pauli and Jung," *Journal of Consciousness Studies* 19, no. 9–10 (2012): 96–120 (25).

196 Patrick Wilcken, *Claude Levi-Strauss: The Poet in the Laboratory* (Bloomsbury, 2011).

197 Frederick W H Myers, "The subliminal Consciousness", *Proceedings of the Society for Psychical Research* Vol VIII Part XXII 1892, Robert Maclehose & Co, Glasgow (1892).

198 Stuart A. Kauffman, *Humanity in a Creative Universe* (New York, NY: Oxford University Press 2016).

199 William James, *The Varieties of Religious Experience* (New York, NY: Penguin Books, 1982).

200 M. Pava, *Jewish Ethics as Dialogue: Using Spiritual Language to Re-Imagine a Better World* (New York, NY: Palgrave Macmillan, 2009).

201 Friedrich Wilhelm Nietzsche, *On The Genealogy of Morals*, trans. Maudmarie Clark and Alan J. Swensen (Indianapolis, IN: Hackett Publishing, 1998).

202 Immanuel Kant, *Groundwork of the Metaphysics of Morals*, ed. Jonathan Bennet, earlymoderntexts.com, last amended September 2008, accessed August 1, 2017, http://www.earlymoderntexts.com/assets/pdfs/kant1785.pdf

203 Jeremy Bentham, *An Introduction to the Principles of Morals and Legislation* (Createspace Independent Publishing Platform, 2016).

204 Thomas Hobbes, *Leviathan: Or the Matter, Forme, and Power of a Common-Wealth Ecclesiasticall and Civill*, ed. by Ian Shapiro (Yale University Press: 2010).

205 Paul Berman, *Terror and Liberalism* (New York, NY: W.W. Norton & Company, 2004).

206 Lynn White, "The Historical Roots of Our Ecological Crisis", *Science*, 1967; 155: 1203–1207.

207 Pierre Hadot, *Philosophy as a Way of Life*, ed. Arnold Davidson (Hoboken, NJ: Wiley-Blackwell, 1995).

208 Robert N. Bellah and Hans Jones, *The Axial Age and its Consequences* (Cambridge, MA: Harvard University Press, 2012).

INDEX

M

Q

R

S

T

Lightning Source UK Ltd.
Milton Keynes UK
UKHW010010071218
333595UK00001B/38/P